Czech

An Essential Grammar

Czech: An Essential Grammar is a practical reference guide to the core structures and features of modern Czech.

It presents a fresh and accessible description of the language and sets out the complexities of Czech in short, readable sections. Explanations are clear and free from jargon. Throughout, the emphasis is on Czech as used by native speakers today.

The *Grammar* is suitable for either independent study or for students in schools, colleges, universities and adult classes of all types.

Features include:

- focus on the morphology, basic syntax and word formation
- clear explanations of grammatical terms
- plentiful illustrative examples
- detailed contents list and index for easy access to information.

Czech: An Essential Grammar will help you read, speak and write Czech with greater confidence.

James Naughton is Lecturer at the University of Oxford, UK.

Routledge Essential Grammars

Essential Grammars are available for the following languages:

Chinese
Czech
Danish
Dutch
English
Finnish
Modern Greek
Modern Hebrew
Hungarian
Norwegian
Polish
Portuguese
Serbian
Spanish
Swedish
Thai
Urdu

Other titles of related interest published by Routledge:

Colloquial Croatian
Colloquial Czech
Colloquial Serbian

Czech

An Essential Grammar

 James Naughton

 Routledge
Taylor & Francis Group

LONDON AND NEW YORK

First published 2005
by Routledge
2 Park Square, Milton Park, Abingdon, Oxon, OX14 4RN

Simultaneously published in the USA and Canada
by Routledge
711 Third Avenue, New York, NY 10017

Routledge is an imprint of the Taylor & Francis Group, an informa business

© 2005 James Naughton

Typeset in 10/12pt Sabon by Graphicraft Ltd., Hong Kong

British Library Cataloguing in Publication Data
A catalogue record for this book is available from the British Library

Library of Congress Cataloging in Publication Data
A catalog record for this book has been requested

ISBN 0–415–28784–7 (hbk)
ISBN 0–415–28785–5 (pbk)
ISBN 978–0–415–28784–5 (hbk)
ISBN 978–0–415–28785–2 (pbk)

Printed and bound in Great Britain by
CPI Group (UK) Ltd, Croydon, CR0 4YY

Contents

Abbreviations

*	non-standard spoken usage (esp. Prague, Bohemia)
***	markedly vulgar
>	arrow head pointing forward to the perfective verb
<	arrow head pointing back to the perfective verb
+	separates determinate and indeterminate verbs of motion

acc.	accusative case
adj.	adjective
anim.	animate
colloq.	colloquial
dat.	dative case
dim.	diminutive
esp.	especially
f., fem.	feminine gender
gen.	genitive case
impf.	imperfective verb
inan.	inanimate
ins.	instrumental case
lit.	literally translated
loc.	locative case
m., masc.	masculine gender
ma.	masculine animate
mi.	masculine inanimate
n., neut.	neuter gender
nom.	nominative case
pf.	perfective verb
pl.	plural
sg.	singular
voc.	vocative case

Chapter 1

Introduction

This is styled an 'essential' grammar, and is certainly not anything like a comprehensive grammar (**mluvnice**) of Czech (**čeština**) – the Czech language (**český jazyk**), with its strong tradition of writing from the late thirteenth century onwards.

All kinds of choices have had to be made – especially about what to exclude! – either simply for reasons of space, or in order to try not to overburden readers who may still be at an elementary level in their knowledge of the language. (The dangers of over-simplification are of course ever-present, and the author is all too aware that he may have succumbed to these at times – he hopes not too often.)

Efforts have been made to separate the basic, core elements from those which are less central and vital.

Presentation of morphology (declension and conjugation) has been interspersed with material on usage. A work designed for trained linguists would arrange this material somewhat differently, no doubt, but it is hoped that the approach adopted here will be helpful to the general reader as well as informative for the more academic scholar.

I have tried to take account of readers' likely unfamiliarity with various grammatical categories, and with linguistic terminology.

Czech grammatical terms have been infiltrated into the text as well, for those who go on to encounter them in their further studies or hear them from their teachers.

The author has no particular theoretical or systematic approach to offer – this may or may not be a weakness. He has simply tried to steer a reasonably pragmatic course through the often thorny jungle of this language – wielding, as he hopes, a not too crude machete in his fist.

1.1 Standard versus non-standard usage

A few words ought perhaps to be said at the outset about how non-standard spoken Czech is presented here alongside the standard written forms.

The standard written language (**spisovná čeština**) differs in various, at times rather obvious, respects from most Czechs' everyday spoken language.

Wherever this book refers to non-standard forms of everyday colloquial language, it is broadly the spoken language of Prague and Bohemia that is being referred to.

People may refer to this variety as **hovorová čeština** 'colloquial Czech', while linguists often call it **obecná čeština** 'common Czech' (the former term has sometimes been used for a slightly relaxed version of the standard language, avoiding the more literary or 'bookish' features, but still more or less standard in phonetics and grammar).

Non-standard forms are often found in literature – in the texts, especially dialogues, of fiction and plays. They also occur on the radio and TV, especially in less formal contexts, and anyone living in the Czech Republic will soon notice these non-standard features even if they only have a rather basic command of the language.

Differences between written and colloquial usage will be pointed out throughout this book, rather than being hived off into a separate chapter. (Non-standard usage is marked by an asterisk.)

Much less attention is devoted to features which readers would mainly encounter when reading older texts, of the nineteenth century and earlier. Seventeenth-century Czech writings, such as those of Comenius (Komenský) are still very accessible to present-day Czech readers, but this grammar focuses mainly on the present-day language, which is spoken by around 10 million people in the Czech Republic, as well as by lesser numbers scattered over the globe.

Chapter 2

Pronunciation and orthography – výslovnost a pravopis

The relationship between standard Czech spelling and Czech pronunciation is relatively straightforward, compared with a language like English.

Nevertheless, as with all languages, the beginner who wants to be able to pronounce the language properly will benefit from access to a native speaker or at least to some sound recordings.

The following is designed more for the layman than the trained linguist. The reader who wants a more specialised approach will need to consult other sources.

Czech rules about punctuation and capital letters are slightly different from the conventions of English, but the main features are not hard to grasp.

2.1 Vowels – samohlásky

Vowel letters **a, e, i/y, o, u** represent sounds which are quite close to the English vowel sounds in 'tuck, tech, tick, tock, took' respectively.

There's no difference in sound between **i** and **y**, but the spelling affects the pronunciation of preceding **d, t, n** – see below.

With acute signs added (**á, é, í/ý, ó, ú**) these vowels are pronounced with longer duration: roughly like English 'ah, eh, ee, aw, oo'.

The long vowel **ú** is normally spelt **ů** (with a **kroužek** 'little circle') except as the first letter in a word.

Word stress is on the first vowel (long or short).

A, Á:	ano, ale, dal, dál, málo, malá
E, É:	ne, den, nese, krém, malé, milé
I, Í/Y, Ý:	byl/bil, syn, sýr, bílý, milý, malý
O, Ó:	ona, slovo, doma, gól, móda, haló
U, Ú/Ů:	ruka, ruku, domu, dům, úloha, domů

There are also three diphthongs (**diftongy**, sequences of two vowels within a single syllable) in which the first vowel, pronounced as above, moves into a very short u or w sound.

The commonest is OU:

OU: bouda, malou, náhodou, nesou

The other two diphthongs appear in loanwords:

AU: auto car, automobile, **autobus** 'bus', **restaurace** 'restaurant'

EU: pneumatika '(pneumatic) tyre', **neutralita** 'neutrality'

Other vowel letter sequences are pronounced as two syllables:

IE: Anglie 'England', as if spelt **-ije** (for **J** see below)

IO: rádio 'radio', as if spelt **-ijo**

AO: 'a-o' e.g. **kakao** 'cocoa'

2.2 Consonants – *souhlásky*

Consonant letters **b, d, f, g** (as in 'good'), **h, k, l, m, n, p, s** (as in 'sun'), **t** (as in 'stop'), **x** and **z** are pronounced much the same as in English. However:

K, P, and **T** lack the typical English 'post-aspiration', a slight puff of air following them, unless they come at the end of a word:

kilo, ruka, pil, koupil, ten, to, ta

but *are* post-aspirated in final position in words like: **buk, lup, mít**.

H is pronounced further back, more deeply, hollowly, than the English equivalent:

holit, haló, mnoho, nahý

CH must be distinguished from **H**, and is pronounced like Scottish 'loch' (*not* like a regular English CH):

chudý, chyba, ucho, chladno

R is briefly trilled, like a Scottish R, and pronounced in all positions:

rád, ruka, Karel, hora, pár, sestra, horko

Both **R** and **L** can act like vowels, creating syllables of their own:

krk, bratr, plný, nesl

One silly Czech tongue-twister suggests (misleadingly) that the language lacks vowels. The saying literally means 'stick (your) finger through (your) neck/throat':

Strč prst skrz krk.

QU and **W** turn up in occasional loanwords with retained foreign spelling.

western [vestern], **WC** [vétsé], **quasi-** (pronounced and more often spelt **kvazi-**).

S is pronounced [z] in words for '-isms' ending in **-ismus** and in a few other loanwords and names:

Josef [Jozef], **feminismus** [feminizmus] (now also spelt **-izmus**)

The letter **X** occurs in loanwords, where it is mostly pronounced [ks], e.g. **extra** 'extra', except in words beginning in **ex-** plus a vowel, if the **ex-** is not perceived as a tacked-on prefix. Here it is pronounced [gz], e.g. **existovat** 'to exist', **exil** 'exile', **exotický** 'exotic'.

Z is as in English 'zebra', e.g. **zebra, zima** 'winter'

| **2.2.1** | *Soft consonants* – **měkké souhlásky** |

For Czech spelling and grammar it is important to identify the so-called 'soft' consonants as a distinct group.

These are the consonant letters **č, d', ň, ř, š, t', ž** plus letters **c** and **j**.

All the soft consonants except for **c** and **j** are written with a diacritic sign over the letter, generally written and printed ˇ, and called a **háček** 'small hook'.

'Soft' **t** and **d** are also hand-written with a **háček**, but in lower-case print this is printed as **t', d'**, using a closely linked apostrophe. The upper-case printed forms are **Ť, Ď**.

C is pronounced as one sound like ts in ba<u>ts</u> (*not* like **K**):

cesta, noc, práce, pecka = *approx.* [tsesta], [nots], [prátse], [petska]

J is like y in yes:

jeden, já, moje, ahoj

Č, Š and Ž are pronounced much like chin, shin, and vision respectively:

čeká, Čech, Angličan, klíč

šest, máš, špatný, píšeš

žena, život, můžeš, muži

Ď/ď, Ť/ť and Ň/ň are close to the sounds in British English duty, tune, new (when pronounced 'dyooty', 'tyoon', 'nyoo'):

ďábel, Láďa, maďarský

ťuknout, chuť, koťata

píseň, promiň, koňak

The true Czech speciality is Ř, a single sound which is pronounced like an energetic briefly trilled R with additional contact from the tip of the tongue, producing some extra slightly ž-like friction. It can be heard in the name of the Czech composer Antonín Dvořák. It is voiceless at the end of a word (before a pause, see 2.5 below):

Dvořák, řeka, říkat – lékař, keř, nekuř

The sound Ř also occurs after other consonants. It is also voiceless when it comes immediately next to a voiceless consonant:

dříve, zavřít – tři, při, přece, křičet

It also occurs sometimes between two consonants, but does *not* add its own syllable:

hřbi|tov – křti|ny (each two syllables only!)

It is necessary to distinguish Ř from R, e.g. **hořký** 'bitter' but **horký** 'hot', **řvát** 'to roar' but **rvát** 'to tear' (these two words are monosyllabic).

2.2.2 | Consonant clusters

Czech is a language with many consonant-vowel-consonant-vowel sequences and some familiar consonant clusters which should not cause an English speaker any difficulties, e.g.

máme, duby, matka, ostrý

But it does present some clusters which are unfamiliar, especially certain combinations of consonants in word-initial position:

mnoho, hluboký, kniha, psi, chci, chtěl

čtvrt, čtyři, vždyť, vždycky

Initial **J** occurs in spelling before **s**, **d** and **m** in words such as:

jsem 'I am', **jsi** 'you are', **jste** 'you *plural* are', **jdu** 'I go', **jde** 's/he goes', **jmenovat** 'to name'

In careful pronunciation a brief **J** sound may be uttered, not constituting its own syllable, but in ordinary speech this **J** is usually silent. However, it *is* pronounced when these words are negative, with the added negative prefix **ne-**:

nejsem, nejsi, nejste, nejdu, nejde, nejmenovat 'I am not' etc.

In ordinary speech these words, when positive, regularly turn into [sem], [si], [ste], [de] and [menovat]. Beginners can imitate this without sounding sloppy.

In words like **dnes** or **ledna** the D is also not fully articulated.

In words like **ingot** the **N** is pronounced, as in English, like an English ng sound, followed by **G**. Note that a final **G** is pronounced 'k' (with devoicing) in words like **gong** 'gong'.

2.2.3 | Hard and ambivalent consonants

Most 'non-soft' consonants (i.e. those which are not listed above as 'soft') are traditionally labelled 'hard' (**tvrdé**).

Exceptions are the so-called 'ambivalent' consonants (**obojetné souhlásky**), which are **b, p, m, v, f** (the labials, formed with the lips) and **l, s, z**.

These 'ambivalent' consonants only need to be distinguished from the other 'non-soft' consonants for certain grammar and spelling reasons.

2.3 Soft *I* versus hard Y

After soft consonants the 'i' vowel is normally spelt with the letter **i**, called 'soft i' (**měkké i**), e.g. **žil** 'he lived'.

The letter **y**, 'hard y' (**tvrdé y**), is pronounced the same, but only follows 'hard' consonants (or occasionally **c**, e.g. **cynický** 'cynical').

'Ambivalent' (**obojetné**) consonants **b, p, m, v, f** and **l, s, z** are followed by either letter **i** or letter **y**.

Certain words like this are differentiated only by their spelling, not by their pronunciation, e.g. **byl** means 'he was', but **bil** means 'he beat'.

2.4 Consonants before Ě and I/Í

Letter sequences **bě, pě, vě, fě** are pronounced as if they were spelt **bje, pje, vje, fje**. Compare the standard English sounds in 'beauty', 'pure', 'view' and 'few':

běhat, pět, věc, žirafě

The sequence **mě** is usually pronounced **mně** (some speakers say **mje**):

mě (pronounced the same as **mně**), **měsíc, mámě**

The letter Ě also indicates that preceding **d, t** or **n** is to be pronounced **ď, ť, ň**. The vowel itself is simply pronounced like an ordinary Czech E:

dělat, tělo, Němec, vidět pronounced [ďelat], [ťelo], [ňemec], [viďet]

Other consonants are never followed by **ě**, but only by the letter **e**.

Before the 'soft' vowel **i/í** the letters **d, t, n** are also regularly pronounced 'soft', as **ď, ť, ň**.

vidím [viďím], **lidi** [liďi], **rádi** [ráďi]

děti [ďeťi], **tisíc** [ťisíc]

nic [ňic], **oni** [oňi]

Notice what happens to the spelling when different endings are used with words or roots ending in one of these three soft consonants:

loď 'boat', *but* **na lodi** [loďi] 'on a boat', **lodě** 'boats'

vidět 'to see', *but* **vidím** 'I see'

After ordinary **d, t, n** Czech habitually spells a 'hard' **y/ý**. There are therefore sound differences between:

ti kamarádi (soft **ť** and **ď**) and **ty kamarády** (ordinary **t** and **d**)

ti páni (soft **ť** and **ň**) and **ty pány** (ordinary **t** and **n**)

ti studenti (soft **ť** twice) and **ty studenty** (ordinary **t**)

Within foreign loanwords however the rule fails to apply, to avoid re-spelling. So you pronounce a 'hard' **t, d** and **n** in foreign words such as:

diplomat 'diplomat', **politika** 'politics', **nikotin** 'nicotine'

2.5 Voicing and devoicing

This section deals with some details concerning pairs of related consonants and how they are pronounced in particular positions.

In the following pairs the first consonant is normally 'voiced' (produced with an onset of humming vocal cords), the second is its 'voiceless' pair:

b – p	v – f
d – t	ď – ť
g – k	h – ch
z – s	ž – š
dz – c	dž – č

When any of these paired consonants are immediately next to one another, they share the same voice quality, 'voiceless' or 'voiced', regardless of the spelling. The quality takes its cue from the second consonant in the sequence, if there are two (and the last one, if there are more).

Typically, one consonant becomes 'voiceless' to match the next:

včera pronounced [fčera], **těžký** [ťeškí], **lehký** [lechkí], **sladký** [slatkí], **Zuzka** [Zuska]

But sometimes one becomes 'voiced' to match the next:

kde pronounced [gde], **kdo** [gdo], **prosba** [prozba], **leckdo** [ledzgdo]

However, voiced **v** has no effect on preceding consonants:

svůj, svoje, tvůj, tvoje

And words with the group **sh** are most often pronounced [sch] (however, this may be [zh] in Moravia):

na shledanou [naschledanou] 'goodbye'

The 'voiced' members of the list also typically 'devoice' when they come at the end of a word, before a pause:

hrad pronounced [hrat], **sníh** [sňích], **už** [uš], **krev** [kref]

Prepositions, like **v** 'in', **s** 'with', **do** 'into', are pronounced together with the next word. If they contain a vowel, they usually take the stress away from the following word:

v Praze [fpraze] 'in Prague', **z Prahy** [sprahy] 'from Prague'

do Prahy [doprahy] 'to/into Prague'

When a word starts with a vowel, there is in fact a slight glottal stop [ʔ] before the initial vowel. This still applies when the word is preceded by the devoiced consonant of a preposition, especially in careful standard pronunciation:

v Olomouci [fʔolomouci] 'in Olomouc'
but sometimes [volomouci]

2.6   Intonation – *intonace*

Learners will find it easiest to acquire intonation patterns by listening to the language as spoken by native speakers, and there are also regional variants.

However, a few extremely basic points may help, and you might try asking a native speaker to perform the examples below, along with some other similar sentences.

Statements have a basically *falling* (**klesavá**) intonation, preceded by a possible short rise on an emphasised word near the end. Notice also how Czech sentences like to start with known information and put key words of fresh information later. English relies on the intonation more fully for supplying any required emphasis, while Czech is able to adjust the word order with greater freedom:

Petr je tady. Je tady Petr.   Petr is here.

Petr je <u>tady</u>. Je tady <u>Petr</u>.   Petr is <u>here</u>. <u>Petr</u> is here.

Questions opening with *question words* have a similar *falling* pattern to plain statements, again with a short rise on a key word near the end. The question word itself makes it clear that this is a question, so no special pattern is required:

Kde je <u>Petr</u>?   Where is <u>Petr</u>?

An exclamation will produce a greater rise on a key word near the end:

Petr je <u>tady</u>! Je tady <u>Petr</u>!   Petr is <u>here</u>! <u>Petr</u> is here!

Questions without a question word will have either a type of *rising* (**stoupavá**) intonation, or, rather more distinctively (especially in Prague and Bohemia), a characteristic *low-to-high rising* and then *falling* (**stoupavě klesavá**) pattern or cadence across the final key word or phrase:

Je tady <u>Petr</u>? Je Petr <u>tady</u>?/   Is <u>Petr</u> here? Is Petr <u>here</u>?
Petr je tady?

The question intonation patterns indicate incompleteness – the reply should complete the whole by supplying the requested answer.

Similarly, *non-final clauses* in a sentence will also have a (less prominent) form of *rising* intonation (e.g. preceding a comma which marks a pause), likewise indicating incompleteness:

Petr je tady, ale Jana je doma.   Petr is here, but Jana is at home.

2.7   The alphabet

Alphabetical order in Czech is much the same as in English, but note that:

* **ch** comes after **h** in the dictionary (e.g. **duch** *after* **duha**)

* **č, ř, š, ž** also count as separate letters (after **c, r, s, z**)

Other letters (**d'**, **ň**, **á** etc.) are NOT treated separately. The position of **ch** after **h** is the difference most likely to throw new learners.

Letters may be read out as follows, e.g. when pronouncing abbreviations or spelling out a word:

a [á], **b** [bé], **c** [cé], **č** [čé], **d** [dé], **d'** [d'é], **e** [é], **f** [ef], **g** [gé], **h** [há], **ch** [chá], **i** [í] = **měkké** [í], **j** [jé], **k** [ká], **l** [el], **m** [em],

n [en], **ň** [eň], **o** [ó], **p** [pé], **q** [kvé], **r** [er], **ř** [eř], **s** [es], **š** [eš], **t** [té], **t'** [t'é], **u** [ú], **v** [vé], **w** = **dvojité** [vé], **x** [iks], **y** = **tvrdé** [ý]/**ypsilon**, **z** [zet], **ž** [žet].

OSN = [ó-es-en], = **Organizace spojených národů**, the United Nations

ČKD = [čé-ká-dé] = **Českomoravská-Kolben-Daněk**, name of a large firm making rolling stock, trams etc.

2.8   Capital letters

Czech uses fewer capital letters than English, especially in names for places, institutions etc. consisting of more than one word.

Often only the first word is capitalised, e.g.

Žitná ulice – Žitná Street

Ministerstvo školství – the Ministry of Education

Pražský hrad – Prague Castle

Staroměstská radnice – the Old Town Hall

Karlův most – the Charles Bridge

Karlova univerzita – the Charles University

Tichý oceán – the Pacific Ocean

Divoký západ – the Wild West

Středozemní moře – the Mediterranean Sea

However, more than one word is regularly capitalised in names of
towns, quarters of towns, and cities, continents, and countries:

Karlovy Vary – Carlsbad

Nové Město – the New Town

Malá Strana – the Lesser Town

Jižní Amerika – South America

Nový Zéland – New Zealand

Unless (!) they contain a general word for state, republic, kingdom etc.:

Spojené státy americké – the United States of America

Česká republika – the Czech Republic

Similarly, when a place name begins with a generic term for a location,
this first word is not capitalised:

mys Dobré naděje – the Cape of Good Hope

ulice Karolíny Světlé – Karolína Světlá Street

With names of houses, restaurants, pubs, streets etc. a preposition which
is part of the name is capitalised if preceded in a sentence by the word
for house etc., but otherwise not.

Such names themselves also now officially have capital letters, as
recommended usage, on the first following word, even if this is not a
proper name. Formerly (before the issuing of this recommendation for
schools in 1993) the following word had either, depending on the name's
origin. City maps still often show the older, more difficult usage:

ulice Na Příkopě – or, as formerly, **Na příkopě** – street name

restaurace U Tří koček – or, as formerly, **U tří koček** – the
Three Cats Restaurant, called 'At the Three Cats'

Seděli jsme u Tří koček. – We sat in the Three Cats

Nowadays **Vánoce** 'Christmas' and **Velikonoce** 'Easter' are capitalised
– until quite recently they were not.

2.9 Non-standard Czech

Non-standard variants of words and forms will be picked out with
asterisks throughout this grammar. Those cited will mainly reflect the
relaxed, informal everyday usage of Prague and Bohemia. Foreigners
using these features may expect sometimes to attract criticism – even
from Czechs who habitually speak like this themselves, or else from
educated Moravians, who sometimes pride themselves on speaking a
more standard variety of Czech than their Prague counterparts (while
also having their own regional dialects).

Learners are advised to be a little cautious about using non-standard
forms until they are competent enough to be able to adapt to the for-
mality or informality of the situation in which they are speaking.

(a) Change of Ý to EJ

In non-standard usage the vowel represented in standard spelling by
long Ý is sometimes altered to EJ. This feature is particularly common
and prominent in the endings of adjectives (see sections 4.1.1, 4.3.3
etc.), but also occurs in other common words. In the wrong context
this usage may come across as vulgar:

dobrý – *dobrej 'good' (masculine singular)

být – *bejt 'to be'

mýt – *mejt 'to wash'

výlet – *vejlet 'excursion, trip'

EJ also occurs sometimes in place of standard Í after C, S, Z:

cítit – *cejtit 'to feel'

sít – *sejt 'to sow'

zítra – *zejtra 'tomorrow'

Also, more exceptionally, lít – *lejt 'to pour'.

(b) Change of É to Ý/Í

Similarly, the vowel represented in standard spelling by É is sometimes
altered to Ý in everyday colloquial usage (sometimes spelt Í in the roots
of words). Again, this is particularly common in the endings of adjectives, e.g.

dobré becomes *dobrý 'good' (neuter sg., feminine pl. etc.)

mléko – *mlíko 'milk'

polévka – *polívka 'soup'

In the case of the last two nouns the standard forms tend to sound a bit stiff and over-formal in everyday situations.

This change to **Ý/Í** is less likely to be perceived as vulgar by speakers than the change to **EJ** above, doubtless because the results stand out less contrastively.

(c)   Shortened [i] vowel

Present tense verb forms ending in -**ím** and adjective case forms ending in -**ým**, -**ím** commonly have a shortened [i] vowel:

> **vím** – **vim** 'I know', **musím** – **musim** 'I must', **malým** – **malym** 'small', similarly **prosím** – **prosim** 'please' (lit. 'I ask, request')

(d)   Initial **VO-** for **O-**

Everyday words with initial **O-** are often pronounced **VO-** (a so-called prothetic **v-**). This usage, though common, is often perceived and criticised as vulgar, and should basically be avoided in more formal contexts:

> **on, ona, oni** – **von, *vona, *voni** 'he, she, they'
>
> **okno** – **vokno** 'window'
>
> **otevřít** – **votevřít** 'to open'
>
> **oba, obě** – **voba, *vobě** 'both'

This usage does not extend to more formal vocabulary, on the whole, e.g. not to **organizace** 'organisation', or even **otec** 'father' (informal usage is **táta, tatínek** 'Dad').

(e)   **OU-** for initial **Ú-**

Certain words with initial **Ú-** retain occasional colloquial variants with initial **OU-**, though this feature is much less frequent than it was in the nineteenth century, e.g.

> **úhoř** – **ouhoř** 'eel'
>
> **úřady** – **ouřady** 'offices, bureaucracy'

(f)   Instrumental plural -**ama** etc.

Another prominent non-standard usage is the colloquial instrumental plural of nouns, ending in -**ama**, -**ema**, -**ma** (see section 3.4.8 etc.). Adjectives and pronouns have non-standard endings here also, e.g.

s *těma *malejma *dětma 'with those small children' – standard Czech has: **s těmi malými dětmi**.

Other non-standard features are pointed out elsewhere throughout the book.

Chapter 3

Nouns – podstatná jména

We may like to think of a noun (**podstatné jméno, substantivum**) as basically a word for a living being or thing, including places, e.g. 'boy, dog, Charles, Lucinda, table, house, London'.

However, nouns are also words for processes, qualities, abstract ideas and the like, which we treat (in language, at least) as if they *were* 'things', e.g. 'love, levitation, playfulness, courage, existence'.

3.1   Gender – *rod*

Czech nouns have a feature of grammar (shared with other European languages, such as German, French and Latin) which we call *gender*. Grammatical gender does partly agree with our English idea of natural gender – men, boys and bulls are 'masculine'; women, girls and milk-bearing cows are 'feminine' – but in Czech, grammatical gender applies to inanimate and abstract nouns as well, and these are *not* by any means all 'neuter'.

Czech nouns are divided into three genders, masculine, feminine and neuter (**mužský rod, ženský rod, střední rod**), but in some situations we have to distinguish between masculine animates (**mužský rod životný**) and masculine inanimates (**mužský rod neživotný**).

Why is this gender classification so important?

One reason is that when describing a noun with an adjective or adding a word such as 'that' to it, you need to know a noun's gender, because the ending of the adjective is affected by it, e.g.:

ten velký hrad	'that large castle'	basic phrase using the masculine noun **hrad**
ta velká řeka	'that large river'	basic phrase using the feminine noun **řeka**
to velké město	'that large town'	basic phrase using neuter noun **město**

In addition, categorising Czech nouns by gender helps to identify what endings they will use in different grammatical cases (for what 'cases' are, see below).

Very basic family terms show the general animate pattern, with feminines ending in -a, e.g.

> masculine: **otec** 'father', **syn** 'son', **bratr** 'brother', **dědeček** 'grandfather', **vnuk** 'grandson'

> feminine: **matka** 'mother', **dcera** 'daughter', **sestra** 'sister', **babička** 'grandmother', **vnučka** 'grand-daughter' – plus **rodina** 'family'

3.1.1 | Rules for gender

Nouns for male persons are normally masculine, e.g. **muž** 'man', **kluk** 'boy'. Nouns for female persons are normally feminine, e.g. **žena** 'woman', **dívka** 'girl'.

Czech habitually distinguishes gender when labelling people by nationality, occupation etc., where English does not necessarily do so (with exceptions for occupations like 'actor' and 'actress'), e.g.

> masculine: **Angličan** 'Englishman', **Čech** 'a Czech man', **překladatel** 'translator'

> feminine: **Angličanka** 'Englishwoman', **Češka** 'a Czech woman', **překladatelka** 'translator'

With some words for animals the gender is clearly specified for us by the meaning, e.g. **býk** 'bull'. But assignation to gender is not as easy where we do not habitually identify the actual sex, e.g. **myš** 'mouse', which happens to be feminine.

Words for the young of animals are usually neuter, e.g. **štěně** 'puppy', **kotě** 'kitten'. This even includes **děvče**, one of the more usual words for 'girl' (alongside **dívka**, which is feminine).

For other kinds of nouns you need to learn the gender as you go along. Luckily, most of the time there are some quite good rules about how to decide, or guess, this, according to how the noun ends.

Masculine animate nouns for human beings are usually deducible from the meaning, although it is also useful to know that their feminine equivalents will usually end in either -ka or -(k)yně.

Masculine animate nouns may end in various ways, usually in a consonant, also in -a, much less often -e or even -o, e.g.

> **pán** 'master, gentleman', **kluk** 'boy', **bratr** 'brother', **kamarád** 'friend' (compare **kamarádka** 'female friend'), **student** 'student' (**studentka** 'female student'), **muž** 'man', **otec** 'father', **učitel**

'teacher' (**učitelka** 'female teacher'), **předseda** 'chairman' (**předsedkyně** 'chairwoman'), **kolega** 'colleague' (**kolegyně** 'female colleague'), **soudce** 'judge' (**soudkyně** 'female judge'), **Ivo** 'the personal name Ivo'.

A pretty reliable rule of thumb for determining the gender of nouns *other than* human masculine animates, is as follows:

Masculine	Most nouns ending in a consonant, e.g. **hrad** 'castle', **kufr** 'suitcase', **vlak** 'train', **stroj** 'machine', **čaj** 'tea'
	[*Some* ending in a 'soft' or 'ambivalent' consonant are *feminine*, e.g. **píseň** 'song', **tramvaj** 'tram'
Feminine	Most nouns ending in **-a**, **-e** or the suffix **-ost** meaning '-ness', e.g. **voda** 'water', **lekce** 'lesson', **radost** 'joy, happiness'
	[A *few* ending in **-e** are *neuter*, e.g. **moře** 'sea', **pole** 'field'
Neuter	Most nouns ending in **-o** or **-í**, e.g. **město** 'town', **auto** 'car', **stavení** 'building', **náměstí** 'square'

Nevertheless, the gender of some nouns still has to be learnt individually.

A few animate nouns which refer to either males or females are grammatically feminine, e.g. **osoba** 'person, character' (and grammatical 'person') and **stráž -e** 'guard'.

3.2   The plural – *množné číslo*

Most nouns have forms for both the singular (**singulár, jednotné číslo**) and the plural (**plurál, množné číslo**).

The plurals of nouns will be covered in proper detail later in this chapter. This is just an overview:

The commonest basic (nominative) plural ending for masculine inanimate and feminine nouns is **-y**, e.g. **rohlík – rohlíky** 'rolls', **řeka – řeky** 'rivers'.

But masculine animate nouns typically have plural **-i**, e.g. **kamarád – kamarádi** [-ďi] 'friends'. (Some have plural **-ové** or **-é**, e.g. **pánové** 'men, gentlemen', **učitelé** 'teachers'.)

Neuter nouns in **-o** have plural **-a,** e.g. **pivo – piva** 'beers'.

Nouns (other than masc. anim.) ending in a 'soft' consonant or -e mostly have plural **-e,** e.g. **tramvaj – tramvaje** 'trams, tramcars', **ulice – ulice** 'streets', **večeře – večeře** 'suppers' (i.e. sometimes basic plural = basic singular).

Some nouns are 'plural-only', often as in English, e.g. **kalhoty** 'trousers', **nůžky** 'scissors'. Also (unlike English): **noviny** 'newspaper', **záda** 'back'.

3.3 Cases – *pády*

Czech nouns change their endings for various purposes, not just for the plural, producing what are called different 'cases'. To go through the various cases of a noun is called to 'decline' it, and the resulting table is a 'declension'.

Cases are initially one of the hardest things for English speakers to master in the language. There are seven different cases in Czech, called *nominative, accusative, genitive, dative, locative, instrumental* and *vocative.* Cases have both singular and plural forms.

Here is a summary of what each case (**pád**) is used for, with the names **Jana** and **David** used as typical feminine and masculine examples.

The *nominative,* or basic (dictionary, default) form of a Czech noun, is used for the subject, agent, doer of a verb.

Jan|a běží.	**David běží.**	Jana/David runs.
Jan|a je chytrá.	**David je chytrý.**	Jana/David is clever.

The *accusative* is primarily used for the object of a verb (the recipient of its action or state). It is also used after certain prepositions, e.g. **pro** 'for'.

Hledám Jan|u.	**Hledám David|a.**	I am looking for Jana/ David. = I am seeking Jana/David.
Dopis pro Jan|u.	**Dopis pro David|a.**	A letter for Jana/David.

The *genitive* primarily means the same as English 'of'. It also follows many prepositions, including basic ones such as **do** 'into', **z/ze** 'out of', **od** 'from (a person)'.

Fotografie Jan|y.	**Fotografie David|a.**	A photograph of Jana/ David.
Dopis od Jan|y.	**Dopis od David|a.**	A letter from Jana/David.

The *dative* primarily means 'to/for'. It also follows a few prepositions, especially **k/ke** 'towards'.

Napsal Jan|ě dopis.	**Napsal David|ovi dopis.**	He wrote a letter to Jana/David. = He wrote Jana/David a letter.
Jde k Jan|ě.	**Jde k David|ovi.**	S/he goes towards Jana/David.

SAME ENDINGS

The *locative* often denotes a fixed location, and is used only after prepositions. It follows prepositions such as **v/ve** 'in', **na** 'on', **o** 'about (a theme, subject)'. (The dative and locative singular endings are often the same.)

Dopis o Jan|ě.	**Dopis o David|ovi.**	A letter about Jana/David.

The *instrumental* means 'by/with (a means or instrument)'. It also follows prepositions **s/se** 'with (= accompanied by)' and prepositions of relative location such as **za** 'behind/beyond', **před** 'in front of'.

Jde tam s Jan|ou.	**Jde tam s David|em.**	S/he is going there with Jana/David.

Lastly, the *vocative* is used for addressing or calling people, e.g. **Jano!** Jana! **Adame!** 'Adam!'. (There is no distinct vocative in the plural – just use the nominative plural form for this.)

Jan|o! Pojd' sem!	**David|e! Pojd' sem!**	Jana/David! Come here!

See Chapter 8 on cases and prepositions for more details on usage.

3.4 Hard and soft declensions

In order to assign the correct case endings to a noun it is necessary to work with the correct declension type.

The main types may be classified as belonging either to a 'hard' pattern (**tvrdý vzor**) or a 'soft' pattern (**měkký vzor**). The 'soft' types in particular share some strong similarities.

Declension type depends on the consonant (and vowel) ending:

'Hard' consonants are **d, t, g, h, k, n, r.** 'Ambivalent' labials **b, p, m, v,** liquid **l,** and sibilants **s, z** mostly count as 'hard', but not always (examples below).

'Soft' consonants are **č, ď, ň, ř, š, ť, ž** (diacritic letters), **c** and **j** (but **c** is occasionally 'hard').

Hard nouns regularly end in a 'hard' or 'ambivalent' consonant, **-a,** or **-o.**

Soft nouns regularly end in a 'soft' consonant, **-e, -ost** or **-í.**

3.4.1 | The genitive as a marker of declension

Dictionaries and glossaries habitually give the genitive sg., along with the gender, to mark the declension type, e.g. **žen|a -y** f. 'woman, wife'.
 Typical *hard* types have genitive sg. **-a** (masculine animate or neuter), **-u** (masculine inanimate) or **-y** (feminine).
 The most typical *soft* types have genitive sg. **-e.**

3.4.2 | Fleeting -E-

Many nouns ending in a consonant drop a final **-e-** syllable when case endings are added.
 In Czech this is called **pohybné -e-.** Fleeting **-e-** is particularly regular with suffixes **-ek, -ec** and (mostly feminine) **-eň.**
 Dictionaries should give the genitive sg., e.g. **dědeček – dědečka** 'grandfather', **Němec – Němce** 'a German', **píseň – písně** 'song', also **Karel – Karla** = 'Charles'.

3.4.3 | Vowel shortening

Sometimes the vowel in the body of a noun undergoes shortening (**krácení**) before any case endings, e.g. **mráz – mrazu** 'frost'. Again, dictionaries should indicate this by giving the genitive sg. Long **ů** shortens to **o**, e.g. **dům – domu** 'house', **stůl – stolu** 'table'. Note also **vítr – větru** 'wind', **sníh – sněhu** 'snow'.

3.4.4 *Summary of hard and soft types*

In these tables of declension types the most essential ones are in block capitals. The nouns adopted as models are often used in Czech textbooks. The genitive sg. is indicated for each type. Further examples of each are given in the next two sections.

Hard types

Masculine Animate	–	type **PÁN -a** 'gentleman, master' (a few ending in -o, e.g. **Iv|o -a**)
	-a	type **předsed|a -y** 'chairman'
Masculine Inanimate	–	type **HRAD -u** 'castle'
Feminine	**-a**	type **ŽEN|A -y** 'woman, wife'
Neuter	**-o**	type **MĚST|O -a** 'town'

Soft types

Masculine Animate	–/-e	type **MUŽ -e** 'man', type **soudc|e -e** 'judge'
Masculine Inanimate	–	type **STROJ -e** 'machine'
Feminine	**-e/–**	types **RŮŽ|E -e** 'rose' and **PÍ|SEŇ -sně** 'song'
	-ost	type **kost -i** 'bone' [some ending in other consonants]
Neuter	**-e**	type **moř|e -e** 'sea'
		type **kuř|e -ete** 'chicken' (esp. young of animals)
	-í	type **staven|í -í** 'building'

3.4.5 *Identifying hard types*

Masculine animate:

type **PÁN -a** 'master'	Most masculine animates ending in 'non-soft' consonants, e.g. **kluk** 'boy', **bratr** 'brother', **student** 'student', **býk** 'bull'
	[a few ending in -o, e.g. the name **Ivo**]

type **předsed|a -y** 'chairman'	Masculine animates ending in **-a**, e.g. **kolega** 'colleague', **komunista** 'a communist', **táta** 'dad', and many familiar forms of personal names, e.g. **Tonda** = 'Tony'

Masculine inanimate:

type **HRAD -u** 'castle'	Most inanimates ending in 'non-soft' consonants, e.g. **strom** 'tree', **papír** 'paper', **koncert** 'concert'.
	Some have gen. sg. **-a**, e.g. **les -a** forest.

Feminine:

type **ŽEN|A -y** 'woman'	Most nouns ending in **-a**, e.g. **řeka** 'river', **hora** 'mountain', **sestra** 'sister', **škola** 'school'

Neuter:

type **MĚST|O -a** 'town'	Most nouns ending in **-o**, e.g. **auto** 'car', **okno** 'window'

3.4.6 Identifying soft types

Masculine animate:

type **MUŽ -e** 'man'	Masculine animates ending in 'soft' consonants (**c, č, d', j, ň, ř, š, t', ž**), e.g. **otec – otce** 'father', **novinář -e** 'journalist'
	Those ending in the suffix **-tel**, e.g. **učitel -e** 'teacher', **překladatel -e** 'translator'
	A few others ending in 'ambivalent' consonants, e.g. **král -e** 'king'
	Proper names ending in **-s, -x, -z**, e.g. **Francouz -e** 'Frenchman', **Alois -e, Klaus -e, Marx -e**
type **SOUDC|E -e** 'judge'	A few masculine animates ending in **-e**, e.g. **průvodce** 'guide', **správce** 'caretaker', **vůdce** 'leader'

Masculine inanimate:

type **STROJ -e** 'machine'	Masculine inanimates ending in 'soft' consonants, e.g. **kon|ec -nce** 'end', **klíč -e** 'key', **stroj -e** 'machine', **čaj -e** 'tea', **nůž – nože** 'knife'
	A few ending in 'ambivalent' consonants, e.g. **py|tel -tle** 'sack', **zřetel -e** 'viewpoint'

Feminine:

type **RŮŽ|E -e** 'rose'	Most nouns ending in **-e**, e.g. **ulice** 'street', **duše** 'soul', **země** 'earth, land', **přítelkyně** 'female friend'
type **PÍ|SEŇ -sně** 'song'	Feminine nouns ending in 'soft' consonants, e.g. **tramvaj -e** 'tram', **skří|ň -ně** 'cupboard', **věž -e** 'tower'
	A few ending in 'ambivalent' consonants, e.g. **postel -e** 'bed', including a group ending in **-ev**, e.g. **lá|hev -hve** 'bottle', **mr|kev -kve** 'carrot'
type **KOST -i** 'bone'	Feminine nouns ending in the suffix **-ost**, e.g. **radost -i** 'joy, gladness'
	A few others, e.g. **část -i** 'part', **moc -i** 'power', **noc -i** 'night', **věc -i** 'thing', **řeč -i** 'speech', **sůl – soli** 'salt', **myš -i** 'mouse'

Neuter:

type **MOŘ|E -e** 'sea'	A few neuters ending in **-e**, e.g. **pole** 'field', **srdce** 'heart'
	Nouns ending in **-iště**, e.g. **letiště** 'airport'
type **KUŘ|E -ete** 'chicken'	Nouns for the young of animals ending in **-e**, e.g. **kotě** 'kitten', **štěně** 'puppy', also **děvče** 'girl'
	A few others ending in **-e**, e.g. **rajče** 'tomato'

type **STAVEN|Í -í** 'building'   Most nouns ending in **-í**, e.g. **náměstí**
'square', **překvapení** 'surprise',
vzdělání 'education'

3.4.7 | *Case numbering*

In Czech schools cases are habitually named by number in a particular
order. They also have Czech names similar to ours:

první pád '1st case'   = **nominativ** nominative   nom.

druhý pád '2nd case'   = **genitiv** genitive   gen.

třetí pád '3rd case'   = **dativ** dative   dat.

čtvrtý pád '4th case'   = **akuzativ** accusative   acc.

pátý pád '5th case'   = **vokativ** vocative   voc.

šestý pád '6th case'   = **lokál** locative   loc.

sedmý pád '7th case'   = **instrumentál** instrumental   ins.

The order of cases adopted in this grammar is different. One reason is
to harmonise better with English learning habits for other inflected
languages such as Russian and Latin. But this order also keeps together
two pairs of cases which are often identical: (a) nominative and accusative, (b) dative and locative sg.

nom., acc., gen., dat., loc., ins., voc.

Only acc. and voc. are 'out of order', from the traditional Czech standpoint.

The Czech numbers have been added to the tables, for reference
purposes.

Native speakers of course do not recite tables in order to speak their
own language. They go directly to the forms required.

3.4.8 | *Declension of hard types – summary*

The table summarises the case forms of the main hard types. Each will
be considered in more detail further below. Only a few variants have
been indicated here, for clarity's sake.

Where accusative = nominative, the accusative form is not shown.

The order masculine, feminine, neuter is traditional, although the
masculine and neuter types have various case endings in common.

(Masculine animate type **předseda** will be treated separately below.)

25

Sg.	Masc. Anim.	Masc. Inan.	Fem.	Neut.
I nom.	**PÁN**	**HRAD**	**ŽENA**	**MĚSTO**
4 acc.	**PÁNA** = gen.		**ŽENU**	
2 gen.	pána	hradu	ženy	města
3 dat.	pánovi	hradu	ženě	městu
6 loc.	(o) pánovi	(o) hradě, -u	(o) ženě	(o) městě, -u
7 ins.	pánem	hradem	ženou	městem
5 voc.	pane!	hrade!	ženo!	= nom.
Pl.				
I nom.	**PÁN|I, -ové**	**HRADY**	**ŽENY**	**MĚSTA**
4 acc.	**PÁNY**			
2 gen.	pánů	hradů	žen	měst
3 dat.	pánům	hradům	ženám	městům
6 loc.	(o) pánech	(o) hradech	(o) ženách	(o) městech
7 ins.	pán|y, *-ama	hrad|y, *-ama	žen|ami, *-ama	měst|y, *-ama

3.4.9 | Declension of soft types – summary

The main soft-stem types have much in common: genitive sg. in -e, dative/locative sg. -i, etc. The less essential type **moře** is also very similar.

Other types are treated separately below.

Sg.	Masc. Anim.	Masc. Inan.	Fem. -e	Fem.	Neut.
1 nom.	**MUŽ**	**STROJ**	**RŮŽE**	**PÍSEŇ**	**moře**
4 acc.	**MUŽE** = gen.		**RŮŽI**		
2 gen.	**muže**	**stroje**	**růže**	**písně**	**moře**
3 dat.	**muž|i, -ovi**	**stroji**	**růži**	**písni**	**moři**
6 loc.	**(o) muž|i, -ovi**	**(o) stroji**	**(o) růži**	**(o) písni**	**(o) moři**
7 ins.	**mužem**	**strojem**	**růží**	**písní**	**mořem**
5 voc.	**muži!**	**stroji!**	= nom.	**písni!**	= nom.
Pl.					
1 nom.	**MUŽ|I, -ové**	**STROJE**	**RŮŽE**	**PÍSNĚ**	**moře**
4 acc.	**MUŽE**				
2 gen.	**mužů**	**strojů**	**růží, ulic**	**písní**	**moří, letišť**
3 dat.	**mužům**	**strojům**	**růžím**	**písním**	**mořím**
6 loc.	**(o) mužích**	**(o) strojích**	**(o) růžích**	**(o) písních**	**(o) mořích**
7 ins.	**muž|i, *-ema**	**stroj|i, *-ema**	**růž|emi, *-ema**	**písn|ěmi, *-ěma**	**moř|i, *-ema**

3.4.10 Dative/locative ending -Ě or -E

The dative/locative singular ending -ě or sometimes -e is standard with feminine nouns type **žena**. The same ending also occurs in the locative *only* with certain common masculine inanimates type **hrad** and neuters type **město**.

The effect of this case ending on preceding consonants needs to be studied carefully.

Labials (**b, p, f, m, v**) and dentals (**d, t, n**) simply change their pronunciation as indicated by the spelling form -ě:

Ostrava – v Ostravě 'in Ostrava', **mapa – na mapě** 'on the map', **ryba – o rybě** 'about the fish', **voda – ve vodě** 'in the water', **máma – mámě** 'to Mum', **kavárna – v kavárně** 'in the café'.

Consonants r and the so-called 'velars' alter as follows, with the spelling -e:

-ra → -ře	**sestra – sestře** 'to (my) sister', **klášter – v klášteře** 'in a monastery'
-ka → -ce	**řeka – v řece** 'in the river', **rok – v roce** 'in the year'
-ga, -ha → -ze	**Olga – Olze** 'to Olga', **Praha – v Praze** 'in Prague'
-cha → -še	**střecha – na střeše** 'on the roof'

After l, s, z, and rarely soft consonants č, j, ř, š, ž, this ending is also spelt -e, e.g. škola – ve škole 'in school', les – v lese in the forest.

3.5   Masculine types

3.5.1 │ *Masculine type pán*

The commonest type of masculine animate noun ends in a hard consonant, e.g. **pán** 'master, man, gentleman'.

	Sg.	Pl.
1 nom.	**pán**	**páni, pánové**
4 acc.	**pána** = gen.	**pány**
2 gen.	**pána**	**pánů**
3 dat.	**pánovi**	**pánům**
6 loc.	**(o) pánovi**	**(o) pánech**
7 ins.	**pánem**	**pán|y** (*-ama)
5 voc.	**pane! kluku!**	

Note the irregular shortening in vocative **pane!** The short-vowel form **pan** is otherwise used for 'Mr', e.g. **pan Novotný** 'Mr Novotný'.

Remember that the accusative singular of masculine animate nouns is regularly the same as the genitive.

The dative/locative regularly ends in **-ovi**, but when two (or more) are used in a series, all except the last normally use the shorter ending **-u**:

pan Novák – panu Novákovi to/for Mr Novák

Adam Novák – o Adamu Novákovi about Adam Novák

The vocative ending **-u!** is used after velars **k, g, h, ch**, e.g. **kluk – kluku!** 'boy!' (note also **synu!** 'son!'). The consonant **r** becomes **ř** before vocative **-e!** if it follows a consonant, e.g. **Petr – Petře!**, but *not* after a vowel: **profesor – pane profesore!** 'Professor!' In the minor sub-type **Iv|o -a**, vocative = nominative.

The nominative plural sometimes ends in **-ové** or **-é**, instead of **-i**, see below.

Only masculine *animate* nouns distinguish between nominative and accusative in the plural (and the accusative plural form is just like an *inanimate* nominative):

To jsou studenti – Češi, Irové a Angličané. These are students – Czechs, Irish and English.

Učím studenty – Čechy, Iry a Angličany. I teach students – Czechs, Irish and English.

Nominative plural -i:

The basic nominative plural ending for this type is **-i**. Note how this ending changes the pronunciation of preceding **d, t, n** to **ď', ť', ň**:

To je kamarád – To jsou kamarádi [-ďi]. That's a friend – Those are friends.

To je student – To jsou studenti [-ťi]. That's a student – Those are students.

Before **-i** you also have to make changes to velars **k, h, ch** and to **r**:

k>c **kluk – kluci** 'boys'

h>z **vrah – vrazi** 'murderers'

ch>š **Čech – Češi** 'Czechs'

r>ř **doktor – doktoři** 'doctors'

Nominative plural -ové:

The ending **-ové** is typically used for human beings, hence **vůl – vola** 'ox' has the ordinary plural **voli** in the sense of 'oxen' but **vůl – volové** means 'idiot(s)'. As a stylistic variant **-ové** may also add an air of solemnity:

páni for 'masters' has an alternative form pánové 'masters, gentlemen', also generally used in the phrase dámy a pánové 'ladies and gentlemen'.

Those with nominative plural -ové include most nouns ending in g and nouns for human beings ending in ambivalent consonants (b/p, v/f, m, l, sometimes s, z): biolog|ové 'biologists', Arab|ové 'Arabs', ekonom|ové 'economists', filozof|ové, generál|ové, Ital|ové.

Some words for animals have alternative forms here, e.g. motýl|i, less often motýl|ové 'butterflies'.

With nouns ending in -ch (but not hoch – hoši 'boys') the ending -ové is sometimes optional, e.g. Češi/Čech|ové 'Czechs', mniši/mnich|ové 'monks', but only duch|ové 'spirits' and živočich|ové 'animals'.

Plural -ové is sometimes favoured with nouns ending in -ek, -ěk, though both forms occur, but is a bit less frequent with -ik, e.g. předek – předkové/předci 'ancestors', svědek – svědkové/svědci 'witnesses', but more often historik – historici 'historians' and politik – politici 'politicians' (alongside -ové).

Amongst other examples are syn – synové 'sons' and one-syllable nationality nouns such as Brit|ové 'the British', Skot|ové 'Scots', Ir|ové 'Irish', Rus|ové 'Russians', Řek|ové 'Greeks'. Similarly, bůh – bohové 'Gods' (less often bozi), vrah – vrazi/vrahové 'murderers'.

Nominative plural -é:

Some nouns have the nominative plural ending -é, mainly nouns with the suffix -an, but this tends to be replaced in relaxed speech by -i: Američan – Američané (-i) 'Americans', Angličan|é (-i) 'English people', Slovan|é (-i) 'Slavs'.

Other examples are host – hosté (-i) 'guests', soused – sousedé (-i) 'neighbours', Žid – Židé 'Jews' (-i may be treated as insulting), anděl – andělé, manžel – manželé 'married couple' (manželové 'husbands'), Španěl – Španělé 'Spaniards'.

Plural of personal names:

Surnames have a special plural ending -ovi (acc. -ovy) for the family as a group, e.g. Novákovi 'the Nováks', and then Nováků, Novákům etc.

Otherwise personal names use the nom. pl. ending -ové, e.g. Čapkové, Václavové, Bohumilové, Lucemburkové.

Locative plural variants:

Masculine nouns ending in velars k, g, h, ch have loc. pl. -ích, preceded by consonant changes k->c and h/g->z, ch->š: kluk – kluci, o klucích 'about the boys', Čech – Češi, o Češích 'about the Czechs'. In non-standard spoken usage the ending -ách sometimes occurs instead, e.g. o *klukách (not with Češi 'Czechs', however – Čechách is the loc. pl. of Čechy 'Bohemia').

The ending -ech is *not* to be used ever after velars, but it *is* used after r, e.g. **profesoři – o profesorech** 'teachers, professors'.

3.5.2 | Masculine type hrad

Type **hrad** 'castle' represents the commonest type of masculine inanimate noun, ending in a hard consonant.

	Sg.	Pl.
I nom. 4 acc.	**hrad**	**hrady**
2 gen.	**hradu**	**hradů**
3 dat.	**hradu**	**hradům**
6 loc.	**(na) hradě, (o) hradu**	**(o) hradech**
7 ins.	**hradem**	**hrad|y** (*-ama)
5 voc.	**hrade!** etc. (like pán)	

In the language as a whole, the majority of nouns of this type always (or usually) have the loc. sg. ending in -**u**. In addition, most abstract nouns, less basic and more recent nouns conform to this pattern, e.g. **sport – o sportu** 'about sport', **kufr – v kufru** 'in the suitcase', **hotel – v hotelu** 'in the hotel', **klub – v klubu** 'in the club'. Most nouns with a final velar **k, g/h, ch** and **r** also have this ending, e.g. **park – v parku** 'in the park', **taxík – v taxíku** 'in a taxi', **roh – na rohu** 'on the corner'.

However, the alternative locative sg. ending -**e/ě** (with its sound changes detailed in 3.4.10 above) remains standard usage with many basic nouns of this type, especially in common phrases, e.g. **hrad – na hradě** 'in (lit. "on") the castle', **les – v lese** 'in the forest', **most – na mostě** 'on the bridge', **sklep – ve sklepě** 'in the cellar', **stůl – na stole** 'on the table'.

Occasionally this ending even occurs after velars and **r**, e.g. **rok – v roce** 'in the year', **jazyk – v jazyce** 'in the language' (or **v jazyku**, and **na jazyku** for 'on the tongue'), **papír – na papíře/papíru** 'on paper', **kožich – v kožiše/kožichu** 'in a fur coat'.

However, even where locative -**ě/-e** occurs, -**u** is often either possible or equally frequent, especially after **s** and **t**: **byt – v bytě/v bytu** 'in the flat', **dopis – v dopise/v dopisu** 'in the letter', **autobus – v autobuse, v autobusu** 'in the bus'.

There is also a tendency to prefer locative -u after prepositions other than v 'in' and na 'on, at', e.g. na hradě 'at the castle' but more usually o hradu 'about the castle'.

A special group of basic nouns of this type have genitive sg. -a. They include place names (and some other nouns) with the suffixes -ín, -ýn and -ov, e.g. Berlín, Londýn, Smíchov. They generally also have the locative sg. ending -e/ě, e.g. Berlín – do Berlína – v Berlíně, les – lesa – v lese 'forest', svět – světa – na světě 'world', ostrov – ostrova – na ostrově 'island', dvůr – dvora – na dvoře 'yard, court', kostel – kostela – v kostele 'church'. However, the months of the year ending in -en and únor all have genitive -a but locative -u, e.g. leden – ledna 'January', v lednu 'in January', v únoru 'in February'.

In standard usage nouns ending in velars k, g, h, ch have locative pl. -ích, with sound changes, just like animates, e.g. zámek – zámky, na zámcích 'at the chateaux'. However, the feminine ending -ách often replaces this in everyday domestic words or foreign borrowings: kousek – pl. kousky, v kouskách/v kouscích 'in pieces', tepláky – v teplákách 'in a tracksuit', doky – v docích/v dokách 'in the docks'.

Locative pl. -ích also occurs after l, s, z, especially in les – v lesích 'forests' (nearly always), hotel – v hotelích/-ech 'hotels', kostel – v kostelích/-ech 'churches'.

3.5.3 | *Masculine types* muž/soudce *and* stroj

Animate types muž 'man, husband' and soudce 'judge', and inanimate type stroj 'machine' have a majority of endings in common. Type soudce only differs from muž where shown.

	Sg.		Pl.	
1 nom.	muž, soudc|e	stroj	muži, soudci (-ové)	stroje
4 acc.	muže = gen.		muže	
2 gen.	muže	stroje	mužů	strojů
3 dat.	muž|i, -ovi	stroji	mužům	strojům
6 loc.	(o) muž|i, -ovi	(o) stroji	(o) mužích	strojích
7 ins.	mužem	strojem	muž|i (*-ema)	stroj|i (*-ema)
5 voc.	muži! *but* soudce!	stroji!		

Nouns ending in **-ec** have vocative **-če**, e.g. **chlapec – chlapče!** 'boy!'

Animates sometimes replace dative/locative sg. **-i** by **-ovi**, especially names, e.g. **Miloš – (o) Milošovi**, but **(o) Miloši Benešovi** (where **Miloš** is within a series).

Some animates have nominative pl. **-ové**, e.g. **otec – otcové** 'fathers', **král – králové** 'kings', **soudce – soudci** or **soudcové** 'judges', **zpravodaj -ové** 'news reporters'.

Animates ending with the suffix **-tel** have nom. pl. **-é**, e.g. **učitel – učitelé** 'teachers'. Note irregular **přítel** – nominative pl. **přátelé** (!) 'friends', genitive pl. **přátel**, and **obyvatel**, genitive pl. **obyvatel** 'inhabitants'.

3.5.4 | Masculine type **předseda**

Type **předseda** 'chairman' broadly follows feminine type **žena** in the singular (see next section), except for its typically masculine dative/locative **-ovi** (always). The plural follows **pán**, but often with nominative pl. **-ové** or **-é**.

	Sg.	Pl.
1 nom.	**předseda**	**předsedové**
4 acc.	**předsedu**	**předsedy**
2 gen.	**předsedy**	**předsedů**
3 dat.	**předsedovi**	**předsedům**
6 loc.	**(o) předsedovi**	**(o) předsedech**
7 ins.	**předsedou**	**předsed|y** (*-ama)
5 voc.	**předsedo!**	

After a soft consonant the genitive sg. is spelt **-i**, mostly with familiar forms of personal names, e.g. **Péťa – Péti** 'Pete'.

Many have nominative plural **-ové**: **předseda – předsedové** 'chairmen', **kolega – kolegové** 'colleagues'. Others have nominative plural **-é**, especially nouns with the suffix **-ista**, though in fact this tends to be replaced by **-i** in ordinary speech: **turista – turisté** (**-i**) 'tourists', **komunista – komunisté** 'communists' (**-i** may sound disrespectful).

The locative pl. ending **-ech** is regularly replaced by **-ích** after velars **g, h, ch, k**, e.g. **kolegové – o kolezích** 'about colleagues'.

3.6 Feminine types

3.6.1 Feminine type žena

Type **žena** 'woman, wife' includes a very large number of both animate and inanimate feminine nouns ending in **-a**.

	Sg.	Pl.
1 nom.	**žena**	**ženy**
4 acc.	**ženu**	
2 gen.	**ženy**	**žen**
3 dat.	**ženě**	**ženám**
6 loc.	**(o) ženě**	**(o) ženách**
7 ins.	**ženou**	**žen|ami** (*-ama)
5 voc.	**ženo!**	

Note the 'zero' ending (i.e. no ending at all) of the genitive plural, e.g. **ženy – žen** 'women', **koruny – korun** 'of crowns', **jahody – jahod** 'of strawberries'. Occasionally there is vowel shortening with these, as in **mouchy – much** 'of flies', **síly – sil** 'of forces'.

Where a noun with the 'zero' ending would end in two consonants an **-e-** is often inserted between the consonants, **sestry – sester** 'of sisters'. This is particularly regular with nouns ending in a consonant + **-ka: švestky – švestek** 'of plums'. But it does not apply with some 'pronounceable' combinations, such as **-st-** as in **cesta – cest** 'roads, journeys'.

After a soft consonant the genitive sg. (and nominative/accusative pl.) ending is spelt **-i**, for spelling reasons. This mostly occurs with forms of personal names, e.g. **Táňa – Táni, Dáša – Dáši**, but also e.g. **skica** -i 'sketch'.

Dative/locative sg. **-i** also occurs sometimes with nouns of this type after a soft consonant, e.g. **gejša** 'geisha' dative/locative sg. **-i/-e**.

3.6.2 Feminine types růže and píseň

There are only a few differences between types **růže** and **píseň**, so they are taken together here.

	Sg.	Pl.
I nom.	**růže – píseň**	**růže – písně**
4 acc.	**růži** but **píseň**	
2 gen.	**růže – písně**	**růží – písní**
3 dat.	**růži – písni**	**růžím – písním**
6 loc.	**(o) růži – písni**	**(o) růžích – písních**
7 ins.	**růží – písní**	**růž|emi – písn|ěmi** **(*-ěma)**
5 voc.	**růže!** = nom., but **písni!**	

Feminines ending in **-ie**, pronounced [ije], also follow type **duše**, e.g. **Anglie – do Anglie, v Anglii** 'to England, in England'. So do the rarer feminines ending in **-ia**, e.g. **Slavia** [slávija], **do Slavie** (football team).

Feminine nouns ending in **-ice** and (optionally) **-yně** have 'zero' genitive plurals, just like type **žena**: **ulice – ulic** 'streets', **učebnice – učebnic** 'textbooks', **kolegyně – kolegyň** 'female colleagues'. There can be two forms for foreign words ending in **-ice** (**edice – edic** or **edicí** 'edition', similarly **definice** 'definition', **pozice** 'position' etc.). Note also: **chvíle – chvil** 'whiles, moments', **míle – mil** 'miles', **košile – košil** 'shirts', **neděle – neděl** 'weeks', but **nedělí** 'Sundays'.

A group of nouns ending in **-ev** belong here, e.g. **láhev** – genitive **láhve/lahve** 'bottle', **mrkev – mrkve** 'carrot', **církev – církve** 'church (the institution)'. Some end in **-l**, e.g. **postel -e** 'bed'.

3.6.3 | Feminine type **kost**

These regularly end in the suffix **-ost**, meaning '-ness', e.g. **radost** 'joy, gladness'. Some other nouns also belong to this group, which is conventionally listed as type **kost** 'bone'.

	Sg.	Pl.
1 nom.	**kost**	**kosti**
4 acc.		
2 gen.	**kosti**	**kostí**
3 dat.	**kosti**	**kostem**
6 loc.	**(o) kosti**	**(o) kostech**
7 ins.	**kostí**	**kost|mi** (*-ma)
5 voc.	**kosti!**	

The typical genitive/dative/locative singular is the same as the nominat-ive/accusative plural: **kosti** [kost'i] 'of/to a bone' or 'bones'.

Nouns of this type not ending in **-st** often tend to switch at least optionally or partially to type **píseň** endings in the less common plural dative, locative and instrumental cases.

Various at least reasonably common further nouns ending in **-st** de-cline entirely like type **kost**, e.g. **bolest** 'pain', **část** 'part', **čest** – gen. **cti** (!) 'honour', **nenávist** 'hatred' (and **závist** 'envy'), **neřest** 'vice', **oblast** 'area', **pověst** 'tale, rumour, reputation', **propast** 'chasm, abyss', **slast** 'delight, bliss', **srst** 'animal's coat, hair', **strast** 'sorrow, suffering' (and **soustrast** 'sympathy'), **vlast** 'homeland'. (Note that **most -u** 'bridge' belongs to masculine type **hrad**.)

The same applies to **řeč** 'speech', **věc** 'thing', **moč** 'urine', **obuv** 'foot-wear', **rtut'** 'mercury', **Budapešt'** 'Budapest' and **Bukurešt'** 'Bucharest'.

Various others decline in the plural like type **píseň**, except for nom./acc. pl. **-i**, e.g. **chot'** 'spouse', **chut'** 'taste, appetite', **lež** – **lži** 'lie', **mysl** 'mind', **noc** 'night' and **půlnoc** 'midnight', **sůl** – **soli** 'salt', **stat'** 'article', **ves** – **vsi** 'village'. Some nevertheless have ins. pl. **-mi**, e.g. **myš** 'mouse', **od\|pověd'** 'answer' (and related words, e.g. **zpověd'** confession'), **směs** 'mixture', **smrt** 'death', **veš** – **vši** (ins. pl. **vešmi**) 'louse', **rukovět'** 'hand-book', **závět'** 'last will and testament'.

A number have dat. and loc. pl. *either* **-em** or **-ím**, **-ech** or **-ích**, but retain ins. pl. **-mi**, e.g. **obět'** 'sacrifice', **zed'** – **zdi** 'wall', **lest** – **lsti** 'trick, ruse', **mast** 'ointment', **past** 'trap', **pěst** 'fist', **pamět'** 'memory'.

Moc 'power', **nemoc** 'illness', **pomoc** 'help' and **velmoc** 'great power' are the same, except that they have ins. pl. **-emi**.

A residual group may decline throughout like type **píseň**, retaining only gen. sg. and nom. -acc. pl. **-i** as alternative endings alongside **-e/ě**, e.g. **čtvrt** 'quarter' and **čtvrt'** 'district, quarter', **hut'** 'ironworks', **lod'** (ins. pl. **loděmi/lod'mi**) 'boat', **nit** 'thread', **ocel** 'steel', **pečet'** 'seal', **pout'** 'pilgrimage', **řit'** 'anus', **trat'** 'track', **zášt'** 'hatred', **závrat'** 'giddiness, vertigo'.

3.7 Neuter types

3.7.1 Neuter type město

Type **město** 'town' represents the commonest type of neuter noun, ending in -o.

	Sg.	Pl.
1 nom.	**město**	**města**
4 acc.		
2 gen.	**města**	**měst**
3 dat.	**městu**	**městům**
6 loc.	**(o) městě**	**(o) městech**
7 ins.	**městem**	**městy** (*-ama)
5 voc.	= nom.	

As with masculine inanimate nouns type **hrad,** locative **-ě/e** is standard usage with many common hard-stem neuters, e.g. **divadlo – v divadle** 'in the theatre', **auto – v autě** 'in the car', **Brno – v Brně** 'in Brno', **město – ve městě** 'in (the) town'. Examples with sound changes: **jádro – v jádře** 'in the core', **břicho – v břiše** 'in the belly', **jaro – na jaře** 'in spring'.

However, as with masculine inanimates, the majority of nouns have locatives ending in **-u.** This includes (with few exceptions) nouns with a final velar **k, g/h, ch,** e.g. **Německo – v Německu** 'in Germany', **ucho – v uchu** 'in the ear', also most abstract nouns, and less basic or more recent vocabulary: **rádio – v rádiu** 'on ("in") the radio'. Even where **-ě/ -e** is regularly used, **-u** may be equally possible: **kino – v kině, v kinu** 'in the cinema', especially in non-set phrases, e.g. **ve městě** 'in town' but **o městě/o městu Čáslav** 'about the town [of] Čáslav'.

The 'zero' ending for the genitive plural is the same as for feminines: **auta – aut** 'cars', **města – měst** 'towns', **slova – slov** 'words'. Vowel shortening occurs in a few words, e.g. **léta – let** 'summers, years', **díla –**

děl 'works (of art)'. Inserted **-e-** occurs here as for feminine nouns: **jablka – jablek** 'apples', **okna – oken** 'windows'.

In standard usage neuters ending in velars have the locative pl. ending **-ách**: **vajíčka – ve vajíčkách** 'in the eggs' (exceptions are **jablka – o jablkách** or **jablcích** 'apples', and in normal standard written usage **střediska – ve střediscích** 'centres', **stanovisko – v stanoviscích** 'standpoints').

3.7.2 | Neuter type moře

There is a relatively minor group of neuter nouns ending in -e, e.g. **moře** 'sea'.

	Sg.	Pl.
I nom.	**moře**	**moře**
4 acc.		
2 gen.	**moře**	**moří**
3 dat.	**moři**	**mořím**
6 loc.	**o moři**	**o mořích**
7 ins.	**mořem**	**moř|i** (*-ema)
5 voc.	= nom.	

Nouns with the suffix **-iště** belong to this group and have a zero genitive plural, e.g. **letiště – letišť** 'airports', similarly **hřiště** 'playing field, sports ground', **bydliště** 'place of residence'.

Other common examples: **pole** 'field', **srdce** 'heart', **kafe** 'coffee' (colloquial), **lože** 'bed' (formal, geological), **nebe** 'sky, heaven' (plural usually **nebesa**), **ovoce** 'fruit', **slunce** 'sun', **vejce** 'egg' (gen. pl. **vajec**). Also: **poledne** 'midday' (and **dopoledne** 'morning', **odpoledne** 'afternoon'), **Labe** 'the Elbe river', **kanape** 'sofa', **citoslovce** 'interjection' and **příslovce** 'adverb'.

3.7.3 | Neuter type kuře

This declension type is mostly used for nouns denoting the young of animals, and is traditionally represented by **kuře** 'chicken'.

	Sg.	Pl.
1 nom.	**kuře**	**kuřata**
4 acc.		
2 gen.	**kuřete**	**kuřat**
3 dat.	**kuřeti**	**kuřatům**
6 loc.	**o kuřeti**	**kuřatech**
7 ins.	**kuřetem**	**kuřat|y** (*-ama)
5 voc.	= nom.	

Neuter words for the young of animals regularly belong to this group, e.g. **štěně** 'puppy', **hříbě** 'foal', **kotě** 'kitten', **tele** 'calf' (plural **štěňata, hříbata, kot'ata, telata**). (Their diminutives end in -átko: **kot'átko, štěňátko** 'little kitten, little puppy'.) Other animal words in this type include **zvíře** 'animal', **prase** 'pig'.

Note also the human nouns **děvče** 'girl' (dim. **děvčátko**) and **dítě** – **dítěte** 'child'. The usual plural for 'children' is **děti**, which is treated as feminine (see 3.8.2 below). Other human examples include **kníže** 'prince, duke', **hrabě** 'count' (these two are treated as masculine in the singular!), **vnouče** 'grandchild' and **dvojče** 'twin'.

Only a few inanimate nouns belong to this neuter type, including especially: **rajče** – **rajčete**, pl. **rajčata** 'tomato', **doupě** 'den', **koště** 'broom', **poupě** 'bud'.

3.7.4 | Neuter type stavení

The relatively common neuter type **stavení** 'building' has only one different case form in the singular (the instrumental), and three in the plural. A large number of nouns of this type are derived from verbs, e.g. **vzdělání** 'education' or **mytí** 'washing'.

	Sg.	Pl.
1 nom. 4 acc.	**stavení**	**stavení**
2 gen.	**stavení**	**stavení**
3 dat.	**stavení**	**stavením**
6 loc.	**(o) stavení**	**(o) staveních**
7 ins.	**stavením**	**staven|ími** (*-íma)
5 voc.	= nom.	

Other common examples are **nádraží** 'station', **náměstí** 'square', **století** 'century', **výročí** 'anniversary', **období** 'period, era'. The plural of **století** is either **století** or **staletí**.

Some are collective nouns, e.g. **kamení** 'stone', **uhlí** 'coal', **stromoví** 'trees'. Also **zelí** 'cabbage', **září** 'September', **pondělí** 'Monday'.

3.8 Other miscellaneous types

3.8.1 The dual – hands, legs, eyes and ears

Ruka 'hand', **noha** 'leg', **oko** 'eye' and **ucho** 'ear' have special forms called the 'dual' (**duál, dvojné číslo**), used for the plural of these paired parts of the body. All count as feminine in the plural.

	ruce 'hands'	nohy 'legs'	oči 'eyes'	uši 'ears'
1 nom. 4 acc.	**ruce** 'hands'	**nohy** 'legs'	**oči** 'eyes'	**uši** 'ears'
2 gen.	**rukou**	**nohou**	**očí**	**uší**
3 dat.	**rukám**	**nohám**	**očím**	**uším**
6 loc.	**(v) ruk|ou** **(-ách)**	**(na) noh|ou** **(-ách)**	**(v) očích**	**(v) uších**
7 ins.	**rukama**	**nohama**	**očima**	**ušima**

Adjectives and determiners qualifying these nouns in the instrumental plural switch their own endings to -ma instead of -mi: **těma čtyřma velkýma nohama** 'with those four big legs'. This *is* standard correct written usage (with other nouns these are colloquial forms).

In figurative senses standard plural forms occur, e.g. **dvě ucha** 'two handles', **hrnec s dvěma uchy** 'a pot with two handles', but **mechanické ruce** 'mechanical arms'.

Diminutives for hands, legs, eyes and ears also have dual instrumental plural forms, e.g. **ručička**, pl. **ručičky – ručičkama, nožička** – pl. **nožičk|y -ama**, **očičko** – pl. **očičk|a -ama**, and **ouško** – pl. **oušk|a -ama**.

The genitive/locative ending -ou is also used optionally by neuter nouns **rameno** 'shoulder', **koleno** 'knee'. It is also standard with the plural-only neuter noun **prsa** 'chest' (contrast with **prs -u** masc. 'breast').

3.8.2 | Lidé *people and* děti *children*

A standard noun for a 'human being, person', whether male or female, is **člověk -a**, grammatically masculine animate. It will also often translate as 'man'. Colloquial English today sometimes uses 'guy' to refer to either sex in this way.

Note the forms sg. dat./loc. **člověku**, voc. **člověče!**

The noun **lidé** 'people', also masculine animate, serves as its plural. It declines mostly like feminine nouns type **kost**, and colloquially the accusative form **lidi** is also used for the nominative.

Similarly **děti** 'children', which actually counts as grammatically *feminine*, serves as the plural of the neuter noun **dítě -ěte** 'child'.

1 nom.	**lidé**, *****lidi m.**	**děti** f.
4 acc.	**lidi**	**děti**
2 gen.	**lidí**	**dětí**
3 dat.	**lidem**	**dětem**
6 loc.	**(o) lidech**	**(o) dětech**
7 ins.	**lidmi**, *****lidma**	**dětmi**, *****dětma**

The diminutives **lidičky** 'people' and **dětičky** 'children' have feminine plural forms like **žena**: nom./acc. **dětičky**, gen. **dětiček**, dat. **dětičkám** etc.

However, the singular noun **lid -u** 'the people' is masculine *inanimate*, as is **národ -a** 'nation', e.g. **milujeme český lid/národ** 'we love the Czech people'.

| 3.8.3 | *Types* **kámen** *and* **břemeno** |

Several masculine inanimate nouns ending in **-en** have some optional soft-type endings in the singular, e.g. **kámen -e/-u** 'stone'.

Others are **hřeben** 'comb', **ječmen -e/-a** 'barley', **kmen** 'stem, trunk', **kořen** 'root', **křemen** 'flint', **plamen** 'flame', **pramen** 'source, spring', **řemen** 'strap'. Also **loket -kte, -ktu** 'elbow'.

A few neuters ending in **-eno** have similar optional endings and high-flown nom./acc. variant forms ending in **-mě**, e.g. **břemeno/břímě** 'burden'.

Similarly: **plemeno/plémě** 'tribe', **rameno/rámě** 'arm, shoulder', **semeno/sémě, símě** 'seed'.

The regular modern singular forms are common, and the plurals are regular.

	Sg.	Pl.
1 nom.	**kámen/břemeno, břímě**	**kameny/břemena**
4 acc.		
2 gen.	**kamene, -u/břemene, -a**	**kamenů/břemen**
3 dat.	**kameni, -u/břemeni, -u**	**kamenům/břemenům**
6 loc.	**(o) kameni, -u/ břemeni, -u**	**(o) kamenech/ břemenech**
7 ins.	**kamenem/břemenem**	**kameny/břemeny (*-ama)**
5 voc.	**kameni!/= nom.**	

| 3.8.4 | *Other irregular nouns* |

Some other common nouns with irregularities are particularly noted here:

Masculine:

Bůh – Boha 'God'   dat./loc. **Bohu,** voc. **Bože!**; pl. nom. **bohové/bozi**

bratr -a 'brother'	pl. regular nom. **bratři**, etc., but as 'brethren' also pl. nom./acc./gen. **bratří**, dat. **bratřím**, loc. **bratřích**, ins. **bratřími**
kněz -e 'priest'	pl. nom./acc./gen. **kněží**, dat. **kněžím**, loc. **kněžích**, ins. **kněžími**
kůň – koně 'horse'	pl. nom./acc. **koně**, gen. **koní**, dat. **koním**, ins. **koňmi,** or regular **koňů** etc.
rodič -e 'parent'	pl. nom./acc. **rodiče**, gen. **rodičů** etc.
syn -a 'son'	sg. voc. **synu!**; pl. nom. **synové**
den – dne 'day'	sg. dat./loc. **dnu/dni, ve dne**; pl. **dny (dni)**, gen. **dnů (dní)**, dat. **dnům**, loc. **dnech**, ins. **dny**
týden – týdne 'week'	sg. dat./loc. **týdnu**; pl. **týdny**, gen. **týdnů** etc.

Feminine:

dcera -y f. 'daughter'	sg. dat./loc. **dceři**
paní -í f. 'Mrs, lady'	sg. invariable; pl. nom./acc./gen. **paní**, dat. **-ím**, loc. **-ích**, ins. **-ími**
studna -y/studně -ě f. 'well'	sg. dat./loc. **studni**, pl. gen. **studní/ studen**

3.8.5	*Latin/Greek and related types*

A number of nouns of Latin/Greek origin partially respect their linguistic antecedents in the way they decline.

Most often these are *neuter* nouns ending in (a) -**um**, (b) -**eum**, -**ium**, -**io**/-**eo**, and (c) -**ma**:

a **vízum** 'visa'	sg. gen. **víza**, dat./loc. **vízu**, ins. **vízem**; pl. nom./acc. **víza**, gen. **víz**, dat. **vízům**, loc. **vízech**, ins. **vízy**
b **muzeum** 'museum'	sg. gen. **muzea**, dat./loc. **muzeu**, ins. **muzeem**; pl. nom./acc. **muzea**, *but* gen. **muzeí**, dat. **muzeím**, loc. **muzeích**, ins. **muzei**

c **drama** 'drama' gen. **dramatu** (!), dat./loc. **dramatu**, ins. **dramatem**;
pl. nom./acc. **dramata** etc. (like **víza**)

Similarly: (a) **centrum** 'centre', **datum** 'date', (b) **gymnázium** 'grammar school', **stipendium** 'grant, scholarship', **studium** 'study', **rádio** 'radio', **studio** 'studio', **sympozion/sympozium** -zia, (c) **dogma** 'dogma', **klima** 'climate', **schéma** 'scheme', **téma** 'theme'.

Some *masculine* foreign nouns ending in (d) **-us**, **-os** and (e) **-ius** behave similarly.

d **cyklus** 'cycle' sg. gen. **cyklu**, dat./loc. **cyklu**, ins. **cyklem**;
pl. nom./acc. **cykly**, gen. **cyklů** etc.

Kristus – acc./gen. **Krista**, dat./loc. **Kristovi**, ins. **Kristem**

e **génius** 'genius' sg. gen. **génia**, dat./loc. **géniovi**, ins. **géniem**, voc. **génie**
pl. nom./acc. **géniové**, acc. **génie**, gen. **géniů**, dat. **géniům**, loc. **géniích**, ins. **génii**

Similarly (d) **romantismus** -smu and other '-isms' (now sometimes also spelt -izmus), **kosmos** – **kosmu** 'cosmos'.

Others however have regular declensions, e.g. **cirkus** – **cirkusu** 'circus'. 'Virus' exhibits various possibilities: **virus** – **viru**, or **virus** – **virusu**, or **vir** – **viru**.

Some others: **prézens** – **prézentu**, 'the present (tense)', **ion/iont** – **iontu** 'ion', **pankreas** – **pankreatu** 'pancreas'.

Feminine examples include: **bronchitis/bronchitida** – **bronchitidy** 'bronchitis', **sfinx/sfinga** – **sfingy** 'sphinx', and **idea** 'idea', which offers a mixture of forms:

idea 'idea' sg. acc. **ideu**, gen. **idey/ideje**, dat./loc. **ideji**, ins. **ideou/idejí**, voc. **ideo!** pl. nom./acc. **idey/ideje**, gen. **idejí**, dat. **ideám/idejím**, loc. **ideách/idejích**, ins. **ideami/idejemi**

Similarly: **Korea**, **Odyssea** 'Odyssey'.

Nouns ending in -ja also produce variants: **sója** 'soya' has genitive sg. -i (sometimes -e) and dative/locative sg. -i, **Trója** 'Troy' has genitive sg. **do Tróje**, dative/locative **k/v Tróji**.

Note also **Nikaragua** – regular, except for sg. dat./loc. **Nikaragui**, pl. gen. **Nikaraguí**. Similarly **Samoa**, **Managua**, **boa**.

Another awkward feminine noun is **revue**, pronounced [revý], which may decline sg. dat./loc. **revui**, ins. **revuí**, pl. **revue revuí revuím revuích revuemi**.

3.8.6 | Foreign proper names

Foreign names of more recent origin can also present problems. Some nouns ending in -y or -i decline almost like adjectives in the singular, e.g.

Verdi – acc./gen. **Verdiho**, dat. **Verdimu**, loc./ins. **Verdim**, pl. nom. **Verdiové**, acc. **Verdie**, gen. **Verdiů**, dat. **-ům**, loc. **-iích**, ins. **-ii**

Similarly **Montgomery -yho, pony -yho** 'pony' (or **poník -a**), sometimes the same is applied to names ending in -e, e.g. **Rilke** – **Rilkeho**/'properly' **Rilka**, similarly **Goethe** – **Goetha**.

Silent final consonants (e.g. in French) are pronounced before case endings, e.g. **Manet** [mane] – **Maneta** [maneta], **Manetovi** [manetovi]. Silent final e is dropped, e.g. **Shakespeare** – **Shakespeara, Shakespearovi**, similarly **Cambridge** – **do Cambridge** [kembridže], **v Cambridgi** [kembridži].

Russian names ending in -oj and -ij are declined like adjectives, e.g. **Tolstoj** – **Tolstého, Tolstému** and **Gorkij** – **Gorkého, Gorkému, Dostojevsk|ij -ého**.

3.9 Adjectival nouns – *zpodstatnělá přídavná jména*

Adjectival nouns are simply identical in form to adjectives of a particular gender and decline accordingly. Animates will normally have masculine and feminine variants:

Masculine   **vrátný** 'porter', **příbuzný** 'relative', **vedoucí** 'manager', **průvodčí** 'guard, conductor', **účetní** 'accountant', **krejčí** 'tailor', **kočí** 'coachman', **mluvčí** 'spokesman', and a few inanimates, e.g. **zlatý** 'gulden', place name **Slaný**

Feminine   **vrátná** 'female porter', **pokojská** 'room maid', **příbuzná** 'female relative', **švagrová** 'sister-in-law', **vedoucí** 'manageress';

inanimates, e.g. sports and meat dishes: **kopaná** 'football', **košíková** 'basketball', **sekaná** 'meatloaf', **vepřová (pečeně)** 'roast pork';

also **zelená** 'green traffic light', **červená** 'red traffic light';

and phrases **na shledanou** 'goodbye, au revoir', **jako na zavolanou** 'as if summoned, in the nick of time'

Neuter   money: **vstupné** 'entrance fee', **spropitné** 'tip'

varieties of meat: **vepřové (maso)** 'pork', **hovězí** 'beef', **telecí** 'veal'

3.10 Plural-only nouns – *podstatná jména pomnožná*

Czech nouns with plural form but singular meaning include many place names ending in -any (masculine type **hrad**) and -ice (feminine type **růže**). Both types have zero genitive plurals:

Hradčany – Hradčan, Hradčanům, na Hradčanech, Hradčany

Budějovice – Budějovic, Budějovicím, v Budějovicích, Budějovicemi

The gender of nouns with no singular is not always clearcut. Some plural-only nouns have mostly regular masculine type endings, e.g.

teplák|y -ů, (v teplácích/teplákách) 'tracksuit', **šach|y -ů (o šachách)** 'chess', **korál|e -ů** 'coral necklace'

But more often they have regular feminine type endings:

dějin|y 'history' – **dějin, dějinám, dějinách, dějinami**

kalhot|y 'trousers' – **kalhot, kalhotám, kalhotách, kalhotami**

Likewise:

noviny 'newspaper', **plavky – plavek** 'swimsuit', **nůžky – nůžek** 'scissors', **varhany** 'organ', **narozeniny** 'birthday', **křtiny** 'christening', **Alpy** 'Alps', **Andy** 'Andes', **Tatry – Tater** 'Tatra Mountains', **At(h)ény** 'Athens'

Soft type **housle** 'violin' – **houslí, houslím, houslích, houslemi**

Likewise:

berle 'crutches', **jesle** 'crib', **kleště** 'pliers', **pomyje** 'slops', **štafle** 'stepladder'

Some are treated as neuter, with typical nominative plural -a:

játra – jater 'liver', **ústa – úst** 'mouth', **záda – zad** 'back', **prsa – prsou** 'chest' (i.e. **prsa** has a dual type gen./loc. **prsou**)

Other nouns hesitate in standard usage between different endings:

džín(s)y 'jeans' – **džín(s)ů/džín, džín(s)ům/džín(s)ám, džín(s)ech/džín(s)ách, džín(s)ami**

dveře/dvéře f. 'door' – **dveří, dveřím, dveřích, dveřmi**

diminutive:

dvířka '(small) door' – **dvířek, dvířkám/dvírkům, dvířkách, dvířky/dvířkami**

vrata n. 'gate' – **vrat, vratům, vratech, vraty** (regular)

diminutive:

vrátka '(small) gate' – **vrátek, vrátkům/vrátkám, vrátkách, vrátky/vrátkami**

Vánoce (officially feminine) 'Christmas'– **Vánoc, Vánocům, Vánocích, Vánocemi/Vánoci**
(similarly **Velikonoce** 'Easter')

3.11   Indeclinable nouns – *nesklonná jména*

Native nouns are hardly ever indeclinable, except for surnames of the type **Janů, Martinů** etc.

A few feminine personal names end in a hard consonant and are thus indeclinable (or usually so), e.g. **Dagmar, Rút (Ruth), Miriam.**

In general only those foreign nouns which end in a way which prevents the noun from following any set declension pattern are treated as indeclinable.

Unless the noun is animate, the gender of indeclinable nouns is most often neuter. The meaning of most of the words is obvious. These are only a few examples.

Masculine	**atašé, kakadu** (or **-ua**) 'cockatoo'
Feminine	**party, brandy** (also neuter), **whisky, revue**, pronounced [revý] (or else it declines sg. dat./loc. **revui**, ins. **revuí**, pl. **revue, revuí, revuím, revuích, revuemi**)
Neuter	a few foreign nouns ending in **-á, -é, -u, -y, -i**, e.g. **angažmá, aranžmá, apartmá, kupé** 'compartment', **filé, klišé, menu** [meny], **tabu, ragby, šery** or **sherry, alibi, taxi** (or **taxík -u**); also **interview** ([intervjú], neuter/masculine), **blues, rekviem, jidiš**

A few neuters ending in -le, -re or -te are indeclinable except for ins. sg. -em, e.g. **finále** (ins. **finálem**), similarly **skóre** 'score', **penále** 'penalty', **parte** 'death notice'.

Chapter 4

Adjectives and adverbs – přídavná jména a příslovce

4.1 The adjective – *přídavné jméno*

Adjectives are words which describe or qualify nouns, 'big', 'small', 'old' etc.

'Attributive' adjectives belong to the noun phrase itself, e.g. **krásný les** 'a beautiful forest'.

'Predicative' adjectives act as the complement of a verb, typically the verb 'to be', referring back to the noun they qualify, e.g. **les je krásný** 'the forest is beautiful'.

Czech adjectives habitually change their endings to match the *gender*, *case* and *number* of the nouns they refer to. This is called *agreement*. Both attributive and predicative adjectives do this:

krásná řeka – řeka je krásná 'a beautiful river – the river is beautiful'

Adjectival nouns have the form and declension of adjectives, e.g. **vrátný** 'porter (male)', **vrátná** 'porter (female)', also many surnames, e.g. **pan Novotný a paní Novotná** 'Mr Novotný and Mrs Novotná'.

4.1.1 | Basic gender forms of adjectives

The basic, i.e. nominative singular, forms of hard and soft adjectives, along with the demonstrative **ten, ta, to** are as follows. The soft type (-í) does not make any gender distinction here.

The non-standard asterisked forms are common in everyday spoken usage (especially in Prague and Bohemia).

Gender	Nominative singular	
Masculine	**ten krásný (*krásnej) jarní les**	that beautiful spring forest
Feminine	**ta krásná jarní řeka**	that beautiful spring river
Neuter	**to krásné (*krásný) jarní město**	that beautiful spring town

4.1.2 | Position of adjectives

Attributive adjectives are normally placed *before* their nouns, just as in English, e.g. **velký dům** a large house, **velká řeka** a large river, **velké město** a large town.

However, occasionally attributive adjectives are placed *after* their nouns. Czech and English usage sometimes coincides here, e.g. **Karel Veliký** 'Charles the Great', **Rudolf Hrušinský mladší** 'Rudolf Hrušinský junior/the younger'.

They may be placed after the noun for emphasis, or when pointing out a contrast:

Byl to nápad přímo geniální.   It was an absolutely brilliant idea.

Modré šaty ti sluší lépe než šaty zelené.   Blue clothes suit you better than green ones.

Emotive emphatic use can even involve using feminine adjectival agreement with a masculine animate noun:

Ty kluku líná!   You lazy boy!

Adjectives are also placed after the noun in hierarchical terminologies (such as anatomy, zoology, botany and chemistry) and in some traditional phrases, often religious or historical, e.g.

pes domácí 'domestic dog, Canis familiaris', **kyselina sírová** 'sulphuric acid', **mše svatá** 'Holy Mass', **syn Boží** 'God's son', **Království české** 'the Bohemian kingdom'

English noun modifiers

In English it is common for nouns to be used like adjectives, to modify other nouns. In Czech adjectives derived from the nouns have to be used instead.

From place names such adjectives regularly end in **-ský, -cký**. Many others end in **-ový** ('made of, of'), others in **-ný** ('made of, containing, relating to'), and **-ní** ('of the type, used for').

Praha 'Prague' but **Pražský hrad** 'Prague Castle'

(České) Budějovice but **Budějovický kraj** 'the Budějovice region'

dub 'oak', **dubový stůl** 'oak table'

počítač 'computer', **počítačová technologie** 'computer technology'

cihla 'brick', **cihlová zeď** 'brick wall'

kámen 'stone', **kamenná zeď** 'stone wall'

žito 'rye', **žitný chléb** 'rye bread'

koncert 'concert', **koncertní síň** 'concert hall'

hudba 'music', **hudební škola** 'music school', cf. **hudební nástroj** 'musical instrument'

škola 'school', **školní budova** 'school building'

For more about the derivation of adjectives, see 10.4.

Standard adjectives – hard and soft types

Most Czech adjectives belong to one of two types, either 'hard' or 'soft', according to the vowels of their endings.

Adjectives are conventionally cited by their masculine nominative singular form.

If this form ends in the 'hard' long vowel **-ý**, the adjective belongs to the hard type, e.g. **krásný** 'beautiful', **mladý** 'young', **starý** 'old'.

Here are a few common adjectives, all belonging to the basic hard type:

velký	big	**malý**	small
starý	old	**nový**	new
		mladý	young
dobrý	good	**špatný**	bad
		zlý	evil, nasty
krásný	beautiful	**ošklivý**	ugly

pěkný, hezký   pretty, nice

čistý   clean, pure   **špinavý**   dirty

Some colour adjectives (**barva** 'colour'):

bílý 'white', **černý** 'black', **červený** 'red', **fialový** 'purple',
hnědý 'brown', **modrý** 'blue', **oranžový** 'orange', **růžový** 'pink',
šedý/šedivý 'grey', **zelený** 'green', **žlutý** 'yellow'

If an adjective ends in the 'soft' long vowel -í, it belongs to the soft
type, e.g. **cizí** 'foreign', **inteligentní** 'intelligent'.

Soft adjectives for seasons and points of the compass, with their nouns:

zima – **zimní** 'winter', **léto** – **letní** 'summer', **jaro** – **jarní** 'spring',
podzim – **podzimní** 'autumn'

sever – **severní** 'north', **jih** – **jižní** 'south', **východ** – **východní**
'east', **západ** – **západní** 'west'

There is also a special category of possessive adjective ending in -**ův** or
-**in**, similar in function to personal nouns with 'apostrophe s' in English, e.g. **bratrův** 'brother's', **sestřin** 'sister's', see 4.6 below.

Only a few foreign loanword adjectives lack adjectival suffixes and
are thus indeclinable (invariable), e.g. **blond** 'blond(e)' (**má blond vlasy**
'she has blond hair'), **fajn** (**fajn kluk** 'a good lad, guy'), **prima** (**prima
kluk** 'a first-class, great guy'), **khaki, senza** (= **senzační** 'sensational').

There is also an indeclinable type of family-name possessive, used
regionally, ending in -**ovic**, e.g. **Mikulovic rodina** 'the Mikula family'.

Certain types of pronoun attach themselves to nouns in the same
way as adjectives, e.g. possessives such as **můj** 'my', and demonstratives
such as **ten** 'that'.

The basic demonstrative **ten** is particularly common as the first element in noun phrases containing adjectives, so its forms have been
added to the main tables below.

4.3.1 | Standard case forms of adjectives

Adjectives have a whole set of case forms in the singular and plural.
Most of the case endings are different from those of nouns, as the
examples in the tables show.

Nominative forms are also used for the vocative case.

Masculine *animate* forms only differ from masculine *inanimate* ones
in the *accusative singular* (= genitive) and in the *nominative plural*.

Neuter forms only differ from masculines in the nominative/accusa-
tive (singular and plural).

Note how the long vowel in the endings of soft adjectives is always **í**, which means that many case and gender forms turn out the same.

Examples = 'that good/foreign student, house, car, woman'

Sg.		
1 nom.	**ten** *dobrý/cizí* **student, dům; to** *dobré/cizí* **auto**	**ta** *dobrá/cizí* **žena**
4 acc.	**toho** *dobrého/cizího* **studenta** (acc. = gen.) but otherwise acc. = nom.	**tu** *dobrou/cizí* **ženu**
2 gen.	**toho** *dobrého/cizího* **studenta, domu, auta**	**té** *dobré/cizí* **ženy**
3 dat.	**tomu** *dobrému/cizímu* **studentovi, domu, autu**	**té** *dobré/cizí* **ženě**
6 loc.	**(o) tom** *dobrém/cizím* **studentovi, domě, autě**	**(o) té** *dobré/cizí* **ženě**
7 ins.	**tím** *dobrým/cizím* **studentem, domem, autem**	**tou** *dobrou/cizí* **ženou**

Plural cases of adjectives do not distinguish between genders, except in the nominative/accusative forms:

Pl.	
1 nom.	**ti** *dobří/cizí* **studenti; ty** *dobré/cizí* **domy, ženy; ta** *dobrá/cizí* **auta**
4 acc.	**ty** *dobré/cizí* **studenty;** otherwise acc. = nom.
2 gen.	**těch** *dobrých/cizích* **studentů, domů, aut, žen**
3 dat.	**těm** *dobrým/cizím* **studentům, domům, autům, ženám**
6 loc.	**(o) těch** *dobrých/cizích* **studentech, domech, autech, ženách**
7 ins.	**těmi** *dobrými/cizími* **studenty, domy, auty, ženami**

4.3.2 | Masculine animate nominative plural

Consonant changes occur before the masculine animate nominative
plural ending -í, just as with masculine animate *nouns* before -i:

 e.g. **mladý kluk – mladí kluci** = [mla<u>ď</u>í kluci]

Note the standard mutations **h – z**, **ch – š**, **k – c** and **r – ř**:

 e.g. **nahý – nazí** 'naked', **tichý – tiší** 'quiet', **velký – velcí** 'great,
 big', **dobrý – dobří** 'good'

(Similarly the relative pronoun **který – kteří** 'who, which'.)
 But also note the changes **-cký** to **-čtí** and **-ský** to **-ští**:

 e.g. **anglický – angličtí** 'English', **německý – němečtí** 'German',
 český – čeští 'Czech', **francouzský – francouzští** 'French'

4.3.3 | Non-standard case forms – colloquial usage

In colloquial usage the long vowel ý may become *ej (but not in the
instrumental sg.) and é may become *ý. This affects many endings of
hard-type adjectives.

 The instrumental plural has a form ending in *-ma, instead of -mi
(*dobrejma, also soft-type *cizíma).

 Genderless nominative/accusative plural forms of adjectives are also
commonly used, e.g.

 *ty *velký *americký/*český/cizí kluci (acc. **kluky**), **holky, auta**

Do not use the asterisked forms in standard writing as they will be
regarded as incorrect, and note that non-standard forms may sound
'vulgar' in the wrong context.

Sg.		
1 nom.	**ten *dobrý*/*dobrej student, dům; to *dobré*/*dobrý auto**	**ta *dobrá* žena**
4 acc.	**toho *dobrého*/*dobrýho studenta** (acc. = gen.) but otherwise acc. = nom.	**tu *dobrou* ženu**
2 gen.	**toho *dobrého*/*dobrýho studenta, domu, auta**	**té *dobré*/*tý *dobrý ženy**

53

3 dat.	tomu *dobrému*/*dobrýmu* studentovi, domu, autu	té *dobré*/*tý* *dobrý* ženě
6 loc.	(o) tom *dobrém*/*dobrým* studentovi, domě, autě	(o) té *dobré*/*tý* *dobrý* ženě
7 ins.	tím *dobrým* studentem, domem, autem	tou *dobrou* ženou

Pl.

1 nom.	ti *dobří* studenti; ty *dobré* domy, ženy; ta *dobrá* auta/*ty *dobrý* studenti, domy, ženy, auta
4 acc.	ty *dobré*/*dobrý* studenty, domy, ženy, auta
2 gen.	těch *dobrých*/*dobrejch* studentů, domů, aut, žen
3 dat.	těm *dobrým*/*dobrejm* studentům, domům, autům, ženám
6 loc.	(o) těch *dobrých*/*dobrejch* studentech, domech, autech, ženách
7 ins.	těmi *dobrými (cizími)* studenty, domy, auty, ženami/*těma *dobrejma (*cizíma)* *studentama, *domama, *autama, *ženama

Forms **tím, malým** and soft-type **cizím** are commonly pronounced with a shortened vowel.

4.4 Adjective *rád*

The adjective **rád** 'glad' is a special so-called short-form adjective which occurs only in the nominative, often in conjunction with **být** 'to be' and idiomatically with **mít** 'to have', in the sense of 'to like (something)':

Jsem rád(a).	I am glad (masc., fem.)
Mám to rád(a).	I like it.
Nemám to rád(a).	I don't like it.

Its forms neatly match the endings of the third-person pronouns, standard hard-type nouns, and past-tense forms of verbs:

On/student byl rád.	He/the student was glad.
Ona/žena byla ráda.	She/the woman was glad.
Ono/děvčátko bylo rádo.	It/the little girl was glad.
Oni/studenti byli rádi.	They/the students were glad.
Ony/ženy byly rády.	They/the women were glad.
Ona/děvčátka byla ráda.	They/the little girls were glad.

Colloquially the last two can be replaced by masculine plural forms:

Oni (= ženy, děvčátka) byli rádi.

Rád is often used along with verbs in the sense of 'like doing':

| **Rád(a) zpívá.** | He/she likes singing. |

It also has a negative form **nerad,** with a shortened vowel:

| **Nerad(a) zpívá.** | He/she doesn't like singing. |

(For more about 'like' and 'prefer' see 7.22.4)

4.5　Short-form adjectives – *jmenný tvar*

Certain other adjectives also have a predicative 'short form' (**jmenný tvar**), alongside their usual 'long forms'. Many more are obsolete today, but you will find them in older texts.

The masculine sg. short form is formed by removing the final vowel of the long form, e.g. **hotov** 'ready', short form of **hotový** 'ready, prepared'. Root vowel a may lengthen, e.g. **starý – stár** 'old', **mladý – mlád** 'young'.

Sometimes an -e- syllable is inserted in a consonant group, e.g. **mrtvý – mrtev** 'dead', **šťastný – šťasten** 'happy', which is lost in other gender/number forms.

Short forms usually occur in the nominative, occasionally also in the accusative:

Sg.	nom.	m. **šťasten**	f. **šťastna**	n. **šťastno**
	acc.	not used	f. **šťastnu**	n. ditto
Pl.	nom.	ma. **šťastni**	mi./f. **šťastny**	n. **šťastna**
	acc.	ma. **šťastny**	mi./f. ditto	n. ditto

Accusative short forms occur, nowadays rarely, where a verb is modified by an accusative adjective, as well as the noun (accusative complement):

Rád tě vidím zdrávu (= zdravou). I am happy to see you (fem.) well (i.e. glad to see in a well state).

Rád tě vidím zdravého. I am happy to see you well (no masculine sg. short form).

Amongst those short-form adjectives still used in set phrases or in more formal style, are:

zdráv 'well' (temporary state, **zdravý** = 'healthy' – general state), **laskavý – laskav** 'kind', **bosý – bos** 'barefoot', **jistý – jist** 'certain', **zvědavý – zvědav** 'curious', **mrtvý – mrtev, mrtva** 'dead', **šťastný – šťasten, šťastna** 'happy', **spokojený – spokojen** 'contented', **živý – živ** 'alive'

Buďte tak laskav(a) (or hodný, -á) a zavřete okno. Be so kind and close the window.

Buď zdráv(a)! Look after yourself! Goodbye!

Je živ(a) a zdráv(a). He/She is alive and well.

Nejsem si jist(a) (or jistý, -á). I'm not sure.

Jsem zvědav(a) (or zvědavý, -á), co tomu řekne. I'm curious/ wonder what s/he'll say.

Byl(a) na místě mrtev, mrtva (or mrtvý, -á). S/he was dead on the spot.

Chodí bos, -a. S/he is walking about barefoot.

The old neuter sg. forms have given rise to a special group of adverbs, e.g. **daleko** 'far away', **blízko** 'nearby', **dávno** 'a long time ago' etc.

Relics of other case forms occur in various adverbs made with prepositions, e.g. **doleva** 'to the left', **doprava** 'to the right', **vlevo** 'on/to the left', **vpravo** 'on/to the right', **zčistajasna** 'suddenly, out of the blue'.

Sometimes the neuter sg. forms have become nouns, e.g.

dobro 'good' (i.e. 'that which is good'), **zlo** 'evil', **nekonečno** 'the infinite, infinity'.

4.6 Possessive adjectives – *přivlastňovací přídavná jména*

If the adjective ends in **-ův** or **-in**, it belongs to the special possessive type, used similarly to nouns with 'apostrophe s' in English.

Those ending in **-ův** refer to possession by a particular masculine person, e.g. **bratrův** 'brother's', **Karlův** 'Charles's'.

Those ending in **-in** refer to possession by a particular feminine person, e.g. **sestřin** 'sister's', **Libušin** 'Libuše's'.

Basic gender/number agreement is just like **rád, ráda, rádo**.

Petrův, Evin bratr	Peter's, Eva's brother
Petrova, Evina sestra	Peter's, Eva's sister
Petrovo, Evino auto	Peter's, Eva's car
Petrovi, Evini bratři	Peter's, Eva's brothers
Petrovy, Eviny sestry, domy	Peter's, Eva's sisters, houses
Petrova, Evina auta	Peter's, Eva's cars

The other standard singular case forms resemble those of hard-type nouns of the same gender, except for the instrumental **-ým**.

Certain non-standard forms are also in common everyday use. These match the colloquial forms of standard adjectives, e.g. *****Petrovýho**, **Petrovýmu**, **Petrovým** and *****Evinýho** etc., where *****-ým** is generally pronounced *****-ym**.

Sg.		
1 nom.	*Petrův, Evin bratr, dům;* *Petrovo, Evino auto*	*Petrova, Evina* sestra
4 acc.	*Petrov|a, Evin|a|*-ýho* **bratra** otherwise acc. = nom.	*Petrovu, Evinu* sestru
2 gen.	*Petrov|a, Evin|a|*-ýho* bratra, auta	*Petrov|y, Evin|y|* *-ý sestry*
3 dat.	*Petrovu, Evinu|*-ýmu* bratrovi, autu	*Petrově, Evině|* *-ý sestře*
6 loc.	*o Petrově, Evině|*-ým* bratrovi, autě	*o Petrově, Evině|* *-ý sestře*
7 ins.	*Petrovým, Eviným* bratrem, autem	*Petrovou, Evinou* sestrou

The plural forms, apart from the nominative and accusative, are just like standard hard-type adjectives:

Pl.

1 nom.	*Petrovi, Evini* **bratři**	
	Petrovy, Eviny **domy, sestry**	
	Petrov|a, Evin|a/*-y* **auta**	
4 acc.	*Petrovy, Eviny* **bratry**; others = nom.	
2 gen.	*Petrových, Eviných/**-ejch* **bratrů, sester** etc.	
3 dat.	*Petrovým, Eviným/**-ejm* **bratrům, sestrám** etc.	
6 loc.	*Petrových, Eviných/**-ejch* **bratrech, sestrách** etc.	
7 ins.	*Petrovými, Evinými* **bratry, sestrami/***-ejma* **bratrama, sestrama**	

Adjectives with the suffix -in require consonant mutations r – ř and h – ž (optionally g – ž), ch – š and k – č:

sestra – sestřin 'sister's', **matka – matčin** 'mother's', **Olga – Olžin/Olgin** 'Olga's'

4.6.1 | *Use of possessive adjectives*

Possessive adjectives regularly occur in street and place names.

Karlův most 'Charles Bridge', **Karlovo náměstí** 'Charles Square', **Karlova (ulice)** 'Charles Street' (named after the fourteenth-century Emperor Charles IV)

Bydlí ve Smetanově ulici.	S/he lives in Smetana Street.
Bydlí ve Smetanově [č. (= číslo)] 12 (= dvanáct).	S/he lives at [number] 12 Smetana Street.

Mánesův most 'Mánes Bridge' (after the nineteenth-century painter), **Libušina (ulice)** 'Libuše Street' (after the legendary pagan princess), **Nerudova (ulice)** 'Neruda Street' (after the nineteenth-century writer), **Masarykovo nádraží** 'Masaryk Station' (after the first President), **Smetanovo nábřeží** 'Smetana Embankment' (after the nineteenth-century composer).

The word **ulice** 'street' is generally omitted on town plans, when writing addresses etc.

Multiple-word names and adjectival names cannot form possessive adjectives. You use the genitive case instead:

(ulice) Boženy Němcové 'Božena Němcová Street', **(ulice) Karoliny Světlé** 'Karolina Světlá Street', **Vrchlického sady** 'Vrchlický Gardens' (all named after nineteenth-century writers).

Similarly: **bratrova kniha** (my) 'brother's book', *but* **kniha mého mladšího bratra** 'my younger brother's book'.

4.7 The adverb – *příslovce*

Adverbs are words without gender, case or number. They qualify other words or whole clauses.

Often they are derived from adjectives, especially *adverbs of manner*. English often uses the suffix '-ly' for this, while Czech regularly uses the suffix -e/ě, e.g.

pěkný 'nice, pretty' – **pěkně** 'nicely, prettily', **hlučný** 'noisy, loud' – **hlučně** 'noisily, loudly', **strašný** 'terrible, awful' – **strašně** 'terribly, awfully'

Adverbs of manner answer the question **jak?** 'how?'

Related non-specific adverbs of manner include **nějak** 'somehow', **jaksi** 'in some way or other' (see 4.12.3), and demonstratives **tak** 'like so, thus', **takhle/takto** 'like this, this way'.

A principal function of adverbs is to qualify verbs or whole clauses, where adjectives qualify nouns, e.g.

adjective: **pěkná/strašná píseň**   'a nice/terrible song'

adverb: **Eva zpívá pěkně/strašně**   'Eva sings nicely/terribly'

But adverbs can also qualify adjectives, quantity words, and even other adverbs, e.g.

strašně dobrá píseň 'a terribly good song', **přibližně dvacet lidí** 'approximately twenty people', **zpívá strašně dobře** 's/he sings terribly well'

4.7.1 Adverbs of degree

Adverbs of degree indicate degrees of quality or intensity, e.g.

strašně milý člověk	a terribly likeable person
Mám strašně moc práce.	I have an awful lot of work.
Mluví strašně rychle.	S/he speaks terribly quickly/fast.

Many such adverbs are 'primary' adverbs, or not derived from adjectives in the regular way, e.g. **velmi** 'very', **příliš** 'too, excessively', **tak** 'so', **docela** 'quite':

velmi milý člověk 'a very likeable person', **jsem velmi rád** 'I am very glad', **velmi to pomohlo** 'it helped a lot/very much', **mluví příliš/tak/docela rychle** 's/he speaks too/so/quite quickly', **příliš mnoho lidí** 'too many people'

4.7.2 | *Modal adverbs etc.*

Many adverbs have modal or similar adjusting functions in a clause, indicating probability, certainty, approximation, and so on:

snad 'perhaps', **asi** 'probably', 'about (approximately)', **možná** 'maybe', **jistě** 'certainly'

They may also indicate restriction, addition, or express an emotional attitude:

jen, **jenom** 'only', **také**, colloq. **taky** 'also', **právě** 'just, only', **tedy**, colloq. **teda** 'then, in that case', **přece** 'after all', **vždyť** 'besides'

Ale to přece není pravda! But that just isn't true! (objecting)

Vždyť nemáme čas! Besides/After all we do not have time! (exclaiming)

Czech grammars and dictionaries use the term **částice** 'particle' for some of these usages, sometimes inconsistently. Further consideration is beyond the scope of this volume.

4.7.3 | *Adverbs of time and place*

Adverbs of time and place indicate when or where an action takes place, e.g. **včera** 'yesterday', **dnes** 'today', **zítra**, *zejtra 'tomorrow', **ted'**, *ted'ka 'now', **už** 'now, already', **už ne(-)** 'no longer', **ještě** 'still', **ještě ne(-)** 'not yet', **potom, pak** 'then, next', **tady** 'here', **tam** 'there', **venku** 'outside'. A phrase or clause can have the same function, e.g. **minulý měsíc** 'last month', **když jsme přišli domů** 'when we arrived home', **za stromem** 'behind a tree'.
The Czech term may be one word, where English has two, e.g. **doma** 'at home'.

| *Interrogative adverbs*

Other basic adverbs ask questions, typically about manner, time or place:

jak? 'how', **kdy?** 'when', **kde?** 'where'

4.8 Standard adverbs ending in -ě/e

Czech adverbs are regularly derived from adjectives by changing the final vowel of the adjective to **-ě/-e**.

In producing these adverbs the same consonant changes occur as in the dative/locative of feminine nouns (cf. **řeka** river – **v řece** in the river, see 3.4.10).

pěkný – pěkně	nice, pretty – nicely, prettily
krásný – krásně	beautiful – beautifully
dobrý – dobře	good – well
špatný – špatně	bad – badly
strašný – strašně	awful – awfully
hrozný – hrozně	terrible – terribly
lehký – lehce	light, easy – lightly, easily
těžký – těžce	heavy, difficult – heavily, with difficulty
tichý – tiše	quiet – quietly
hlučný – hlučně	noisy – noisily

4.9 Adverbs ending in -cky, -sky

Adjectives in **-ský** or **-cký** regularly form adverbs in **-sky, -cky**. So does **hezký** 'nice, pretty'. Many are language adverbs:

Nemluví česky.   S/he doesn't speak Czech.

Mluví cynicky/hezky.   S/he speaks cynically/nicely.

4.9.1 *Language adverbs*

To say 'know (a language)' you use **umět** 'know how to' followed by special language adverbs ending in **-sky** or **-cky** (short **-y**), e.g.

česky '(in) Czech', **anglicky** 'English', **německy** 'German', **slovensky** 'Slovak', **maďarsky** 'Hungarian', **polsky** 'Polish', **rusky** 'Russian', **francouzsky** 'French'.

Pan Beneš umí jenom česky.   Mr Beneš only knows Czech.
Ale Věra umí anglicky.   But Věra knows English.

Similarly, with **mluvit** 'to speak': **Jan mluví německy** 'Jan speaks German'.

4.10   Adverbs ending in -o

Some common adverbs, e.g. of time and place, end in -o:

dlouhý 'long' – **dlouho** 'for a long time' (*but* **krátký** 'short' – **krátce** 'briefly'), **dávný** – **dávno** 'long ago', **daleký** 'distant' – **daleko** 'far away', **blízký** 'near' – **blízko** 'near by', **vysoký** 'high' – **vysoko** 'high up', **nízký** 'low' – **nízko** 'low down'

Forms in -o often occur with the verb 'to be', often with **je to** 'it is':

Je to daleko.	It's far (away). It's a long way.
Je to blízko.	It's near (by).
Už je to dávno.	It's a long time ago now.

Sometimes English speakers might think an adjective was required:

Praha je daleko.	Prague is far away, a long way off.
Vesnice je blízko.	The village is near.

4.10.1   Parallel adverbs ending in -o and -ě/e

Sometimes adverbs ending in -o coexist with forms ending in -e/ě, related to the same adjective, but with different usages, e.g. **dlouho** 'for a long time' and **dlouze** 'in a long/long-drawn-out manner'.

Similarly, **blízko** 'near by' and **blízce** 'closely', e.g. **blízce příbuzný** 'closely related', **blízce souviset** 'to be closely dependent'.

Also **dalece** 'far, extensively': **Jak dalece tomu rozumí?** 'How far does s/he understand this?'

Often the -o forms occur with the verb 'to be'. Thus, alongside **hlučně** 'noisily' one finds **hlučno** in such contexts:

Mluvili hlučně.	They spoke noisily.	Adverbs ending in -o
V sále bylo hlučno.	It was noisy in the hall.	

4.10.2 Adverbs and the weather

Statements about **počasí** 'the weather' often begin:

Je ...	It is ...
Bylo ...	It was ...
Bude ...	It will be ...

Quite a lot of weather phrases use adverbs, as the complement of the verb 'to be'. Often the forms ending in **-o** are used here, but not always. The choice is a matter of usage.

Bylo teplo, horko.	It was warm, hot.
Je chladno. Bude zima.	It is cool. It'll be cold.
Je pěkně/hezky.	It's nice/lovely weather.
Bude krásně.	It's going to be beautiful.
Bylo ošklivo.	It was nasty weather.
Venku je tma.	Outside it's dark.
Je ještě světlo.	It is still light.
Dnes bude slunečno.	Today it will be sunny.
Bude jasno.	It will be bright.
Bude polojasno. Místy přeháňky.	It will be 'semi-bright', fair. Showers in places.
Je oblačno, zataženo.	It's cloudy, overcast.
Je mlha. Je mlhavo.	There's a mist. It's misty/foggy.
Je větrno.	It's windy.
Je sucho. Je mokro.	It's dry. It's damp.
Bude bouřka.	There'll be a thunderstorm.

Other weather expressions use verbs:

Prší. Pršelo.	It's raining. It was raining.
Sněží. Sněžilo.	It's snowing. It was snowing.
Mrzne. Mrzlo.	It's freezing. It was freezing.
Svítí slunce.	The sun is shining.
Fouká vítr.	A wind is blowing.

4.10.3 | *Adverbs in idioms expressing feeling*

Note the idiomatic phrase **je jí smutno**, lit. 'it is to her sad', which means 'she's feeling sad, she's in a sad state of mind'. Similarly, you say **je mi smutno**, lit. 'it is to me sad', 'I'm feeling sad.'

Similar phrases with the verb 'to be' with the dative of a pronoun and an adverb include:

Je mi pěkně/hezky/krásně.	'It is to me fine/great.' = I feel fine/great.
Bylo mi špatně.	I felt 'bad' = ill, sick.
Není vám zima?	Aren't you cold? Don't you feel cold?
Není ti teplo?	Aren't you warm?

4.11 Looking happy/sad etc.

The verb **vypadat** 'to look' is often followed by an adverb form ending in -ě/e, instead of an adjective.

Vypadá smutně/vesele/ustaraně/podezřele. 'S/he looks sadly/happily/worriedly/suspiciously.' = S/he looks sad/happy/worried/suspicious.

4.12 Interrogatives, place and motion

4.12.1 | *Where? Where to? Here/there*

Certain basic adverbs distinguish between 'place' and 'motion towards a place'.

Amongst the most common are words for 'where' and 'here'.

Kde je Honza?	Where is Honza?
but: **Kam jde?**	Where is he going?
Je tady. Je zde.	S/he is here.
but: **Jde sem.**	S/he is coming here.

The adverb **zde** is generally restricted to formal style, though a pupil may say it for example when the register is taken at school.

The usual colloquial word **tady** has a parallel colloquial emphatic form **tadyhle** 'here, over here', also non-standard *tajdle.

Another alternative expression is **tu** 'here', emphatic **tuhle**. The former can be used as an unstressed enclitic:

Karel tu není.   Karel isn't here.

The basic word **tam** for 'there' makes no distinction between place and motion to the place:

Je tam.   S/he is there.

but also: **Jde tam.**   S/he goes there.

Tam also has the more emphatic colloquial form **tamhle** 'there, over there'.

4.12.2 Which way? Where from?

A further group of words speak of 'motion by a certain route' and 'motion from a place':

Kudy šli?   Which way did they go?
Šli tudy.   They went this way.
Šli tamtudy.   They went that way.

Odkud jste?   Where are you from?
Nejste odtud/odsud (*vocad').   You are not from here.
Jste odtamtud.   You are from over there.

4.12.3 Somewhere, sometime(s), nowhere, never

The element **ně-** added to interrogatives gives the idea of 'some':

nějak 'somehow', **někde** 'somewhere', **někdy** 'sometime(s)', **někam** 'to somewhere', **někudy** 'by some route', **odněkud** 'from somewhere'

The suffix **-si** produces rather similar adverbs meaning 'some . . . or other':

jaksi 'somehow or other', **kdesi** 'somewhere or other', **kamsi** 'to somewhere or other', **kdysi** 'at some time or other (in the past), once', **odkudsi** 'from somewhere or other'

The contrasting element **ni-** gives the idea of 'no', and requires a negative verb, e.g.

nijak 'in no way', **nikde** 'nowhere', **nikam** 'to nowhere', **nikdy** 'never'

Nikdy tam nechodím. I never go there.

For related words see 5.6.3–5.6.4, 5.6.7, 5.8.

4.12.4 Elsewhere, everywhere

Another two groups are formed with the elements **jin-** meaning 'other' and **vš-** meaning 'every, all'. The second group is less complete:

jinde 'elsewhere', **jinam** 'to elsewhere', **jinudy** 'by another route', **odjinud** 'from elsewhere'

všude 'everywhere', **odevšad** 'from everywhere'

4.13 More adverbs of place and motion

Other adverbs also make the distinction between 'place' and 'motion to a place':

Sedí doma.	S/he is sitting at home.
but: **Jde domů.**	S/he is going home.
Je venku.	S/he is outside.
but: **Jde ven.**	S/he is going out.
Je uvnitř.	S/he is in/inside.
but: **Jde dovnitř.**	S/he goes in/inside.
Je nahoře.	S/he's upstairs, up above.
but: **Jde nahoru.**	S/he goes up(stairs).
Je dole.	S/he's downstairs, below.
but: **Jde dolů**	S/he goes down(stairs).

Most of these also have adverbs denoting 'motion away from, out of a place':

zvenčí/zvenku 'from outside', **zevnitř** 'from inside'

shora/seshora/odshora 'from above', **zdola/zezdola/odzdola** 'from below'

but: **z domova** 'from home' (two words)

Other similar words make no distinction between 'place' and 'motion':

Je pryč.   S/he is away.   **Jde pryč.**   S/he goes away.

Je zpátky.   S/he's back.   **Jde zpátky.**   S/he goes back.

4.14   Other forms of adverb

Occasionally the forms of adverbs are unexpected.

Rychlý – rychle 'quick – quickly' is regular, but note **pomalý – pomalu** 'slow – slowly'.

Note also **pozdní – pozdě** 'late – adv. late', and **raný – brzo/brzy** 'early – adv. early'

Adjectives ending in **-cí** based on present participles sometimes form adverbs. These use the suffix **-ně**:

vroucí – vroucně 'fervent – fervently'

4.15   Comparison of adjectives – *stupňování*

In English we regularly make comparative adjectives by attaching 'more' or adding the suffix '-er' to adjectives.

In Czech you usually form the comparative (**komparativ, druhý stupeň** 'second degree') by replacing **-ý** with **-ější/-ejší**, e.g. **pěkný – pěknější** 'pretty – prettier, more pretty'.

Certain (especially some very common) adjectives have a shorter ending **-ší**.

zajímavý – zajímavější   interesting – more interesting

nový – novější   new – newer

but:

starý – starší   old – older

mladý – mladší   young – younger

Both types decline like regular soft adjectives:

Hledám staršího, zajímavějšího muže.
I'm looking for an older, more interesting man.

Bydlím ve starším, v novějším domě.
I live in an older, newer house.

'Than' in comparisons is **než**:

Jeho auto je novější než moje.	His car is newer than mine.
Pavel je starší než já.	Pavel is older than me.
Pavel je mladší než Petr.	Pavel is younger than Peter.

To say 'much' with comparatives add **mnohem/o moc**. Both mean literally 'by much',

| **Zuzana je mnohem/o moc** | Zuzana is much younger than |
| **mladší než Věra.** | Věra. |

Daleko 'far' may also be used with comparatives:

| **Petr je daleko lepší než já.** | Petr is far better than I/me. |

4.15.1 Irregular comparatives

Four essential comparatives are irregular:

malý – menší	smaller
velký/veliký – větší	bigger, greater, larger
dobrý – lepší	good – better
špatný/zlý – horší	bad/evil – worse

4.15.2 Consonant changes etc.

Certain consonant changes regularly take place in the formation of comparatives. These are not quite identical to those changes you met before, e.g. in forming basic adverbs.

r – ř:	**chytrý – chytřejší**	cleverer
	mokrý – mokřejší	wetter
h – ž:	**ubohý – ubožejší**	more wretched
ch – š:	**suchý – sušší**	drier
k – č:	**divoký – divočejší**	wilder
	hezký – hezčí	nicer, prettier
ck – čť:	**cynický – cyničtější**	more cynical
sk – šť:	**lidský – lidštější**	more humane

Adjectives based on present participles use the suffix **-nější**:

vroucí – vroucnější 'fervent – more fervent' (compare the adverb **vroucně**)

4.15.3 Essential adjectives and comparatives

The following basic examples are grouped by meaning. Some are slightly irregular, and some end in -čí, instead of -ší.

vysoký – vyšší	higher
hluboký – hlubší	deeper
nízký – nižší	lower
široký – širší	wider
úzký – užší	narrower
těžký – těžší	heavier, more difficult
lehký – lehčí	lighter, easier
krátký – kratší	shorter
dlouhý – delší	longer
blízký – bližší	nearer
daleký/vzdálený – vzdálenější	further away, more distant

NB další = 'further' in the sense of 'next in line'. In a shop for example: Další, prosím! 'Next (customer), please!'

tenký – tenčí	thinner (slice, layer)
hubený – hubenější	thinner (person, body)
tlustý – tlustší	fatter, thicker
měkký – měkčí	softer
tvrdý – tvrdší	harder
chudý – chudší	poorer
bohatý – bohatší	richer
drahý – dražší	dearer, more expensive
levný – levnější	cheaper
laciný – lacinější	cheaper
tmavý – tmavší	darker (tma darkness)
světlý – světlejší	lighter (světlo light)
tichý – tišší	quieter (ticho silence)
hlučný – hlučnější	noisier (hluk noise)
slabý – slabší	weaker
silný – silnější	stronger

jednoduchý – jednodušší	simpler
prostý – prostší	simpler, plainer
složitý – složitější	more complicated
čistý – čistší	cleaner
špinavý – špinavější	dirtier

4.15.4 *Superlative prefix* nej-

To say 'newest', 'oldest', 'youngest', 'most intelligent' etc. you simply add **nej-** to the comparatives. The resulting form is called the superlative (**superlativ, třetí stupeň** 'third degree').

nejnovější 'newest', **nejstarší** 'oldest', **nejmladší** 'youngest', **nejinteligentnější** 'most intelligent', **nejlepší** 'best', **nejhorší** 'worst'

Pavel je starší než já.	Pavel is older than me.
Ale Petr je nejstarší z nás. (note: **z** +gen. = 'of, out of')	But Petr is the oldest of us.
Ivan je můj nejlepší kamarád.	Ivan is my best friend.

The superlative may be intensified with **zdaleka** 'by far':

| **Petr byl zdaleka nejlepší.** | Petr was by far the best/much the best. |

(But – with comparatives: **byl daleko/mnohem lepší** 'he was far/much better')

4.16 Comparison of adverbs

To say 'more quickly', 'most quickly' etc. you use the comparative adverb ending **-ěji/-eji**, then add the prefix **nej-** for the superlative:

| **Pavel běhá rychleji než já.** | Pavel runs more quickly (quicker, faster) than me. |
| **Ale Petr běhá nejrychleji.** | But Peter runs most quickly (quickest, fastest). |

Adverbs in -ce have the comparative ending -čeji:

Marie zpívá sladce, pěkně.   Marie sings sweetly, nicely.

Ale Jan zpívá sladčeji, pěkněji.   But Jan sings more sweetly, more nicely.

In spoken usage adverbs sometimes have the comparative ending *-ějc:

Přijdu později/*pozdějc.   I'll come later.

Mluvte pomaleji/*pomalejc.   Speak more slowly.

4.16.1 | Common adverbs and their comparatives

Learn these common irregular examples:

dobře – lépe/líp 'well – better', špatně, zle – hůř(e) 'badly – worse'

Umí to líp/hůř než on.   S/he knows it better/worse than him.

Věra zpívá dobře, líp než já.   Věra sings well, better than me.

Karel zpívá špatně, hůř než já.   Karel sings badly, worse than me.

málo – méně/míň 'little – less', mnoho/hodně – víc(e) 'much/a lot – more'

Učí se víc(e), méně/míň.   He's studying more/less.

blízko – blíž(e) 'near – nearer', daleko – dál(e) 'far away – further'

Bydlí blíž/dál.   He lives nearer/further away.

dlouho – déle, colloq. dýl 'for a long time – longer'

Nechci tady zůstat déle/dýl.   I don't want to stay here longer.

vysoko – výš(e) 'high up – higher', nízko – níž(e) 'low down – lower'

Letadlo letí výš/níž.   The plane is flying higher/lower.

hluboko – hloub(ěji) 'deeper'

Šli hlouběji do lesa.   They went deeper into the forest.

draho/draze – dráž(e) 'dearly – more dearly'

Je tam draho/dráž.   It's expensive/more expensive there.

brzo – dřív(e) 'soon – sooner', pozdě – později 'late – later'

Přijel dřív než ona.   He arrived sooner than her.

Karel přijel později.   Karel arrived later.

spíš(e) – nejspíš(e) 'more likely – most likely'

Nejspíš nepřijde.   Most likely s/he won't come.

Chapter 5

Pronouns – zájmena

Pronouns are either very basic 'noun-like' words which denote or point to particular persons or things within the actual or speech context ('I', 'you', 'she') or else, in an 'adjective-like' way, they modify a noun in order to specify more narrowly what the noun is in a given context ('this book', 'that book', 'his book' etc.)

Often a particular word can be used in both ways.

5.1 Pronoun types

In their 'noun-like' role pronouns act as a kind of shorthand reference to persons or things within the actual or speech context, e.g. the personal pronouns **já** 'I', **ty** 'you sg.', **on** 'he', **ona** 'she'.

Interrogative pronouns ask questions about a person or thing, e.g. **kdo?** 'who?', **co?** 'what?'

'Adjective-like' pronouns (sometimes called 'determiners' in recent English grammars) identify more precisely what their noun is or refers to in the given context. They regularly precede any standard adjectives which may also be present, e.g. **tahle dobrá kniha** 'this good book', **moje nová kniha** 'my new book'.

They can also act as interrogatives: **která nová kniha?** 'which new book?', **jaká kniha?** 'what kind of book?'

English definite and indefinite articles ('the' and 'a') are similar to these, but Czech has no direct equivalent for them. When translating from Czech into English, you need to add whatever article is required (if any) according to the context:

Mám kufr.   I have a suitcase.

Kufr je tady.   The suitcase is here.

Often the same word can be either 'noun-like' or 'adjective-like' in the way it behaves.

73

This applies perhaps most obviously to demonstratives – basically words like 'this' or 'that' which *point* to people or things:

Co je to?   What is that? [noun-like **to**]

To auto je moje.   That car is mine. [adjective-like **to**]

Some Czech pronouns have forms which decline like standard adjectives, for example **který** m., **která** f., **které** n. 'which?' (which is also used as the relative pronoun 'who, which').

Others have special declensions, e.g. **já** 'I' and **ten, ta, to** 'that'.

5.2   Personal pronouns – *osobní zájmena*

A personal pronoun refers to a person (or thing) already mentioned or known from the context of the speech or text.

'I' and 'we' are first-person pronouns, referring to the speaker or a group including the speaker. 'You' is a second-person pronoun, referring to the person(s) being spoken to or addressed. 'He', 'she', 'it' and 'they' are third-person pronouns, referring to other persons or things being spoken about.

The basic Czech personal pronouns are (in their subject/nominative forms):

já I	**my** we
ty you (singular)	**vy** you (plural, or formal singular)
on, ona, ono he, she, it	**oni** they

In Czech, subject pronouns are regularly omitted as the subjects of verbs, except where necessary or for emphasis, see further below.

5.2.1 | *Saying 'you'*

There are two basic words for 'you', **ty** and **vy**.

Ty and its matching verb forms are used to address a child or a person you are on familiar terms with:

Jak se máš?   How are you?

A jak se máš ty?   And how are *you?*

Vy and its matching verb forms are used to address (a) more than one person, (b) one person who is a stranger, not well acquainted with you, or a more senior person whom you wish to address with polite respect:

Jak se máte?   How are you? (can be sg. or pl.)

A jak se máte vy?   And how are *you*?

The easiest and safest rule is to address adult strangers as **vy**, switching to **ty** as appropriate if and when they suggest it to you.

Amongst personal friends, especially those roughly your own age, **ty** is normal usage, but use the **vy** forms when addressing strangers on the street, parents of friends, shop assistants, bank clerks, and so on.

The verbs **tykat** 'to say **ty**' and **vykat** 'to say **vy**' can be used when discussing this topic in conversation.

Proč mi vykáš?   Why are you saying **vy** to me?

Všichni mu tykají.   Everyone says **ty** to him.

In letter writing, all forms of the second-person pronouns are normally spelt with a capital letter, as are any corresponding possessives: **Ty/Vy** 'you', **Tobě/Vám** 'to you', **Tvůj/Váš** 'your' etc.

Milá paní Novotná!	Dear Mrs Novotná,
Děkuji Vám za Váš milý dopis.	Thank you for your kind letter.
S pozdravem,	Yours sincerely,
Josef Jungmann	

5.2.2 | Third-person subject pronouns

In everyday usage the nominative forms of the noun-like personal pronouns **on** 'he' and **ona** 'she' normally only refer to animate beings.

Similarly, the form **ono** 'it' as a noun-like pronoun may refer to a neuter animate noun, such as **dítě** 'child', **kotě** 'kitten', but will only rarely refer to a particular inanimate thing of neuter gender.

Podívej se na to dítě. Ono spí!   Look at that child. It is asleep.

Oni 'they' is regularly used as a subject pronoun for all genders in the everyday spoken language.

But in standard written Czech **oni** has three gender forms, parallel to those of the past-tense verb forms (see 7.5):

ma. **oni byli**, mi./f. **ony byly**, n. **ona byla** = 'they were'

Thus, the form **ony** is used for a uniformly feminine (and occasionally masculine inanimate) 'they', e.g. to refer to **ženy** women. (Note how all these plural endings match – **ony, ženy, byly**.)

The rarer neuter plural form **ona**, identical to **ona** 'she', is mostly only used when referring to neuter animate beings, e.g. **kot'ata** kittens.

The third person pronouns also have widespread non-standard subject forms with an initial **v-**:

***von** 'he', ***vona** 'she', ***vono** 'it', ***voni** 'they'

Use of these may attract disapproval – they may be regarded as somewhat vulgar, especially in more polite or formal contexts.

5.2.3 | Use and omission of subject pronouns

The subject pronouns **já, ty, on** etc. are only needed for extra emphasis or contrast, or in combinations.

Já mám kufr, ale ona nemá.	I have a suitcase, but she hasn't.
Ty, já a Petr to uděláme spolu.	You, I and Petr will do it together.

Mostly the verb is sufficient to indicate the subject, and you can simply omit the subject pronoun:

Mám kufr.	I have a suitcase.
Má kufr.	S/he has a suitcase.
Máme kufry.	We have suitcases.
Mají kufry.	They have suitcases.
Znáš tuhle knihu?	Do you know this book?
Ano, je dobrá.	Yes, it is good.
Znáš její romány?	Do you know her novels?
Ano, jsou dobré.	Yes, they are good.

Third-person subject pronouns **on, ona, ono** 'he, she, it' and **oni, ony, ona** 'they' are rarely used for things or abstracts. Mostly no subject pronoun is needed for these, but for emphasis you can use the appropriate form of the demonstrative pronoun **ten** m., **ta** f., **to** n.:

| **Ano, ta je dobrá.** | Yes, that one/it (e.g. **ta kniha** 'that book') is good. |
| **Ano, ty jsou dobré.** | Yes, those/they (e.g. **ty romány** 'those novels') are good. |

Normally **ona je dobrá** will mean 'she is good', not 'it is good'.

5.2.4 | Empty subject words 'it' and 'there'

There is generally no subject pronoun present in Czech for 'it', if the thing has already been specified:

| **Kde je auto? – Je tady.** | Where is [the] car? [It] is here. |

But also, where English has an empty subject word 'it', such as in statements about the weather, no subject word should be used in Czech:

| **Je zima.** | It is cold. |
| **Prší.** | It is raining. |

A similar context arises where an English 'it' refers to a following infinitive:

| **Pracovat ve sněhu je těžké.** | It is difficult to work in the snow. |

(English omits this 'it' if the order of elements is changed: 'To work in the snow is difficult.' 'Working in the snow is difficult.')

English also has an empty grammatical subject word 'there', indicating existence or occurrence, where there is also no equivalent in Czech, e.g.

| **V Praze jsou stovky kostelů.** | In Prague there are hundreds of churches. |
| **Najednou se ozvala rána.** | Suddenly a shot rang out. Suddenly there rang out a shot. |

This use of 'there' is different from the adverbial use of 'there'. Sometimes in English both occur together, but Czech will only have a single adverb of place:

| **Je tam velký hotel.** | There is a large hotel there. |

5.2.5 | Expressive use of ono/vono etc.

The neuter third-person pronoun **ono/*vono** 'it' can be used as an expressively emphatic empty 'it' subject for a verb which does not otherwise have a subject pronoun, with exclamatory or explanatory effect:

Prší! Vono prší!   It's raining! Well, it's raining!

Vono pršelo, víš.   Well, it was raining, you know.

It can also buttress the neuter demonstrative **to** 'that':

Vono to není pravda, víš.   That's not actually true, you see.

The third-person subject pronoun forms can also be used emphatically with nouns or pronouns of matching gender:

Von Karel je prostě génius!   He Karel is simply a genius!

| 5.2.6 | *Declension of personal pronouns* |

This section onwards assumes you understand the basics about the Czech case system, as discussed in the chapter on nouns. Pronouns have no distinctive vocative case – just use nominative forms instead, e.g. **Ty!** You!

Where more than one form is given below, those following a dash are reserved for use after prepositions or may be used as stressed forms. Forms which are more or less restricted to formal written style are shown in square brackets.

The first table gives forms for 'I', 'you', 'we', and also the reflexive pronoun 'oneself', since it closely matches the other two:

1 nom.	**já** I	**ty** you	– (one)self
4 acc.	**mě**, [mne] me	**tě** – **tebe**	**se** – **sebe**
2 gen.	**mě**, [mne]	**tě** – **tebe**	**se** – **sebe**
3 dat.	**mi/mně** – **mně**	**ti** – **tobě**	**si** – **sobě**
6 loc.	**o mně**	**o tobě**	**o sobě**
7 ins.	**mnou**	**tebou**	**sebou**

1 nom.	**my** we	**vy** you (plural, formal sg.)
4 acc.	**nás** us	**vás**
2 gen.	**nás**	**vás**
3 dat.	**nám**	**vám**
6 loc.	**o nás**	**o vás**
7 ins.	**námi/*náma**	**vámi/*váma**

In the tables of third-person pronouns which follow, the most common forms are those listed first (before and after the dash). The forms after the dashes beginning with **n-** are obligatory after prepositions, but are not used on their own. The stressed variants used in isolation begin with a **j-** instead.

I nom.	**on** he		**ona** she	**ono** n. it
4 acc.	**ho, [jej] – něj, něho/jeho** him		**ji – ni** her	**ho, [je] – něj, [ně]**
2 gen.	**ho, [jej] – něj, něho/jeho**		**jí – ní**	**ho – něj, něho/jeho**
3 dat.	**mu – němu/jemu**		**jí – ní**	**mu – němu/jemu**
6 loc.	**(o) něm**		**(o) ní**	**(o) něm**
7 ins.	**jím – ním**		**jí – ní**	**jím – ním**

In the accusative case the forms **něho/jeho** 'him' are masculine animate only.

The feminine accusative **ji – ni** 'her' has a short vowel, while the other case forms of **ona** have a long vowel, **jí – ní**.

Most of the neuter sg. forms are the same as the masculine ones, except for the older accusative forms **je – ně**. These are identical to the accusative plural forms for 'them', and usually avoided in ordinary speech.

I nom.	**oni [ony** mi./f., **ona** n.**]** they
4 acc.	**je – ně** them
2 gen.	**jich – nich**
3 dat.	**jim – nim**
6 loc.	**o nich**
7 ins.	**jimi – nimi** and */dual **jima – nima**

Subject forms, when used, are always stressed. Non-stressed ('enclitic') forms come roughly second position in a sentence, but after any auxiliaries, e.g. **jsem/jsi, jsme/jste,** and the reflexive pronoun **se/si**:

Kdo mě hledá?	Who is looking for me?
Kdo ti to řekl?	Who told you that? Who said that to you?
Zeptali jsme se ho, jestli nás viděl v kině.	We asked him whether he saw us in the cinema.

An extra -e is added to some prepositions before **mě/mne**, **mně** and **mnou** 'me':

beze mě (beze mne), ode mě (ode mne), ze mě (ze mne) 'without, from me, out of me'

ke mně, ve mně 'towards me, in me'

se mnou, přede mnou, nade mnou, pode mnou 'with, in front of, above, below me'

5.2.7 | Stressed personal pronouns

The longer personal pronoun forms required for use after prepositions can also be used on their own as stressed forms, when referring to animate beings. In this context the third-person forms used for emphasis begin with **j-** instead of **n-**, e.g. masculine animate acc./gen. **jeho** and dat. **jemu**.

Emphatic or stressed pronouns often come at the beginning of a sentence. The ordinary forms are used for emphasis where there are no special ones:

Tebe hledal?	Was he looking for you?
Mě (Mne) nehledal.	He wasn't looking for me.
Nás nehledal.	He wasn't looking for us.
Jeho nevidím.	'Him I don't see.' I don't see him.
Jemu nic neřeknu.	I won't say anything to him.

In practice the form **jeho** occurs much more often as the possessive 'his': **jeho kniha** 'his book'.

5.2.8 | Non-subject 'it'

Outside the subject position, inanimate nouns are properly referred to by the corresponding gender of pronoun.

To je krásná zahrada.	That's a lovely garden.
Vidíš ji? Podívej se na ni.	Do you see 'her'/it? Look at 'her'/it.
To je krásný dům.	That's a lovely house.
Vidíš ho? Podívej se na něj.	Do you see him/it? Look at it.
To je krásné auto.	That's a lovely car.
Vidíš ho? Podívej se na něj.	Do you see it? Look at it.

The accusative form **něho** is never inanimate: use **něj** for this.

But the less specific use of neuter **to** 'this' is also often appropriate, here referring to the sight, the scene, rather than grammatically to the noun which was used:

Podívej se na to.	Look at it/this.

5.3 Reflexive pronoun *se* – *zvratné zájmeno*

The pronoun **se** 'self, oneself' refers back to any person of subject. Some verbs are always reflexive – that is to say, they always have **se** attached, e.g. **ptát se** 'to ask'.

Other verbs are reflexive only in certain senses, e.g. **učit se** 'to study', literally 'to teach oneself', alongside non-reflexive **učit** 'to teach'.

5.3.1 Reflexive si

The dative of **se** 'oneself' is **si**, meaning 'to/for oneself'.

Many verbs commonly appear with **si** attached:

Kupuji si svetr.	I buy (for) myself a sweater.
Kupuješ si svetr.	You buy yourself a sweater.
Kupuje si svetr.	S/he buys herself/himself a sweater.
Kupujeme si svetr.	We buy ourselves a sweater.
Kupujete si svetr.	You buy yourselves a sweater.
Kupují si svetr.	They buy themselves a sweater.

Try not to confuse this word when you hear it with **jsi** meaning 'you are'.

Jsi doma?	Are you at home?

5.3.2 | *Each other*

Se 'oneself' can also mean 'each other', in a reciprocal sense:

Mají se rádi.   They like each other.

Nemají se rádi.   They don't like each other.

5.3.3 | *Declension of the reflexive pronoun*

Se (dative si) has further (strong) case forms parallel to those of **ty** 'you':

acc./gen.	**pro sebe**	for oneself
	od sebe	from oneself
dat./loc.	**(k) sobě**	to(wards) oneself
	o sobě	about oneself
ins.	**s sebou**	with oneself

Máš před sebou těžkou úlohu.   You have a hard task in front of yourself.

Vařím pro sebe.   I cook for myself.

5.4 Demonstratives – *ukazovací zájmena*

Demonstratives, e.g. 'this, that', as both 'adjective-like' or 'noun-like' pronouns, indicate that the nouns they refer to are located somewhere within the actual or speech context.

5.4.1 | *Demonstrative ten, ta, to*

The basic Czech demonstrative **ten, ta, to** broadly corresponds to English 'that/those'. It points to something or someone visibly not too far away in the immediate physical environment:

Kdo je ten kluk? Vidíš ho?   Who is that boy? Do you see him?

Co je ta kniha?   What is that book?

Čí je to auto?   Whose is that car?

The same demonstrative can also point backwards within a speech or textual context ('anaphoric reference'). Here it often matches English 'this/these' as well as 'that/those':

Kam jsi dala ty peníze?   Where have you put that/this money?

Potkal jsem dívku a ta   I met a girl, and that/this girl was very
dívka byla velmi krásná.   beautiful.

Sometimes it also points forwards ('cataphoric reference'). Here it usually corresponds to 'that/those', or simply 'the':

Omlouváme se těm studentům, kteří nedostali náš dopis.
We apologise to those/the students who did not get our letter.

Ten, to, ta declines as follows:

Sg.	ma. ‖ mi.	f.	n.
1 nom.	**ten**	**ta**	**to**
4 acc.	**toho ‖ ten**	**tu**	**to**
2 gen.	**toho**	**té, *tý**	**toho**
3 dat.	**tomu**	**té, *tý**	**tomu**
6 loc.	**(o) tom**	**(o) té, *tý**	**(o) tom**
7 ins.	**tím**	**tou**	**tím**

Pl.	ma. ‖ mi.	f.	n.
1 nom.	**ti, *ty ‖ ty**	**ty**	**ta, *ty**
4 acc.	**ty**	**ty**	**ta, *ty**
2 gen.		**těch**	
3 dat.		**těm**	
6 loc.		**(o) těch**	
7 ins.		**těmi**, */dual **těma**	

Note how in the plural both **ti** and **ta** may be replaced by **ty** in colloquial usage to produce a single nom./acc. pl. form.

Kde jsou ti (*ty) kluci?   Where are those boys?

5.4.2 | Declension of onen and jeden

The less common, often formal demonstrative **onen, ona, ono** meaning 'that, the aforesaid, the one referred to' also declines like **ten, to, ta** – compare **onoho – toho, onomu – tomu,** and **oné – té,** and in the plural **oni – ti, ony – ty, oněch – těch** etc.

Toho/Onoho léta bylo chladno.	That summer (genitive) it was cold.

The two are sometimes used contrastively, e.g. **v té nebo oné formě** 'in this or that form'.

Jeden, jedna, jedno 'one' declines the same way (see also 6.1.1 and 6.12), with standard forms (as in the table above):

sg. **jednoho, jednomu, jednom, jedním** and **jednu, jedné, jednou**

pl. **jedni** 'some', **jedny, jedněch, jedněm, jedněmi** (plural cases used for 'one' with plural-only nouns, e.g. **jedny kalhoty** 'one pair of trousers')

5.4.3 | 'This' (Here) versus 'that' (there)

For a more definite 'this (here)' you add an invariable **-hle** to the case forms of **ten, ta, to**, producing **tenhle, tahle, tohle**. Colloquially, this also occurs as *tendle, *tadle, *todle. In formal standard Czech the invariable suffix **-to** is added instead.

Tenhle (tento) časopis je velmi dobrý.	This magazine is very good.
Tahle (tato) kniha je velmi dobrá.	This book is very good.

For greater emphasis you can add another **ten, ta, to** after **-hle**, producing the forms **tenhleten, tahleta, tohleto** (*tendleten, *tadleta, *todleto):

Tenhleten časopis se mi moc líbí.	I like this magazine very much.
Tahleta kniha je moc dobrá.	This book is very good.

Sometimes **tuhle-** or **tadyhle-** 'here' is prefixed to **ten, ta, to** to emphasise the location instead:

Tuhleten časopis je lepší.	This magazine here is better.
Přečti si tadyhletu povídku.	Read this story here.

For an emphatic 'that (there)' add **tam-** or **tamhle-** on the front of **ten,
ta, to**:

Tam(hle)ta kniha není moc dobrá.	That book there is not very good.
Vidíte tam(hle)toho studenta?	Do you see that student there?
Vidíte tam(hle)tu knihu?	Do you see that book there?

The less common demonstrative **onen** (see above) is sometimes used in a similar way, when pointing to a place, e.g. **za oním/tamtím vysokým stromem** 'behind yonder/that tall tree (over there)'.

5.4.4 | *To, tohle etc.*

The neuter sg. noun-like demonstrative pronoun **to** corresponds to the English noun-like pronoun 'that'. It consists of the neuter sg. forms of the demonstrative tabled above.

It may also correspond to English 'it' or 'this' at times, depending on the precise context.

To refers to things or persons which are not defined – or not yet defined – by particular nouns. It often occurs in questions, and in defining statements, which may be answers to such questions. In such contexts English often uses 'it', which is less emphatic than 'that'. When speaking of a person English also often uses 'he' or 'she', where Czech puts **to** 'that':

Co je to?	What is that? What is it?
Co to je?	What *is* that? (emphasis)
To je pomeranč.	That is an orange. It's an orange.
Kdo je to?	Who is that? Who is it? Who is he?
To je Filip.	That is Filip. It's Filip. He's Filip.
Kdo je to?	Who is that? Who is it? Who is she?
To je Eva.	That is Eva. It's Eva. She's Eva.

NB: In the past tense the form of **byl** 'was' agrees with the noun defined, while **to** is again unaffected:

To byl Filip.	That was Filip.
To byla Eva.	That was Eva.

Singular **to** is also used when identifying plural things or persons:

Co to jsou?	What are those?
To jsou pomeranče.	Those are oranges.
To byli jeho kamarádi.	Those were his friends.

To is often used as an equivalent for 'that' when commenting on a situation or a set of circumstances, again something which is not defined by a particular noun:

To je dobré.	That's good.
To je smutné.	That's sad.
To nepomůže.	That won't help.
Nechci tomu věřit.	I do not want to believe that.
Nebudeme o tom mluvit.	We won't talk about that.

To also often corresponds to the less emphatic English 'it' in this kind of context, especially in the lighter non-initial position:

Je to smutné, ale . . .	It is sad, but . . .
Nepomůže to.	It won't help.

For an emphasised 'this', referring to location nearby, the suffixed pronouns **tohle** (also *todle), or **toto** (formal style) can be used:

Co je tohle? (Co je toto?)	What is this?
Kdo je tohle?	Who is this?
Tohle je Pavel.	This is Pavel.
Tomuhle nevěřím.	I don't believe this (dat.).
Tohohle si vážím.	I respect this.

There is also a stronger colloquial form **tohleto** (*todleto) with an extra declinable -to added, which also produces other case forms:

Co je tohleto (*todleto)?	What is this?
O tomhletom nebudeme mluvit.	We won't speak about this.
ve srovnání s tímhletím	in comparison with this

Tuhleto and **tadyhleto** also occur for 'this thing here'.

Conversely, for a more emphatic 'that, that over there', the suffixed forms **tamto** and (colloquially) **tamhleto** may be used:

Co je tam(hle)to?	What is that? What is that over there?

5.4.5 | Further use of ten, ta, to *as pronouns*

Demonstratives can also be used as slightly emphatic third-person noun-like pronouns, referring to people and things already defined, and using the appropriate gender.

Ten nám nic neřekl.	That one (he) didn't tell us anything.
Ta nám nic neřekla.	That one (she) didn't tell us anything.
Ti nám nic neřekli.	Those ones (they) didn't tell us anything.

Vemte si nějaké pomeranče. Tyhle(ty) jsou moc dobré.
Take some oranges. These ones (here) are very good.

The demonstrative can also indicate a switch of grammatical subject, by referring unambiguously to the nearest preceding noun:

Anna tam šla. A ona tam potkala Janu, a ta jí řekla, že jde zítra domů.
Anna went there. And she (i.e. Anna) met Jana there, and she (i.e. that one, Jana) told her she was going home tomorrow.

5.4.6 | Demonstrative takový

Another demonstrative is **takový**, formed like a normal hard-stem adjective, and derived from the adverb **tak** 'so, like this'. It basically means 'such' or 'of that type'.

In practice **takový** corresponds to a whole variety of words and phrases in English – 'suchlike, of that kind, that kind of, like that, a kind of . . .' etc.

It is attached to nouns used variously to denote people or things as being of a certain quality:

Takoví přátelé jsou nebezpeční.	Such friends are dangerous.
Takové auto jsem dlouho neviděl.	I haven't seen a car like that for a long time.

In a slightly different sense:

Filozofie jako taková ho nudí.	Philosophy as such bores him.

Takový may also anticipate the kind of person or thing defined in the noun or adjective which follows:

Takový Dostojevskij by to napsal líp.	Someone like Dostoevsky would have written that better.
Je takový divný.	He is kind of strange.
Byla tam taková bouda.	There was a kind of a hut there.

It can also be used in exclamations:

Taková krása! Taková škoda!	Such beauty! Such a pity!

Just as **tak** 'so' has more emphatic variants **takhle**, formal **takto** 'like this, in this way', **takový** also has its own emphatic variant **takovýhle** (formal **takovýto**) 'this kind of, of this kind', using the same suffixes and referring to a closer, immediate context.

Takovíto/Takovíhle přátelé jsou nebezpeční.	Friends like these (ones here, in this context) are dangerous.
Takovýhle případ jsem ještě nezažil.	I have never experienced such a case like this.

5.4.7 | *English definite and indefinite article*

Czech has no direct equivalents for the definite article 'the' and indefinite article 'a, an'. You just decide what is meant from the context.

Mám kufr.	I have a suitcase.
Kufr je tady.	The suitcase is here.
Pavel je jméno jeho otce.	Pavel is the name of his father.

But sometimes another word may take their place, the number **jeden** 'one' for the indefinitive article, for example, or the demonstrative **ten** for the definitive article.

Jeden můj kamarád mi to řekl.	A friend of mine/One of my friends told me.
Myslíš tu paní, kterou jsme viděli včera?	Do you mean the/that lady we saw yesterday?

Ten often stands for 'the' before a *defining* adjective or noun:

Filip byl ten vysoký/ten nejlepší.	Filip was the tall one/the best (one).
Dám si ten menší banán/ten menší.	I'll take the smaller banana/the smaller one.

5.5   Possessives – *přivlastňovací zájmena*

Possessives act typically as adjective-like pronouns, e.g. **můj přítel** 'my friend', **tvůj dobrý přítel** 'your good friend'.

They can also be used in a noun-like fashion, e.g. **ten hotel je můj** 'that hotel is mine' (note how here English uses 'mine' instead of 'my').

Possessives **můj** 'my' and **tvůj** 'your' correspond in their meaning to personal pronouns **já** 'I' and **ty** 'you' (informal sg.).

The possessive **svůj** 'one's own' corresponds to the reflexive pronoun **se, sebe.**

Possessives **náš** 'our' and **váš** 'your' correspond to **my** 'we' and **vy** 'you' (polite sg. and plural).

Tvůj means possession by someone you address as **ty. Váš** means possession by a person or people addressed as **vy** (plural, or formal).

Můj, tvůj and **svůj** share the same case endings. **Náš** and **váš** have another set of shared case endings. (See the table below.)

Jeho 'his/its' and **jejich** 'their' correspond to personal pronouns **on/ono** 'he, it' and plural **oni/ony/ona** 'they' and are indeclinable, i.e. they never alter their forms.

The possessive **její** 'her' corresponds to the personal pronoun **ona.** It declines like a soft adjective.

Mluvíme o jeho bratrovi, o jejich sestře, o <u>jejím</u> autě.
We are talking about his brother, about their sister, about her car.

The possessive can generally be omitted for family members, when it is clear who is meant:

To je bratr.	This is (my) brother.
To je matka.	This is (my) mother.
To je manžel, manželka.	This is (my) husband, wife.

Můj 'my' and **náš** 'our' show some differences in their case forms from normal adjectives.

Here is a full table of case forms, using as examples 'my, our brother/house/car/sister'.

Most of the forms which are not the same as standard hard adjectives are parallel to the endings of the third person pronoun. Compare **jeho** and **našeho, jemu** and **našemu, jí** and **naší,** and so on.

Sg.

1 nom.	**můj, náš bratr/dům** *but* **moje (mé), naše auto**	**moje (má), naše** sestra
4 acc.	**mého, našeho bratra** rest = nom.	**moji (mou), naši** sestru
2 gen.	**mého, našeho bratra**	**mojí (mé), naší** sestry
3 dat.	**mému, našemu bratrovi**	**mojí (mé), naší sestře**
6 loc.	**(o) mém, našem bratrovi**	**(o) mojí (mé), naší** sestře
7 ins.	**mým, naším bratrem**	**mojí (mou), naší** sestrou

Pl.

1 nom.	**moji (mí), naši bratři** rest = acc. pl.
4 acc.	**moje (mé), naše bratry, sestry/moje (má), naše auta**
2 gen.	**mých, našich bratrů, sester** etc.
3 dat.	**mým, našim bratrům, sestrám**
6 loc.	**(o) mých, našich bratrech, sestrách**
7 ins.	**mými, našimi bratry, sestrami**/dual **mýma, našima očima** 'eyes'

The bracketed variants can sound slightly solemn, while the form **mojí** is mildly colloquial.

The forms **mé, mého, mému** and **mém** may be replaced in speech by *mý, *mýho, *mýmu and *mým, and in the plural **mé, mých, mým, mými** by *mý, *mejch, *mejm, *mejma.

Tvůj and **váš** 'your' and **svůj** 'one's own' have precisely parallel forms to **můj, náš**.

Nezná tvého, vašeho bratra.	S/he doesn't know my, your brother.
Hledám tvoji, vaši sestru.	I'm looking for your sister.
Zná tvoje, vaše rodiče?	Does s/he know our parents?

Possessives can be used immediately after demonstratives, unlike English, e.g.

ten můj přítel	that friend of mine
ta vaše nová kolegyně	that new female colleague of yours

The singular phrases **ten můj, ta moje/ten tvůj, ta tvoje** may refer, sometimes disparagingly, to a person's husband and wife, while **naši/vaši** can often be used on their own to refer to parents, or to sports teams, e.g.

Naši šli někam ven.	Our folks have gone out somewhere.
Naši prohráli.	Our team lost.

5.5.1	*Possessive* svůj

The reflexive possessive **svůj** 'my own' etc. (related to **se** 'oneself') only refers to possession by the subject. Its forms are parallel to **můj** and **tvůj**. It means 'my' if the subject is 'I', but 'your' if it's 'you', and so on.

Ztratil(a) jsem svůj sešit.	I've lost my [own] exercise book.
Ztratil(a) jsi svoji tužku?	Have you lost your [own] pencil?
Věra ztratila svoji knihu.	Věra has lost her [own] book.
Karel ztratil svoje pero.	Karel has lost his [own] pen.
Děti ztratily svého kamaráda.	The children have lost their [own] friend.
Ztratili jsme svoje poznámky.	We've lost our [own] notes.

Compare examples where the possessor is *not* the subject of the sentence:

Ztratil moji knihu.	He lost my book.
Irena ztratila její knihu.	Irena lost her (= another person's) book.
Petr ztratil jeho pero.	Petr lost his (= another person's) pen.

The idiomatic negative **nesvůj** meaning 'not himself' occurs in the nominative, with the shorter forms only:

Je nesvá.   She is not herself.

Jsou nesví.   They are not themselves.

5.5.2 Vlastní *own*

The adjectival word **vlastní** 'own' only partially overlaps with **svůj**. It more specifically indicates personal ownership but need not refer to possession by the grammatical subject:

To je jeho vlastní auto. That is his own car.

Má vlastní auto. (Or: **Má svoje auto.** Or, more emphatically: **Má svoje vlastní auto.**) He has his own car. He has a car of his own.

5.6 Interrogatives – *tázací zájmena*

Interrogative pronouns ask about a person or thing, e.g. **kdo?** 'who?' **co?** 'what?'

5.6.1 Kdo – *who?* and co – *what?*

To ask the question 'who?' you use the interrogative pronoun **kdo**. To ask 'what?' you use **co**, e.g.

Kdo je to?   Who is it?

Co je to?   What is it?

Interrogative **kdo** counts as grammatically masculine, as the past tense form shows, while **co** is neuter:

Kdo tam byl?   Who was there?

Co tam bylo?   What was there?

If 'who?' or 'what?' is the object **kdo** becomes **koho**, but **co** is unchanged, being inanimate:

Koho hledáte?   Who are you looking for?

Co hledáte?   What are you looking for?

The case forms of **kdo** and **co** are as follows:

I nom.	**kdo**	**co**
4 acc.	**koho**	**co**
2 gen.	**koho**	**čeho**
3 dat.	**komu**	**čemu**
6 loc.	**(o) kom**	**(o) čem**
7 ins.	**kým**	**čím**

Note how English commonly puts prepositions like 'about' and 'for' at
the end of questions. This is not allowed in Czech:

O čem mluvíte?   What are you talking about? = About
                       what . . .?

O kom mluvíte?   Who are you talking about? = About
                       whom . . .?

Komu vaříš oběd?   Who are you cooking lunch for? = For
                       whom . . .?

The same two words also introduce what are called indirect questions,
where the question is not asked directly, but referred to in a subordinate
clause:

Nevím, kdo to je.   I don't know who that is.

Nevím, co to je.   I don't know what that is.

Note idiomatic use of **co** in:

Co je to za člověka?   What kind of person is that?

Co je to za zvíře?   What kind of animal is that?

5.6.2 Contracted -č, -ň

The masculine third-person pronoun is occasionally contracted to **-ň**
and the interrogative pronoun **co** 'what' to **-č** after certain prepositions
followed by the accusative, and **do** followed by the genitive:

doň, doč; naň, nač; oň, oč; proň, proč; veň, več; zaň, zač

The interrogative **proč?** 'why, for what reason?' is the only high-
frequency item. Much less common is **nač?** 'for what purpose?' There
are also a few fixed idioms using forms with **-č**:

93

Proč mi to říkáte?	Why are you telling me this?
Nač bych tam chodil?	What would I go there for?
Nač si kazit odpoledne?	Why spoil one's afternoon? (= to what purpose)
Děkuji. – Není zač.	Thank you. – It was nothing. (You're welcome.)
Oč běží? O co běží?	What is going on? What is this all about?

The -ň forms are much rarer, and you really only need to recognise them:

Pak se doň zavěsila.	Then she linked arms with him.
Vrhala se naň celým svým tělem.	She hurled herself at him with her whole body.
Je sám, tak přijď si proň.	He's alone, so come for him, i.e. come and fetch him.
Byla na cestě, aby se zaň provdala.	She was on the way to marry him.

5.6.3 | *Someone, something etc.*

Indefinite pronouns refer to or identify a person or thing only vaguely. They are often formed from interrogatives by means of a prefix, e.g. **někdo** 'someone', **něco** 'something'.

Indefinite pronouns are regularly produced by adding the prefix **ně-** 'some-' to an interrogative, e.g. **někdo** 'someone, somebody', **něco** 'nothing'.

Někdo 'someone, somebody' changes to **někoho** if it is the object, but **něco** 'something' remains unchanged:

Je tam někdo?	Is somebody there?
Někoho hledám.	I'm looking for someone.
Něco hledám.	I am looking for something.

The indefinite pronouns have case forms identical to the interrogatives from which they are derived:

někoho, někomu, (o) někom and **někým** 'of someone' etc.

něčeho, něčemu, (o) něčem and **něčím** 'of something' etc.

A rather similar set of words is produced with the suffix **-si** meaning 'some . . . or other':

kdosi 'a certain someone, someone or other', **cosi** 'a certain something, something or other'

There are adverbs of place and time with the same attached elements, e.g.

kde 'where?', **někde** 'somewhere', **kdesi** 'a certain somewhere, somewhere or other'

kdy 'when?', **někdy** 'sometimes, sometime', **kdysi** 'once, at some time in the past'

5.6.4 | *No one – nikdo, nothing – nic*

The negative equivalents of **kdo** and **co** are **nikdo** 'no one, nobody' and (irregular form) **nic** 'nothing'. They require negative verbs as well, so-called double negatives, and the results can be translated into English in two basic ways:

Nebyl tam nikdo.   Nobody was there. There wasn't anybody there.

Nebylo tam nic.   Nothing was there. There wasn't anything there.

Again they have parallel case forms:

nikoho, nikomu, (o) nikom and **nikým** 'of no one' etc.

ničeho, ničemu, (o) ničem and **ničím** 'of nothing' etc.

5.6.5 | *Genitive of quality following co, něco, nic*

When **co**, **něco** and **nic** and other compounds of **co** (e.g. **cokoli** 'anything') are in their basic forms, they are followed by adjectives or adjectival words describing quality in the genitive:

Co je nového?   What's new?

Něco strašného.   Something awful.

Něco takového.   Something of the sort. Something like that.

Není nic nového.   Nothing's new.

(This does not happen with **někdo**, e.g. **někdo nový** 'someone new'.)

In other inflected cases the genitive is not used, which is similar to what happens with numerals and other quantifiers:

Před něčím takovým člověk neví, co má dělat.
Faced with something like that one doesn't know what to do.

| **5.6.6** | *Interrogatives* **jaký**, **jak** *and* **který** |

The common interrogative **jaký -á -é?** asks the question 'what kind of?', in English often 'what . . . like?' It declines like a standard hard-stem adjective:

Jaký je to román?	What kind of novel is it? What is the novel like?
Jaký je?	What is it like?
Jaká je to žena?	What kind of woman is she?
Jaká je?	What is she like?
Jaké je to auto?	What kind of car is it? What is the car like?
Jaké je?	What is it like?

The related interrogative adverb **jak** asks the question 'how?':

Jak to děláte?	How do you do that?

Both can also introduce exclamations:

Jaká škoda!	What a pity!
Jak ten čas letí!	How time flies!

The interrogative **který -á -é** similarly asks the question 'which?' It also declines like a standard adjective. Compare with the above:

Které je to auto?	Which car is it?

These interrogatives can also be used in indirect questions, where the question is referred to in a subordinate clause, e.g.

Nevím, které je to auto.	I don't know which car it is.
Nevím, jaké je to auto.	I don't know what kind of car it is. I don't know what the car is like.
Nevím, jak to děláte.	I don't know how you do it.

| **5.6.7** | *How, what kind of, some, any* |

Various words involving the idea of 'some' are derived from **jak**, **jaký** and **který**, as follows:

jak 'how?', **nějak** 'somehow', **jaksi** 'in some way or other' (adverbs)

jaký 'what kind of?', **nějaký** 'some, any', **jakýsi** 'some certain kind or other of'

který? 'which?', **některý** 'some, certain particular kind(s) of', **kterýsi** 'some particular kind or other of'

Distinguish:

Byly tam nějaké pomeranče?	Were there some/any oranges there?
Byly tam nějaké pomeranče.	There were some oranges there.
Dostali nějaké pomeranče.	They got some oranges.

Byly tam/Dostali jakési pomeranče.
There were some kind (or other) of oranges there. They got some kind of oranges.

Některé pomeranče nejsou sladké.
Some (certain particular kinds of) oranges are not sweet.

Některé (z nich) nebyly sladké. Some (of them) were not sweet.

The indefinite quantifier **několik** may also mean 'some' in the sense of 'a certain number of, several' (rather than 'some kind of'). It is derived from **kolik?** 'how much? how many?', and is followed by the genitive case (details in 6.8):

Bylo tam několik pomerančů a několik jahod.
There were several oranges there and several strawberries.

5.7   Relative pronouns – *vztažná zájmena*

Where English 'who' has nothing to do with a question, but refers to a preceding noun, it introduces what is traditionally called a relative clause. The relative clause further describes this preceding noun, habitually called its antecedent.

5.7.1 *Relative pronoun* který

Který -á -é functions as a relative pronoun 'who, which', as well as an interrogative, as discussed just above.

The gender and number of **který** have to match its antecedent, i.e. the particular noun it refers back to:

97

Mám bratra, který se učí česky. I have a brother who is learning Czech.

Mám sestru, která se učí anglicky. I have a sister who is learning English.

If the noun referred back to is a thing, **který** corresponds to English 'which' (which is often replaced by 'that' or omitted in English):

Auto, které tady vidíte, je výborné.
The car (which) you see here is excellent.

The case of **který** has to correspond to its function within its relative clause. Sometimes in English we also use the form 'whom' to indicate that the relative pronoun 'who' is not the subject of the relative clause. In this example **kterého** is the object of **potkali**, and therefore has to be in the accusative case. Moreover, the antecedent noun **člověk** to which **který** refers is masculine, and so the accusative of **který** has to be the masculine animate accusative singular:

To jen ten člověk, kterého jsme potkali včera.
That is that person [who(m)] we met yesterday.

Use this table to test your knowledge of Czech adjectives. Do you immediately know which gender form is which? If not, go and revise them.

	Sg.	Pl.
I nom.	**který, které, která**	**kteří, které, která**
4 acc.	**který/kterého, které, kterou**	**které, která**
2 gen.	**kterého, které**	**kterých**
3 dat.	**kterému, které**	**kterým**
6 loc.	**(o) kterém, které**	**(o) kterých**
7 ins.	**kterým, kterou**	**kterými,** dual **kterýma**

Spoken Czech often uses the genderless nom./acc. plural form *který.
  Other non-standard usage is the same throughout as for adjectives, e.g.

singular: *kterej = který, *který = které, *kterýho, *kterýmu, *kterym

plural: *který, *kterejch, *kterejm, *kterejma

You will also come across casual forms *kerej, *kerýho etc.

5.7.2 | Colloquial relative co

In colloquial Czech the relative pronoun **který** is often replaced by **co** 'what'. This resembles some people's regional English usage:

To je ten muž, co chodí denně do našeho parku.
That's that man 'what' comes every day to our park.

Co never alters in this usage. You get round any need for a preposition or another case by adding a pronoun phrase as if it was in a separate sentence:

To je ten muž, co jsme o něm včera mluvili.
That's the man 'what' we were speaking about ['him'] yesterday.

= more formal style: . . . **o kterém jsme včera mluvili.**

To je ta žena, co jsme o ní včera mluvili.
That's the woman we were talking about yesterday.

= more formal style: . . . **o které jsme včera mluvili.**

5.7.3 | Relative use of kdo and co after pronouns

When you refer back to a pronoun, rather than a noun, **kdo** can be used as an animate relative, while **co** is inanimate. In colloquial Czech **co** can be used for both:

Ten, kdo (colloq. **co**) **mi to řekl, už odjel.**	The one who told me this has now left.
To, co mi říkáte, je velmi důležité.	That which you are telling me is very important.
Řekni všechno, co umíš.	Say everything you know.

Kdo and **co** may be treated as plural, if the antecedent pronoun is plural. Sometimes **který** is used in such circumstances instead:

Všichni, kdo/kteří ho znali, chválili ho.	All who knew him praised him.
Ti, kdo/kteří ho znali, chválili ho.	Those who knew him praised him.

5.7.4 | Relative což

Note also **což** for 'which', referring back to a whole clause as its antecedent, rather than a particular noun:

Nerad se učí, což mě	He doesn't like studying, which
nepřekvapuje.	doesn't surprise me.

The related temporal relative **načež** 'whereupon' is used rather similarly:

Odešel, načež začalo pršet.	He left, whereupon it started to
	rain.

5.7.5 | Relative pronoun jenž

In formal written style, another relative **jenž** also occurs as a alternative for the standard relative pronoun **který, -á, -é** 'who, which'.

Problém, jenž (= který) stojí před námi, je velmi vážný.
The problem which stands before us is a very serious one.

This pronoun is not normally used in everyday speech.

The case forms of **jenž**, apart from the nominative forms, are basically the same as the personal pronoun forms for 'him, her, it' (the stronger, more conservative forms, where these differ), with -ž stuck on the end.

	ma. || mi. (n.)	f.	m., f., n. pl.
I nom.	**jenž (jež** n.)	**jež**	**již** ma., **jež** others
4 acc.	**jehož || jejž (jež** n.)	**již**	**jež**
2 gen.	**jehož**	**jíž**	**jichž**
3 dat.	**jemuž**	**jíž**	**jimž**
6 loc.	**o němž**	**o níž**	**o nichž**
7 ins.	**jímž**	**jíž**	**jimiž**, */dual **jimaž**

The forms after prepositions have **n-** instead of **j-**, just like the forms of the corresponding personal pronouns.

Muž, do něhož (= do kterého) se zamilovala, byl její lékař.
The man with whom she fell in love was her doctor.

Člověk, jemuž (= kterému) dala peníze, utekl do jižní Ameriky.
The person to whom she gave the money ran away to South America.

5.7.6 | Interrogative and relative 'whose'

To ask the question 'whose?' you use the interrogative **čí?**, which declines just like a soft adjective, although it most often occurs in the nominative or accusative.

Čí je to dopis?   Whose letter is that?

Čí je to auto?   Whose car is that?

For 'whose' at the head of *relative* clauses there are three possibilities, depending on the gender and number of the antecedent noun:

jehož 'whose' (masculine or neuter sg.):

To je muž, jehož mínění si vážím.
That is a man whose opinion I respect. (**vážit si** + gen.)

jejíž 'whose' (feminine sg.):

To je žena, jejíhož mínění si vážím.
That is a woman whose opinion I respect.

jejichž 'whose' (plural, all genders):

To jsou lidé, jejichž mínění si vážím.
Those are people whose opinion I respect.

5.8   Interrogatives and their derivatives

Here is a summary list of interrogatives, including a variety of others not discussed above.

Those which are not pronouns ending in -ý or -í have invariable forms, and can mostly be classified as adverbs, e.g. **kde?** 'where?'

Kolik? 'How much/many?' is a quantifier as well as an interrogative.

co? what	**Co je to?** What is it?
čí? whose?	**Čí je ten kabát?** Whose is that coat?
jak? how?	**Jak se to dělá?** How is that done?
jaký? what kind of?	**Jaké máte auto?** What kind of car do you have?
kam? where to?	**Kam jdete?** Where are you going?
kde? where?	**Kde jste?** Where are you?
kdo? who?	**Kdo jste?** Who are you?

kdy? when?	**Kdy přijedeš?** When will you arrive?
kolik? how much/many?	**Kolik to stojí?** How much does it cost?
	Kolik studentů? How many students?
	(genitive of quantity after **kolik**)
kolikátý? 'what number?'	**Kolikátého je dnes?** What's today's date?
	(genitive date, e.g. **pátého května** 5th May)
který? which?	**Kterou knihu chcete?** Which book do you want?
kudy? which/what way?	**Kudy šli?** Which way did they go?
odkud? where from?	**Odkud jste?** Where are you from?
proč? why?	**Proč mi nepíšeš?** Why don't you write to me?

The plain forms of some interrogatives can also correspond to English senses with an added 'some-' or (with negatives) 'any-' in combination with infinitives, or at least where an infinitive can be understood.

This usage is in fact similar to interrogatives in indirect questions. The first example below concerns the question **kam jít?** where to go? and whether the answer to it is yes or no:

Má kam jít.	S/he has somewhere to go.
Nemá kam jít.	S/he doesn't have anywhere to go.
Nemá kam.	S/he has nowhere (i.e. to go).
Nemá kde bydlet.	S/he doesn't have anywhere to live. She has nowhere to live.
Nemá s kým.	S/he doesn't have anyone to go with.
Má co jíst.	S/he has something to eat.
Nemá co jíst.	S/he doesn't have anything to eat. She has nothing to eat.
Nemá co dělat.	S/he doesn't have anything to do.

Various other closely related words are derived from these interrogatives using certain recurring prefixes and suffixes. This is not a complete list.

ně- some	**něco** something, **někdo** someone
	někde somewhere, **někam** (to) somewhere
	někdy sometimes, at some time
	nějak somehow, **nějaký** some, some kind of
	některý some, certain, esp. plural
ni- no	**nic** nothing, **nikdo** nobody
	nikde nowhere, **nikam** (to) nowhere
	nikdy never
bůhví- God knows	**bůhvíco** God knows what
	bůhvíjak God knows how
	bůhvíkde God knows where
lec- various	**leckdo** some people, **leccos** this and that
málo- few	**málokdo** few people, **málokde** in few places
	málokdy seldom
-pak then	**kdopak?** 'who then?' (emphatic)
	copak 'what then?'
-si some . . . or other	**cosi** something or other
	kdosi someone or other, **kdesi** somewhere or other
	kdysi sometime or other (in the past), once
-koli(v) any	**kdokoli(v)** anyone, anybody, **cokoli(v)** anything
	kdykoli(v) any time
	kdekoli(v) anywhere, **jakýkoli(v)** any kind of

Similarly related are:

jin- other	**jinde** elsewhere, **jinam** (to) elsewhere
	jindy another time, **jinak** otherwise, in another way
vš- all	**všude** everywhere, **vždy(cky)** always
všeli- all kinds of	**všelijak** in all kinds of ways, **všelijaký** all kinds of

5.8.1 | Interrogatives as relatives

Some interrogatives other than those already discussed can also sometimes function as relatives, introducing relative clauses and referring back to an antecedent:

jaký the like of which	**To je přítel, jakých je málo.** That is a friend, the like of which there are few.
kam (to) where	**Chodím (tam), kam chci.** I go where I want.
kde where	**To je dům, kde jsem se narodil.** That is the house where I was born.
kudy by which	**Hledali cestu, kudy šli.** They looked for the way they came.
kdy when	**To je rok, kdy jsem se narodil.** That's the year when I was born.

But note that the basic conjunction for 'when' in an adverbial clause is **když**. Here there is no noun antecedent – unlike the relative clause example just above, where the relative **kdy** referred to **rok**.

Když odešel, začalo pršet.   When he left, it started to rain.

5.9 Sám and Samý

Sám 'himself', **sama** 'herself', **samo** 'itself', also 'alone', has short adjective forms in the nominative and accusative, but long adjective forms in other cases. Long forms also occur sometimes in the accusative.

Sg.	ma. ‖ mi.	f.	n.
nom.	**sám**	**sama**	**samo**
acc.	**sama, samého ‖ sám**	**samu, samou**	**samo**
Pl.			
nom.	**sami ‖ samy**	**samy**	**sama**
acc.	**samy, samé**	**samy, samé**	**sama, samá**

Other forms have standard long adjectival endings, e.g. **samému, samém** etc.

Sám emphasises the subject:

Sám to víš nejlíp.	You know it best yourself.
Napsal to sám král.	The king himself wrote it.
Svědčí o tom sám fakt, že . . .	This is witnessed to by the fact that . . .
Byla poctivost sama.	She was honesty itself.
Sama operace byla jednoduchá.	The operation itself was simple.

It can also express independence, self-reliance:

Udělal jsem to sám, sama.	I did it (by) myself.
Udělal to sám.	He did it (by) himself.
Udělala to sama.	She did it (by) herself.
Opravíme si to sami.	We will correct it (by) ourselves.
Dobré zboží se chválí samo.	Fine goods praise themselves. (saying)

Or it expresses isolation:

Cestoval sám.	He travelled alone.
Zůstal tam sám.	He remained/was left there (by) himself, alone.
Chodí všude sama.	She goes everywhere (by) herself, alone.
Zůstali tam sami.	They were left alone there.
Konečně byli sami.	At last they were alone.

In the isolation sense it is often replaced by the more emphatic **samotný**:

Nechali ho tam sama/ samotného.	They left him there alone/by himself.
Nechali ji tam samu/samotnou.	They left her there alone/by herself.
Nechali děti doma samy/ samotné.	They left the children alone at home.

Colloquially also in the emphatic sense, and corresponding to English 'the very':

Mě samého/samotného to zajímá. That interests me myself.

Combined with the strong forms of the reflexive pronoun **sebe** it emphasises the subject of the verb. Notice how a preposition comes between the two words:

Udělal to sám od sebe.	He did it by himself, off his own bat.
Spoléhej sám na sebe.	Rely upon yourself, lit. 'yourself upon yourself'.
Sám sebe nenávidí.	He hates himself.
Sama sebe nenávidí.	She hates herself.
Sám o sobě není zlý.	He himself, in himself, is not bad/nasty.
Sama o sobě není zlá.	She herself is not bad/nasty.
Pomáhají sami sobě.	They help themselves/each other.
Žili sami pro sebe.	They lived for themselves.
To se rozumí samo sebou.	That is understood by itself. That goes without saying.

Sometimes it agrees in case with **sebe**, emphasising it (rather than the subject of the verb), particularly in the sense of 'the self, one's own self'.

Milovati budeš bližního svého jako sebe samého.	You will love your neighbour (lit. 'near one') as yourself.
Musíte zapomenout na sebe samého.	You have to forget your own self.
Spatřila sebe samu/samou.	She saw herself, her own self.
Strašně ráda poslouchá sebe samu.	She just loves listening to herself, her own voice.

For **ten samý** in the sense of 'the same' see the next section.

The long adjective form **samý** is also used in the sense of 'nothing but':

Kolem nich byla samá voda.	Around them there was nothing but water.
Byli to samí studenti.	They were all students, nothing else but students.
Jsou to samé lži.	Those are nothing but lies.

Both the long or short form, or alternatively **samotný**, may be used in the sense of English 'the very' to emphasise a limit, boundary or quantity:

Sám/Samý/Samotný vrchol hory byl ještě daleko.	The very summit of the mountain was still far off.
Na samém/samotném konci cesty.	At the very end of the road.
Od samého/samotného počátku.	From the very beginning.
Pro samé stromy nevidí les.	S/he can't see the wood for the (very) trees (themselves).
Pro samou práci se nestačí najíst.	With all the work s/he doesn't have time to eat.

5.10 The same

There is more than one way of saying 'the same' in Czech. You can use the adjective-type word **stejný**:

Stále dělá stejné chyby.	He keeps making the same mistakes.
Je to stejný člověk.	It's the same person.
To je stejná píseň.	That is the same song.

Many people also use the phrase **ten samý** for 'the same', 'one and the same', 'the identical', but this usage is often disapproved of in writing:

To je (jedna a) ta samá píseň.	That's (one and) the same song.

For a neuter pronoun meaning 'the same thing' you can use **totéž**, usually in the nominative/accusative only in ordinary usage.

Karel řekl totéž/to samé.	Karel said the same (thing).

| 5.10.1 | *The same* – **týž/tentýž** |

Another adjective form **týž/tentýž** '(one and) the same' is not usual in everyday speech, except for neuter sg. **totéž** in the noun-like sense of 'the same thing'. This rather formal word has these case forms:

	Sg.		Pl.
1 nom.	m. **týž/tentýž**, n. **totéž**	f. **táž/tatáž**	ma. **tíž/titíž** (rest = acc.)
4 acc.	= nom. (ma. = gen.)	**touž/tutéž**	m./f. **tytéž**, n. **táž/tatáž**
2 gen.	**téhož**	**téže**	**týchž**
3 dat.	**témuž**	**téže**	**týmž**
6 loc.	**(o) témž(e)/ tomtéž**	**(o) téže**	**(o) týchž**
7 ins.	**týmž/tímtéž**	**touž/toutéž**	**týmiž**/dual **týmaž**

Note that although the word **též** looks as if it might belong in this table, in fact it is a formal variant for **také** 'also, likewise'.

5.11 *Jiný* etc. – other, another

The Czech equivalents for the English words 'other, another' need a bit of careful attention, even at the simplest level.

The adjectival word **jiný** means 'another, other, different'. **Odlišný** means more specifically 'distinct, different' and is a full adjective with comparative and superlative forms, unlike **jiný**.

Byli tam psi, kočky a jiná zvířata.	There were dogs, cats and other animals there.
To je jiná (odlišná) barva.	That is another (a different) colour.
To je jiná věc.	That's another thing/matter.
Přešli na jiné téma.	They moved on to another topic/ theme.

The 'other' of two is **druhý**, which also means 'the second, next':

Na druhé straně řeky je zámek.	There is a castle on the other side of the river.
Přišel druhý den.	He came the next day.

'Another' or 'other' in the sense of 'additional' is **další**, lit. 'further':

Dáme si další pivo, ne?	We'll have another beer, shall we? (lit. '. . . no?')
Potom přišel další člověk.	Then another person arrived.
Potom tam přišli další lidé.	Then some other people arrived there.

But 'the other(s)' in the sense of 'the remaining, the rest' is the soft adjectival word **ostatní**:

Potom tam přišli ostatní (studenti).
Then the rest (of the students) came. Then the others (the other students) came.

5.12 *Všichni, všechno* – all

The word for 'all' is particularly frequent in the plural. Masculine animate forms are nominative **všichni**, accusative **všechny**, also used for 'everyone':

Všichni ho znali.	Everyone knew him. They all knew him.
Byli tam všichni kluci.	All the boys were there.
Pozvali všechny kluky.	They invited all the boys.

For other genders you use **všechny** (written neuter form **všechna**) for both cases:

Byly tam všechny ženy.	All the women were there.
Pozvali všechny ženy.	They invited all the women.

The commonest singular form is neuter **všechno** 'all, everything'.

Other forms of neuter **všechno** are shorter. In the singular they match **našeho, našemu** etc. 'our':

Mluvila o všem.	She spoke about everything.
Všemu rozuměla.	She understood everything.

109

In the plural the other case forms match **těch, těm, těmi** 'those':

Mluvila se všemi o všech problémech.
She spoke with everyone about all the problems.

Here is the complete table of singular and plural forms:

	Sg.		Pl.
I nom.	m. **všechen**, n. **všechno**	f. **všechna**	ma. **všichni** (rest = acc.)
4 acc.	= nom. (ma. = gen.)	**všechnu**	m./f. **všechny**, n. **všechna**
2 gen.	**všeho**	**vší**	**všech**
3 dat.	**všemu**	**vší**	**všem**
6 loc.	(o) **všem**	(o) **vší**	(o) **všech**
7 ins.	**vším**	**vší**	**všemi**, */dual **všema**

Formal alternatives are neuter **vše** = **všechno** and rarer feminine **vši** = **všechnu**.

Other variants have a colloquial colouring, or are more or less obsolete (†). The commonest is neuter sg. **všecko**:

všecek and †**všecken** = **všechen**

všeck|o -a, -u, -y and †**všeckno** etc. = **všechn|o -a, -u, -y**

všicci and †**všickni** = **všichni**

also plural †**všechněch** and †**všeckněch**, †**všechněm(i)** and †**všeckněm(i)** = **všech, všem(i)**

A complete group of two is described as **oba** m., **obě** f./n. 'both', which declines just like the numeral **dva** m., **dvě** f./n. 'two' (see 6.1.6).

Byli tam oba/oba dva.
They were both there. Both of them were there. The two of them were there.

S oběma/oběma dvěma byly potíže.
There were difficulties with both (of them), with the two of them.

Note also the adjectival word **veškerý** 'the entire', which in formal usage sometimes has short forms, including an odd masculine nom.

sg. **veškeren**, e.g. **veškeren svět** 'the entire world', alongside **veškera**, **veškero** etc.

Zaplatil veškeré výdaje.	He paid all the expenses, the entire expenses.
Věnují veškerý volný čas studiu.	They devote all their spare time, their entire spare time to study.

5.12.1 Všechen, celý – *all, the whole*

Singular forms of masculine **všechen**, feminine **všechna** (acc. **všechnu**) are relatively rare, but are used with nouns for uncountable 'stuff':

Snědl všechen salát, všechnu zeleninu.
He ate up all the salad/vegetable.

For nouns seen as unitary countable items, use **celý** for 'all, (the) whole':

Zůstal tam celý den.	He stayed there all day, the whole day.
Vypili celou láhev.	They drank the whole bottle, all of the bottle.
Celý národ se radoval.	The whole nation rejoiced. All the nation rejoiced.
Celé hodiny nemluvila.	She didn't speak for whole hours on end.
Byl celý bledý.	(Also possible is: **Byl všecek bledý.**) He was all pale, pale all over.

5.13 Každý – *each, every*

The word **každý** 'each, every, everybody' is another quantifier closely related in meaning to **všichni** 'all', but it is singular in meaning and puts the focus on a single example taken out of a whole group. It can be both 'noun-like' and 'adjective-like' in usage:

Každý to říká.	Everyone says it.

Compare:

Všichni to říkají.	They all say it.
Každý den je jiný.	Every day is different.

5.14 *Jediný* – only, sole

The adjectival word **jediný** 'sole, only, one and only, a single' is used to indicate that the things or persons referred to form a complete set in the given context. It emphasises the lack of others.

Je to můj jediný bratr.	He is my only brother.
Byly to jediné básně tohoto autora.	These were the only poems of this author.
Bylo tam jen jediné okno.	There was only a single (one single) window.
Neměli ani jediný dobrý nápad.	They didn't have a single good idea.

5.15 *Žádný* – no, not any

The opposite of 'all' is the adjectival word **žádný** 'no, not any, none'. It is accompanied by a negative verb, and sometimes also stands for **nikdo** 'nobody', where it may be gender-specific:

Nemáme žádný čas.	We have no time. We don't have any time.
Neměli žádné jídlo.	They had no food. They didn't have any food.
To ti žádný neuvěří.	Nobody will believe you (in) this.
To ti žádná neřekne.	No woman will tell you this.

The less common alternative **nijaký** 'no, none . . . of any kind' is more emphatic:

To nemá na to nijaký (vůbec žádný) vliv.
That doesn't have any influence on it (at all).

Chapter 6

Numerals and quantifiers – číslovky

A numeral (**číslovka**) is basically a word which expresses a number (**číslo**), e.g. cardinal numerals **jeden** 'one', **dva** 'two', **tři** 'three', but also ordinal numerals **první** 'first', **druhý** 'second', **třetí** 'third' etc.

Numerals are best considered as a separate class of word in Czech, for various reasons, and the way they behave in connection with nouns and verbs requires some detailed explanation.

A numeral is a precise kind of quantifier. Certain 'indefinite quantifiers' (**neurčité číslovky**) resemble numerals closely in the way they operate, words like **několik** 'several', **mnoho** 'many', **málo** 'few'. These are also discussed in this chapter.

6.1   Cardinal numerals – *základní číslovky*

We look first at the cardinal numerals, corresponding to English 'one, two, three, four, five . . .' In English these precede their nouns just as if they were adjectives: 'one book, three books' etc.

In Czech these numerals hesitate between the role of nouns and the role of adjectives.

Numerals one to four function as if they were adjectives, but Czech numerals from 'five' upwards behave like nouns followed by the genitive case, unless the whole phrase is in a case other than the nominative or accusative. Examples below.

6.1.1   One

The numeral **jeden, jedna, jedno** 'one' declines like the demonstrative **ten, ta, to** (see 5.4.1–5.4.2).

jeden dolar	one dollar
jedna koruna (libra)	one crown (pound)
jedno pivo (euro)	one beer (euro)

Kolik to stojí? Jednu korunu.	How much does it cost? One crown (accusative).
Mám jednoho bratra.	I have one brother.
Mám jednu sestru.	I only have one sister.
Řekl to jednomu člověku.	He said it to one person.
Řekl to jedné kamarádce.	He said it to one (female) friend.

When citing the number one on its own, the feminine form **jedna** is normally used, e.g. **číslo jedna** the 'number one'.

6.1.2 | Two to four

Nominative/accusative **dva** 'two' becomes **dvě** with feminine and neuter nouns. Nominative/accusative **tři** 'three' and **čtyři** 'four' do not alter. With numbers 2–4 plural forms of nominative/accusative nouns are used, as in English:

dvě, tři, čtyři koruny	two, three, four crowns
dvě, tři, čtyři libry, eura	two, three, four pounds, euros
but **dva . . . dolary**	two etc. dollars (*masculine*)

6.1.3 | Five upwards

Unlike the lower numbers, five and above are treated as nouns followed by the genitive case, if the number is in a context requiring the nominative or accusative case:

Mám pět, šest, sedm . . . korun.	I have five, six, seven . . . ['of'] crowns.
osm, devět, deset . . . liber, eura	Eight, nine, ten . . . ['of'] pounds, euros
pět . . . dolarů	five . . . ['of'] dollars

6.1.4 | Numbers 1–20

For the '-teens' basically just add **-náct** to numbers one to nine, but watch out for 14, 15 and 19.

jeden/jedna/jedno	1	jedenáct	11
m. **dva**, f.n. **dvě**	2	dvanáct	12
tři	3	třináct	13
čtyři	4	čtrnáct (!)	14
pět	5	patnáct (!)	15
šest	6	šestnáct	16
sedm	7	sedmnáct	17
osm	8	osmnáct	18
devět	9	devatenáct (!)	19
deset	10	dvacet	20

As we have noted, nominative/accusative forms **pět** = five upwards are followed by the genitive plural. So you say:

Mám čtyři koruny.　　　I have four crowns.

but:

Mám pět korun.　　　I have five crowns.

Nominative/accusative phrases with five upwards are also treated as neuter singular for verb agreement:

Přišlo deset kamarádů.　Ten friends came.
(*but:* **Přišli tři kamarádi.**　Three friends came.)

Přijde osm lidí.　　　Eight people will come.
(*but:* **Přijdou čtyři lidé.**　Four people will come.)

Bylo nás pět.　　　There were five of us.
Je nás pět.　　　There are five of us.
(*but:* **Jsme tři.**　　　We are three.)

If the phrase is qualified, e.g. by **každý** 'every', the qualifier agrees in case with the noun, but precedes the numeral, e.g.

každé dva měsíce　　　every two months

but:

každých šest měsíců　　　every six months

6.1.5 | *Higher cardinal numerals*

The numerals for twenty up to a hundred are:

> 20 **dvacet**, 30 **třicet**, 40 **čtyřicet**, 50 **padesát**, 60 **šedesát**,
> 70 **sedmdesát**, 80 **osmdesát**, 90 **devadesát**, 100 **sto**

The hundreds are:

> 200 **dvě stě** (!), 300 **tři sta**, 400 **čtyři sta** – but then 500 **pět set**,
> 600 **šest set**, 700 **sedm set**, 800 **osm set**, 900 **devět set**

1,000 is **tisíc**, 2,000/3,000/4,000 **dva/tři/čtyři tisíce** – but 5,000/6,000
pět/šest tisíc (NB) and so on.

'A million' is simply **milion**, then dva **miliony** . . . pět **milionů** . . .
Miliarda = 'a thousand million', dvě **miliardy** . . . pět **miliard** . . .

Intermediate numbers are easy enough:

> **sedm set padesát tři** 753

> **devět set devadesát devět** 999

The higher intermediate cardinal numerals, 21–29 etc. are simply combinations of numbers (for 'one' and 'two' always use **jedna** and **dva**):

> **dvacet jedna** 21, **dvacet dva** 22 . . . **dvacet devět** 29

Sometimes reversed forms are used: **jed(e)nadvacet** 'one and twenty',
dvaadvacet 'two and twenty' etc.

6.1.6 | *Case forms of numbers*

In 'non-basic' number phrases – i.e. those which are not nominative-
subject or accusative-object (or accusative after a preposition) – a
numeral goes into the same case as the noun counted.

Jeden, jedna, jedno 'one' declines like the demonstrative **ten, ta, to**
(see 5.4–5.4.1 and 6.1.1), e.g. **po jednom roce** 'after one year'.

Dva, dvě 'two', **tři** 'three' and **čtyři** 'four' have special case forms as
shown in the table below.

Pět 'five' has only one 'non-basic' form **pěti**, and other numbers
5–99 repeat this pattern:

> **šest – šesti** 'six', **sedm – sedmi** 'seven', **osm – osmi** 'eight', but
> **devět – devíti** 'nine' (sometimes **-et** also changes to **-íti** with **deset**,
> **dvacet, třicet, čtyřicet**)

1 nom.	dva m., dvě f., n.	tři	čtyři	pět
4 acc.				
2 gen.	dvou	tří	čtyř	pěti
3 dat.	dvěma	třem	čtyřem	pěti
6 loc.	dvou	třech	čtyřech	pěti
7 ins.	dvěma	třemi	čtyřmi	pěti

Examples:

děti do dvou/tří/čtyř/pěti let children up to two/three/
four/five years

po dvou/třech/čtyřech/pěti letech after two/three/four/five
years

před dvěma/třemi/čtyřmi/pěti lety two/three/four/five years ago

Oba, obě 'both' also has forms like dva, dvě: gen./loc. obou and dat./
ins. oběma, e.g. v obou zemích 'in both countries', s oběma přáteli
'with both friends'.

Sto '100' is invariable in the singular with a noun, but has its usual
neuter endings in the plural. Tisíc '1,000' usually has one 'non-basic'
form tisíci, while milion and higher numerals behave like nouns:

před sto lety 'a hundred years ago', **před dvěma sty lety** 'two
hundred years ago', **před několika tisíci lety** 'several thousand
years ago' (*but*: **před třemi miliony let** 'three million years ago')

Jedna in compounds remains fixed: před dvaceti jedna lety (or reversed
forms may be used: před jednadvaceti lety).

6.1.7 | *Age and years*

When speaking or writing about numbers of years, instead of roků 'of
years' people regularly say and write let (lit. 'of summers'). If asked
Kolik let? 'How many years?' you say:

čtyři roky four years

but:

dvacet let twenty years (Less often:
dvacet roků)

Kolik je ti/vám let?	How old are you? lit. 'How many is to you of years?'
Je mi osmnáct (let).	I am eighteen (years old).
Je mi dvacet jedna (let).	I am twenty-one.

To state 'in' a calendar year you say either **roku** or **v roce** followed by the number as in English:

Narodila se roku 1986 (devatenáct set osmdesát šest).
She was born in 1986.

Autor této učebnice se narodil roku (v roce) 1950 (devatenáct set padesát).
The author of this textbook was born in 1950.

6.2 Ordinal numerals – *řadové číslovky*

Ordinal numerals have regular adjectival forms in Czech and therefore agree with the nouns they qualify in gender and number. Ordinal numerals up to 'twelfth' are clearly derived from the cardinals, except for first and second:

první 'first', **druhý** 'second', **třetí** 'third', **čtvrtý** 'fourth', **pátý** 'fifth', **šestý** 'sixth', **sedmý** 'seventh', **osmý** 'eighth', **devátý** 'ninth', **desátý** 'tenth', **jedenáctý** 'eleventh', **dvanáctý** 'twelfth'

Note that **první** 'first' and **třetí** 'third' are soft adjectives. **Druhý** also means 'other, another, next', see 5.11.

6.2.1 Higher ordinals

The -teenths all end in **-náctý**, parallel to the ordinary numbers:

'thirteenth' **třináctý**, 'fourteenth' **čtrnáctý**, 'fifteenth' **patnáctý**, 'sixteenth' **šestnáctý**, 'seventeenth' **sedmnáctý**, 'eighteenth' **osmnáctý**, 'nineteenth' **devatenáctý**

Then come: 'twentieth' **dvacátý**, 'thirtieth' **třicátý** and 'fortieth' **čtyřicátý**. Followed by: 'fiftieth' **padesátý**, 'sixtieth' **šedesátý**, 'seventieth' **sedmdesátý**, 'eightieth' **osmdesátý** and 'ninetieth' **devadesátý**.

Next: 'hundredth' **stý**, 'two-hundredth' **dvoustý**, 'three-hundredth' **třístý**, 'four-hundredth' **čtyřstý**, 'five-hundredth' **pětistý**, 'six-hundredth' šestistý, 'seven-hundredth' **sedmistý**, 'eight-hundredth' **osmistý**, 'nine-hundredth' **devítistý**.

Finally: 'thousandth' **tisící**, 'two-thousandth' **dvoutisící**, 'three-thousandth' **třítisící** and so on (like the hundredths), plus **miliontý**, **miliardtý**, and **biliontý**!!

For 'twenty-first' you say **dvacátý první** 'twentieth first', and so on, but for the initial parts over a hundred of higher complex ordinals you use ordinary numbers: '1,964th' **tisíc devět set šedesátý čtvrtý**, '5,115th' **pět tisíc sto patnáctý**.

You can also reverse the number order for twenty-first to ninety-ninth: **jednadvacátý** 'twenty-first' ('one and twentieth'), **rok osmašedesátý** 'year sixty-eighth' (= 1968).

To refer to decades as 'the sixties' etc., ordinals are used with plural **léta**, e.g. **šedesátá léta – v šedesátých letech** 'the sixties – in the sixties'.

6.3   X times – *x-krát*

To say 'x times' you can simply add **-krát** to the number:

jedenkrát (or **jednou**) 'once', **dvakrát** 'twice', **třikrát** 'three times' . . . **desetkrát** 'ten times' . . . **stokrát** 'a hundred times'

Similarly: **několikrát** 'several times', **mnohokrát/mockrát** 'many times', **víckrát** 'more times', also **tentokrát** 'this time', **tenkrát** 'that time' (or **tehdy** 'then, at that time').

When ordering things in a café or restaurant you regularly say 'once', 'twice', 'three times' etc. to stipulate the number of items. The item stays in the singular.

dvakrát pivo	two beers, lit. 'twice beer'
třikrát řízek	three schnitzels
pětkrát jahodovou zmrzlinu	five strawberry ice-creams

6.3.1   For the x-th time

'For the first time' is **poprvé**. The rest of this series is formed with **po**-plus the neuter form of the ordinal numeral: **podruhé/po druhé, potřetí/po třetí, po čtvrté** etc.

When listing points in an argument, 'first(ly)', 'secondly', 'thirdly' . . . you say **za prvé, za druhé, za třetí** . . .

Compound adjectives with numbers

Compound adjectives derived from a cardinal numeral plus a noun
regularly use the genitive form of the numeral:

> **dvacetiletý muž** 'a 20-year-old man', **dvoudenní výlet** 'a two-day
> excursion', **osmdesátikilometrová rychlost** '80-kilometre speed'
> (but: **stokilometrová rychlost** '100-kilometre speed')

Talking about numbered items

For items which are numbered, like buses or hotel rooms, Czech uses a
special series of nouns ending in **-ka**. They also mean 'a number three'
etc., referring to a numeral as a written sign (**číslice**).

> 1 **jednička**, 2 **dvojka**, 3 **trojka**, 4 **čtyřka**, 5 **pětka**,
>
> 6 **šestka**, 7 **sedmička**, 8 **osmička**, 9 **devítka**, 10 **desítka**
>
> 11 **jedenáctka**, 12 **dvanáctka**, ...
>
> 20 **dvacítka**, 21 **jednadvacítka**, 22 **dvaadvacítka** (reversed forms)
>
> 30 **třicítka**, 40 **čtyřicítka** 50 **padesátka** ...
>
> 100 **stovka**, 120 **sto dvacítka**, 134 **sto třicetčtyřka**, ...

Jezdím osmičkou nebo třiadvacítkou.	I go by the number 8 or 23.
Jezdím dvacítkou.	I go by the number 20 (e.g. Prague tram).
Nasedla do stoosmnáctky.	She got on a 118 bus.
Bydlí na/ve čtyřce.	S/he's living in room/flat 4.
Zaplatil stovkou.	He paid with a hundred-crown note.

Jedenáctka is also a football 'eleven', **desítka** and **dvanáctka** are respectively 10 and 12-degree beer. Using the local system of 'original gravity',
12 degree equals about 5 per cent alcohol.

Dvojka is also 'second gear' or 'a mark of two'. **Jednička** is the best
Czech school **známka** 'mark', **pětka** 'five', the worst.

Czech money

'Coin' is **mince**, 'money' is **peníze** m. pl. (gen. **peněz**), the abbreviation
Kč = koruna česká 'Czech crown'. The smaller unit **haléř**, colloq. **halíř**
'heller' (100 = **koruna**) is on its way out:

padesát haléřů 50 hellers

dvoukoruna 'a two-crown coin', **pětikoruna** 'a five-crown coin', **desetikoruna** 'a ten-crown coin', **dvacetikoruna**, colloq. **dvacka** 'a twenty-crown coin', **padesátikoruna** 'fifty-crown coin/note'.

'Banknote' is bankovka (banka 'bank'):

stokoruna, colloq. **stovka** 'a hundred-crown note', **dvoustovka** 'two-hundred-crown note', **pětistovka** 'five-hundred-crown note', **tisícovka** 'thousand-crown note'

Mohl byste mi rozměnit pětistovku? Could you change me a 500-crown note?

6.7 Weights and measures

Phrases stating weight or other kinds of measurement are typically followed by 'of' in English, and in Czech by the genitive case.

For describing weight the commonest measure words are **kilo** (kilogram, 2.2 lbs) and **deko/deka** (dekagram, 10 grams), as well as **gram** 'gram'.

Deka is generally invariable, e.g. čtyři, pět, deset deka, however 'one decagram' is regularly **jedno deko**.

For 2 to 4 kilos you say **dvě/tři/čtyři kila**, but for five upwards you just use the basic form kilo, e.g. **pět kilo, deset kilo**.

Půl kila 'half (of) a kilo' is just over one pound. **Čtvrt kila** 'a quarter of a kilo' is just over half a pound. **Deset deka** is a bit under a quarter of a pound.

Koupil kilo/dvě kila cukru.	He bought a kilo/two kilos of sugar.
Koupil pět kilo mouky.	He bought five kilos of flour.
Koupil deset/dvacet deka sýra.	He bought 10/20 dekagrams of cheese.

For liquid measure you generally use **litr** (litre) and **deci** = decilitr (a tenth of a litre). **Deci** is another invariable form.

Koupil litr/dva litry mléka.	He bought a litre/two litres of milk.
Objednala si dvě deci vína.	She ordered two decilitres (fifth of a litre) of wine (a common measure for one person).
Dejte mi deset litrů.	Give me ten [of] litres.

6.8 Indefinite quantifiers – *neurčité číslovky*

Indefinite quantifiers, unlike numerals, give only a general idea of quantity. Czech grammars call them **neurčité číslovky**, lit. 'indefinite numerals'.

Typical examples are **mnoho** 'many', **hodně** 'a lot, lots of' and **málo** 'little, few'.

Their basic nominative/accusative forms are followed by the genitive case, just like cardinal numbers five and above.

Má mnoho (hodně) studentů.	S/he has many (a lot of) students.
Má málo studentů.	S/he has few students.
Mám mnoho/hodně času.	I have much/a lot of time.
Mám příliš mnoho času.	I have too much time.
Mám málo času.	I have little time.

As with numbers five upwards, these phrases count as neuter. Another basic quantity term like this is the interrogative **kolik?** 'how many?':

Kolik tam bylo lidí?	How many ('of') people were there?
Bylo tam málo lidí.	There were few people there.
Bude tam asi šest lidí.	About six people will be there.

Other such words are **několik** 'some, several', **tolik** 'so many', **víc(e)** 'more', **méně/míň** 'less, fewer', **trochu** 'a little, a bit', **moc** 'lots, too many', **pár** 'a couple':

Znám jenom několik/pár Čechů.	I know only some/a couple of Czechs.
Mirek zná víc lidí než já.	Mirek knows more people than me.
Tolik lidí!	So many people!

Some of these quantifiers have a unified 'non-basic' form, like numerals five and above. The following non-basic case forms end in **-a**, e.g.

několik – několika 'several', **kolik – kolika** 'how many', **tolik – tolika** 'so many', **mnoho – mnoha** 'many'

The quantifier now behaves like an adjective:

po mnoha letech 'after many years', **po několika letech** 'after several years'

Other quantifiers are invariable with nouns in all or most cases, e.g. **pár** 'a couple of', **málo** 'few' (except for genitive **mála**):

po pár dnech	after a couple of days

Trochu 'a little, a bit', and **trošku** 'a little bit', generally revert to their original status as feminine nouns **trocha, troška** in other cases:

Mám trochu/trošku peněz.	I have a (little) bit of money.
Přišel s trochou/troškou peněz.	He came with a (little) bit of money.

The interrogative pronoun **co** 'what', used in an exclamatory sense, and **něco** 'something' can also behave as quantifiers, followed by the genitive:

Co tam bylo lidí!	What a number of people there were there!
Ještě mám něco peněz.	I still have a bit of money.

6.8.1 | More and less

As indefinite quantifiers **víc** 'more' and **nejvíc** 'most' indicate degrees up from **mnoho** or **hodně** 'much, a lot'.

Má hodně/mnoho peněz.	S/he works a lot, has lots of money.
Má (nej)víc peněz.	S/he has more, most money.

Similarly, **méně/míň** 'less' and **nejméně/nejmíň** 'least' derive from **málo** 'little':

Pracuje málo, má málo peněz.	S/he works little, has little money.
Má (nej)méně/(nej)míň peněz.	S/he has less, least money.

6.9 Telling the time

The basic measurements for periods of time up to a day are **hodina** 'hour', **minuta** 'minute' and **vteřina/sekunda** 'second'.
   To ask 'What time is it?' you say:

Kolik je hodin?	lit. 'How many is it of hours?'

For one to four o'clock you say:

Je/byla/bude jedna hodina.	It is/was/will be one o'clock.
Jsou/byly/budou dvě, tři, čtyři hodiny.	It is/was/will be two, three, four o'clock.

But from five up you say: Je/bylo/bude [X hodin].

Je pět, šest, sedm, osm (hodin).	It is five, six, seven, eight (o'clock).
Bylo devět, deset, jedenáct, dvanáct (hodin).	It was nine, ten, eleven, twelve.
Je půlnoc.	It's midnight.
Je poledne.	It's midday.

Learn also:

ráno 'in the (early) morning', **dopoledne** 'in the morning', **odpoledne** 'in the afternoon', **večer** 'in the evening', **dnes večer** 'this evening, tonight', **v noci** 'in the night', **ve dne** 'in the day(time)'

Other basic adverbs of time are:

dnes 'today', **včera** 'yesterday', **zítra** (*zejtra) 'tomorrow'

předevčírem 'the day before yesterday', **pozítří** 'the day after tomorrow'

6.9.1 | *At what time?*

To ask 'At what time?' you say:

Kdy přišel?	When did he come?
or: **V kolik (hodin) přišel?**	At what time did he come?

For 'at one o'clock' you say:

V jednu (hodinu).

For 'at two, three, four' you say:

Ve dvě, ve tři, ve čtyři (hodiny).

And for 'at five, six' etc. you say:

V pět, v šest, v sedm, v osm, v devět, v deset, v jedenáct, ve dvanáct (hodin).

Note also:

V poledne. At midday.

but: **O půlnoci.** At midnight.

| 6.9.2 | *More about telling the time* |

Saying the quarter and half hours is a bit tricky. For 'quarter past' you say **čtvrt na . . .** and refer forward to the next hour;

Je (bylo) čtvrt na dvě.	It is (was) quarter past one = 'quarter onto two'.
Je (bude) čtvrt na šest.	It is (will be) quarter past five = 'quarter onto six'.
Je (bylo) čtvrt na jednu.	It is (was) quarter past twelve = 'quarter onto one'.

For 'half past twelve' you say **půl jedné** 'half of one', also referring forward to the next hour:

Je (bylo, bude) půl jedné.	It is (was, will be) half past twelve = 'half of one'.

Otherwise, for 'half past . . .' you say **půl druhé, třetí** etc., using the feminine genitive of the ordinal numeral you've just learnt (to agree with the absent word **hodiny**):

Bylo půl druhé.	It was half past one = 'half of the second (hour)'.
Je (bude) půl třetí.	It is (will be) half past two = 'half of the third'.

(půl čtvrté . . . půl dvanácté)

For 'a quarter to' you say **tři čtvrtě na** ('three-quarters to'):

Je (bylo) tři čtvrtě na jednu.	It is (was) 'three-quarters to' one.
Je (bude) tři čtvrtě na pět.	It is (will be) 'three-quarters to' five.

You can also add five-/ten-minute intervals to the above, using **za** +acc:

Je za pět minut osm.	It is five to eight = 'in five minutes eight'.
Je za deset minut půl osmé.	It is twenty past seven = 'in ten minutes half of the eighth'.

V +acc. is used for 'at'.

Přišli ve čtvrt na dvanáct.	They arrived at a quarter past eleven.
Přišli v půl deváté.	They arrived at half past eight.
Odešli ve tři čtvrtě na pět.	They left at a quarter to five.

For **v půl** (e.g. **deváté**) 'half past (eight)' you can also say **o půl** (**deváté**). Omit **v** 'at' before **za pět/deset minut**:

Za pět minut sedm zastavil před hotelem.
(At) five minutes to seven he stopped in front of the hotel.

6.9.3 | The 24-hour clock

You may find it easier to say the time with numbers alone. This is standard with the 24-hour clock anyway.

Je sedm hodin a patnáct minut.	It is 7 o'clock and 15 minutes.
Je třináct deset.	It is 13.10.
Je pět hodin a deset sekund/ vteřin.	It is 5 o'clock and ten seconds.
Vlak odjíždí (v) osm pět.	The train leaves (at) 8.05.
Chytil rychlík (v) sedmnáct třináct.	He caught the 17.13 express.

6.10 Days of the week, months and date

The days of the week, some named by number, are:

pondělí, úterý, středa, čtvrtek, pátek, sobota, neděle
Monday ('day after Sunday'), Tuesday, Wednesday ('middle day'), Thursday ('4th day'), Friday ('5th day'), Saturday, Sunday ('not doing day')

v pondělí, v úterý, ve středu, ve čtvrtek, v pátek, v sobotu, v neděli 'on Monday' etc.

do/od pondělí, od úterý, od středy, od čtvrtka, od pátku, od soboty, od neděle 'till/from Monday' etc.

The names of the months are completely different from ours:

leden, únor, březen	January, February, March
v lednu, v únoru, v březnu	in . . .
duben, květen, červen	April, May, June
v dubnu, v květnu, v červnu	in . . .
červenec, srpen, září	July, August, September
v červenci, v srpnu, v září	in . . .
říjen, listopad, prosinec	October, November, December
v říjnu, v listopadu, v prosinci	in . . .

To say 'from' and 'until, to' use **od** and **do** +gen.:

od ledna do dubna	from January till April
od března do prosince	from March to December
od září do listopadu	from September till November

The date is always in the genitive, which mostly ends in -**a**, but note: **červenec** -**nce**, **prosinec** -**nce**, **září** -**í** and **listopad** -**u**. The standard question about the date also uses the genitive, with **kolikátý** 'the how-manyeth' asking the question:

Kolikátého je dnes?	What's today's date?
or: **Co je dnes?**	What is today?
Je třicátého ledna.	It's 30th January.
Přijeli prvního května.	They arrived on 1st May.

Květen is sometimes **máj**, as a festival, or in poetry.

6.11   Arithmetic

Simple arithmetical relations are expressed like this:

Tři <u>plus</u> deset je třináct.	Three plus ten is (equals) thirteen.
Dvanáct <u>minus</u> sedm je pět.	Twelve minus seven is five.
Sedm <u>krát</u> čtyři je dvacet osm.	Seven times four is twenty-eight.
Osmnáct <u>děleno</u> třemi je šest.	Eighteen divided by three is six.

6.11.1 *Fractions – zlomky*

A basic fraction (**zlomek**) takes the form of a noun: **polovina** 'half', **třetina** 'a third', **čtvrtina** 'a quarter', **dvě třetiny** 'two-thirds', **tři čtvrtiny** 'three-quarters'. Others in numerical order (all with **-ina**) are **pětina**, **šestina, sedmina, osmina, devítina, desetina/desítina . . . setina** (100th) . . . **tisícina** (1,000th).

Shorter terms **půl** 'half' and **čtvrt** 'quarter' are used for simple measures: **půl roku** 'half a year', **čtvrt litru** a quarter of a litre. **Čtvrt** declines like type **píseň**, e.g. **tři čtvrtě kilometru** 'three-quarters of a kilometre' (nom./acc. **tři čtvrti** also).

Půl, čtvrt and **tři čtvrtě** behave like invariable quantifiers (see 6.8):

před čtvrt hodinou	a quarter of an hour ago
před tři čtvrtě hodinou	three quarters of an hour ago
před půl rokem	half a year ago, six months ago
Psa máme jen půl roku.	We have had the dog for only half ('of') a year.

In singular nominative/accusative phrases with further qualification (e.g. **každý** 'each', **necelý** 'not a whole', i.e. less than) there may be no genitive after **půl** or **čtvrt**. The qualifier must agree with the noun:

Psa máme necelý půl rok/necelého půl roku.
We have had the dog for less than half a year.

Vlak jezdí každou půl hodinu/každé půl hodiny.
The train goes every half hour.

With plural **tři čtvrtě**:

Trvalo to necelé tři čtvrtě roku.	It lasted for less than three quarters of a year.

Noun forms **půlhodina, půlrok, čtvrthodina, čtvrtrok** also occur.

For divisions of a larger whole viewed as items, e.g. half a loaf of bread, the noun terms **půlka** 'a half', **čtvrtka** 'a quarter', can be used, e.g.

půlka chleba/kuřete	half a loaf of bread, half a chicken
druhá půlka roku	the second half of the year

Percentages use the noun **procento**: **jedno procento** '1 per cent', **dvě procenta** '2 per cent', **pět procent** '5 per cent', **sto procent** '100 per cent'.

Decimals are read as follow, using the term **celá** for 'whole number'. (You don't say 'point' – **tečka** is the word for 'period, full stop' – nor do you say **čárka** 'comma', which is how the point is written). Adding the word for 'tenths' etc. is optional:

1,5 = jedna celá pět (desetin)	one whole five (tenths)
3,1 = tři celé jedna (desetina)	three wholes one (tenth)
9,2 = devět celých dvě (desetiny)	nine wholes two (tenths)
0,05 = nula/žádná celá pět setin	zero whole five hundredths
or: **nula celá nula pět**	zero whole zero five

6.12 Collective or set numerals – *souborové číslovky*

Czech has a special series denoting 'x-sets/pairs-of', called collective or set numerals, **souborové číslovky**. Only the lowest ones are used with any frequency.

They are most typically used with plural nouns which designate single items, such as **kalhoty** 'trousers', **noviny** 'newspaper', **nůžky** 'scissors', **dveře** 'door(s)', **brýle** 'glasses, spectacles':

'one' **jedny**, 'two' **dvoje**, 'three' **troje**, 'four' **čtvery**, 'five' **patery**, 'six' **šestery**, 'seven' **sedmery**, 'eight' **osmery**, 'nine' **devatery**, 'ten' **desatery** . . . similarly, **kolikery?** 'how many?' **několikery** 'several'

Kupuju dvoje noviny.	I buy two newspapers.
Mám dvoje brýle.	I have two pairs of spectacles.
Mám jen jedny kalhoty.	I have only one pair of trousers.
Koupil troje startky.	He bought three packets of Start cigarettes.

Singular forms may occur with uncountable nouns, or nouns of the neuter -í type, e.g.

dvoje řízení 'dual control', **dvoje mínění** 'two opinions', **troje teplé prádlo** 'three sets of warm underwear'

Jedny has other plural case forms parallel to **ty** 'those' to accompany such nouns:

jedněch, jedněm, jedněch, jedněmi

Chodil celý rok v jedněch botách.	He went about all year in one pair of shoes.

Jedni ma. also means 'some', in contrast to 'others':

Jedni souhlasili, jiní ne.	Some agreed, others didn't.

Occasionally a related neuter sg. form functions as a noun, e.g. **Čtvero ročních období** 'The Four Seasons'.

6.13 Generic numerals – *druhové číslovky*

So-called generic numerals, **druhové číslovky**, are formed from two upwards, meaning 'x kinds of'.

These are usually regular adjectival forms parallel to the set numerals detailed in the previous section: **dvojí, trojí, čtverý** etc.

These adjectival forms also provide the non-basic case forms for the set numerals, e.g. **ve čtverých ponožkách** 'in four pairs of socks'.

However, in the nominative/accusative we may distinguish:

> **kolikery šaty? – několikery šaty**   how many dresses? – several dresses

and

> **kolikeré šaty? – několikeré šaty**   how many kinds of dresses? – several kinds of dresses

But nominative/accusative generic forms are sometimes used as set numerals, e.g. **několikeré volání o pomoc** 'several calls for help', **tisíceré díky** 'a thousand thanks'.

Chapter 7

The verb – sloveso

Verbs are words which notionally carry out *actions* ('run', 'walk', 'make', 'write') or represent *states* ('sit', 'lie').

7.1 Verb forms and categories

Finite forms of verbs act as central verbs of sentences or clauses. They occur in different *tenses*, representing time as *present*: 'John runs, is running', *past*: 'John ran, has run', or *future*: 'John will run'.

Ordinary *active* verbs have *subjects*, i.e. agents or 'doers', those who carry out the action or state ('John writes'). The *direct object*, if present, is the recipient of the action ('John wrote a <u>letter</u>'). The *indirect object* indicates a person (less often a thing) also affected by the action ('John wrote <u>Anne</u> a letter'). Verbs used with objects are called *transitive*, those without are *intransitive*.

Finite verbs may also distinguish the *person* of their subject. Czech verbs do this much more obviously than English verbs do, but compare the English *first person* form 'I <u>am</u>' from *second person* 'you <u>are</u>' (obsolete 'thou <u>art</u>') and *third person* 'he, she, it <u>is</u>'.

Auxiliary verbs help to form the tenses of other verbs, e.g. 'John <u>is</u> running', 'John <u>has</u> run'. In Czech this also happens in the past tense, and in the conditional.

The verb 'to be' on its own generally acts as a *copula*, connecting the subject with a noun or adjective *complement*, stating a category to which the subject belongs or a quality which it has, e.g. 'John is a teacher', 'John is nice'.

Other, *non-finite* forms of verbs are also regularly formed and used in various other ways. These include *infinitives* ('to write', 'to inflate'), *verbal nouns* ('the writing of books', 'the inflating of balloons') and *participles* (adjective-like forms of verbs, e.g. 'an inflated balloon', 'a slowly inflating balloon').

Modal verbs adjust the sense of other verbs in terms of necessity, desire etc. In Czech, as in English, these other verbs are typically added in the infinitive – in English this is often the infinitive without 'to' ('John can write', 'John must write'), but sometimes also with 'to' ('John wants to write').

Negative verbs in Czech are normally prefixed with ne-, e.g. **dělat** 'to do', **dělám** 'I do/make', **nedělat** 'not to do/make', **nedělám** 'I do not do/make'.

For *passive* verbs see 7.15, under the passive participle etc.

7.2 The infinitive – *infinitiv*

Verbs are conventionally cited and listed in dictionaries according to their infinitive forms, which correspond in meaning and in use to English verbs preceded by 'to'. The infinitive of a Czech verb usually ends in -t preceded by a vowel. The most regular types are:

-at	**dělat** to do	**-ovat**:	**pracovat** to work
-it	**prosit** to ask (request, beg)	**-nout**:	**tisknout** to press/to print
-et	**trpět** to suffer		

A few infinitives end in -st, -zt, -ct (in older formal usage -ci) or a long vowel plus -t:

nést 'to carry', **lézt** 'to climb/to crawl', **moct/moci** 'to be able, can', **spát** 'to sleep', **být** 'to be', **mít** 'to have'

In older formal usage the infinitive regularly ended in -ti instead of -t. You will now encounter this mainly when reading older texts only: dělati, prositi, nésti, býti and so on.

It is also useful to divide verbs into two groups, according to the number of syllables they have in the infinitive form (**slabika** – syllable): *monosyllabic verbs* (**jednoslabičná slovesa**) – verbs with infinitives of only one syllable, after subtracting the final syllable of older infinitive -ti, -ci and any added prefixes, e.g.

nést, lézt, spát, moct/moci, **spát**, but also prefixed compounds such as **od|nést** 'to carry away', **po|moct** 'to help', **za|čít** 'to begin' *polysyllabic verbs* (**víceslabičná slovesa**) – the rest, e.g.

dělat, prosit, pracovat, tisknout etc.

Regular verbs are generally polysyllabic, according to this definition, whereas verbs with forms which cannot be fully predicted from the infinitive are mostly monosyllabic.

Verbs and their infinitives are also categorised according to what is conventionally called their 'aspect', *imperfective* – describing an action in progress – or *perfective* – describing an action as something complete (see 7.6).

7.3 Reflexive verbs – *zvratná slovesa*

Czech verbs are also often 'reflexive'. Reflexive verbs (**zvratná slovesa, reflexíva**) are accompanied either by the accusative form of the reflexive pronoun **se** 'oneself' or by its dative form **si** 'to/for oneself'. This pronoun is the same for any person, so it corresponds to a whole range of words in English: 'myself', 'yourself', 'ourselves', 'yourselves', 'themselves' etc.

Many verbs are only reflexive in certain particular senses, e.g. **učit se** 'to study', literally 'teach oneself', alongside the plain verb **učit** 'to teach'.

Certain very common verbs are permanently accompanied by **se**, and thus *always* reflexive, not always with any obvious logical reason, e.g. **dívat se** 'to look', **ptát se** 'to ask' (a question), **bát se** 'to fear, to be afraid'.

Some verbs with **si** also always occur in this form, e.g. **umínit si** 'to make up one's mind, take it into one's head'. The reflexive pronoun indicates that the action affects the subject, its doer. Particularly common examples where **si** is normally present include **sednout si** 'to sit down' ['for oneself'], **lehnout si** 'to lie down' ['for oneself'].

Other verbs are frequently accompanied by **se** or **si**, but in a much looser way, e.g. **mýt se** 'to wash, wash oneself', and **mýt si ruce** 'to wash one's hands', lit. 'wash to oneself the hands'. Here, unlike in the examples above, the reflexive pronoun can be replaced by another noun or pronoun, without any change in grammar, e.g. **mýt *auto*** 'to wash the car', **mýt *někomu* ruce** 'to wash someone's hands'.

Reflexive forms of verbs are also used in certain passive constructions (see 7.15.4).

Those with the accusative pronoun **se** mostly require non-accusative objects, e.g. **bát se něčeho/psa** 'to be afraid of something/a dog', **ptát se Jany** 'to ask ["of"] Jana'. This logical rule is only regularly broken by a couple of common verbs, e.g. **učit se češtinu** 'to study Czech', **do(z)vědět se něco** 'to get to know, find out something'.

7.4   **The present tense – *přítomný čas***

The one and only Czech present tense corresponds to several present tense forms in English, e.g. 'I make, I am making'.

The personal forms of the present tense are expressed by endings attached to the root of the verb. These personal endings can usually be predicted, if the verb has a polysyllabic infinitive. (Subject pronouns are only added for emphasis or clarification.)

If the verb is perfective (which often means that a perfectivising prefix has been added) the present tense form basically acts as a future tense, e.g. **udělat** is the perfective equivalent of **dělat**, and **udělám** means 'I'll do it, I shall do it', where **dělám** means 'I am doing it, I do it' (more about this later).

7.4.1   **Být – to be**

The present-tense forms of **být** 'to be' (colloquially often ***bejt**) are unlike those of any other verb, but of course absolutely essential. The initial **j** is silent in ordinary pronunciation:

(já)	**jsem** I am	**(my)**	**jsme** we are
(ty)	**jsi**, ***(j)seš** you are (familiar sg.)	**(vy)**	**jste** you are (plural/polite sg.)
(on, ona)	**je** he, she is	**(oni)**	**jsou** they are

As with all tense forms of Czech verbs, the subject pronouns **já, ty** etc. are usually superfluous, except when giving a certain emphasis or in order to make clear distinctions.

Jsem doma.   I am at home.

Já jsem doma, ale ona je v práci.   I'm at home, but she is at work.

The non-standard form ***seš/jseš** is commonly used in everyday speech instead of **jsi** for 'you are'. (But it is never used as an auxiliary form in the past tense.)

Another form **jest** '(it) is' only occurs as an archaism, for example as an equivalent for the abbreviation **tj.** 'i.e.' = **to jest/to je** 'id est, that is', or, solemnly, **tak jest!** 'it is so!'

For the negative, you add **ne-** (as for other verbs), but the negative of **je** is **není**. In these negative forms the **j** is always pronounced:

nejsem I am not	**nejsme** we are not
nejsi you are not (familiar sg.)	**nejste** you are not (plural/polite sg.)
není he, she is not	**nejsou** they are not

Nejsem Čech/Češka.	I am not (a) Czech.
Není doma.	He/she is not at home.
Nejsou doma.	They aren't at home.

7.4.2 Mít – to have

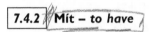

The basic verb **mít** 'to have' has the following personal forms in the present tense:

mám I have	**máme** we have
máš you have (familiar sg.)	**máte** you have (plural/polite sg.)
má he, she has	**mají** they have

Again, the subject pronouns **já, ty, on** etc. are only needed for greater emphasis or contrast.

Má kufr.	She/he has a suitcase.
On má kufr, ale ona nemá.	He has a suitcase, but she hasn't.

Spoken English often uses 'have got' instead of 'have':

Mám zmrzlinu.	I have an ice-cream. I've got an ice-cream.
Mají tři kufry.	They have three suitcases. They've got three suitcases.

To make the verb negative you just add **ne-** to any of the forms:

Nemám kufr.	I don't have a suitcase. I haven't got a suitcase.
Nemají kufry.	They don't have (any) suitcases.

Czech sometimes uses 'have' where English prefers 'is', e.g. **Máte tady dopis** 'There's a letter here for you', lit. 'you have here a letter.'

7.4.3 | Classification of verbs – třídění sloves

Czech grammars continue to disagree about how best to classifiy Czech verbs into types (**třída** – 'class, type', e.g. **pátá třída** 'fifth class, type 5'). The following (basically quite traditional) method matches different third-person singular present-tense endings to the most regular infinitive types:

	infinitive	3sg. present 'he/she/it does'	
Type 5:	**-at**	**-á**	**dělat – dělá** does, makes
Type 4:	**-it, -et**	**-í**	**prosit – prosí** asks
			trpět – trpí suffers
Type 3:	**-ov-at**	**-u-je**	**kupovat – kupuje** buys
Type 2:	**-nout**	**-ne**	**tisknout – tiskne** presses, prints
Type 1:	**-st, -zt, -ct/-ci**	**-e**	**nést – nese** carries

Verbs with infinitives **-st, -zt, -ct** usually belong to Type 1, but you should learn the present-tense types of monosyllabic verbs individually. (Lists will be given later, see 7.23 and 7.24.)

7.4.4 | Present tense – types 5 and 4

These types are characterised by long vowels **-á-** or **-í-** in their endings and have first person singular forms ending in **-ám** or **-ím**.

7.4.5 | Type 5 – dělat

děl|at to do, make	**děl|ám** I do, make **děláš** you do, make **dělá** he/she/it does, makes	**děláme** we do, make **děláte** you pl. do, make **dělají** they do, make

Examples: **říkat** 'to say', **čekat** 'to wait', **dávat** 'to give', **dívat se** 'to look', **hledat** 'to look for', **volat** 'to call'. This is a very common type with few complications.

7.4.6 | Type 4 – prosit, trpět

pros|it	**pros|ím** I ask	**prosíme** we ask
to ask, request	**prosíš** you ask	**prosíte** you pl. ask
	prosí he/she/it asks	**prosí** they ask

Examples: **mluvit** 'to speak', **vařit** 'to cook, boil', **chodit** 'to walk, go', **cítit** 'to feel', **věřit** 'to believe'.

trp|ět	**trp|ím** I suffer	**trpíme** we suffer
to suffer	**trpíš** you suffer	**trpíte** you pl. suffer
	trpí he/she/it suffers	**trpí** they suffer

Examples: **běžet** 'to run', **držet** 'to hold', **slyšet** 'to hear', **sedět** 'to sit', **ležet** 'to lie', **vidět** 'to see'.

7.4.7 | Type 4a – sázet

Subtype with infinitive -et and third person plural -ejí:

sáz|et	**sáz|ím** I plant	**sázíme** we plant
to plant, bet	**sázíš** you plant	**sázíte** you pl. plant
	sází he/she/it plants	**sázejí** they plant

The third person plural -ejí will regularly be matched by imperatives -ej! -ejte! This can sometimes help establish in one's mind whether a particular verb belongs to this subtype.

Most commonly encountered verbs of this subtype are prefixed imperfectives, e.g. **odcházet** 'to go away' (with negative imperative neodcházej!) – the imperfective counterpart of **odejít** 'to arrive'. Similarly, **přinášet** 'to bring', the imperfective counterpart of **přinést** 'to bring'. Likewise, they are often imperfectives derived from a more basic perfective counterpart, e.g. **házet** 'to throw' from pf. **hodit** 'to throw', **vracet** (**se**) 'to return, give back' (reflexive: 'come/go back'), derived from the more basic perfective infinitive **vrátit** (**se**).

Others of this subtype include **umět** 'to know how', **rozumět** 'to understand'.

There are also some perfective verbs derived from adjectives in this category, e.g. **zlidovět** 'to become' **lidový** 'popular' (e.g. of a song becoming a well-known folksong).

Although many people use the third personal plural ending **-í** for these verbs also, this is traditionally regarded as stylistically inferior.

With certain verbs both possible third person plural forms traditionally occur, e.g. **bydlet** 'to live (in a place)', **muset** 'to have to, must', **myslet** 'to think'. These three verbs also have alternative (now less frequently used) infinitives **bydlit**, **musit** and **myslit**.

In non-standard and widespread colloquial usage, particularly in Bohemia, the third person plural ending **-ejí** may be applied to all Type 4 verbs, in a form usually pronounced **-ej**, e.g. *prosej, *trpěj, *uměj.

| **7.4.8** | *Present tense – Types 3, 2 and 1* |

These types have present-tense endings characterised by the vowel **-e-** and first person singular forms ending in **-u/-i**.

| **7.4.9** | *Type 3 – kupovat, hrát* |

Note how the **-ov-** in the infinitive becomes **-u-** before the present-tense endings here.

kup|ov|at	**kup|u|ji, kup|u|ju** I buy	**kupujeme**, ***kupujem** we buy
to buy	**kupuješ** you buy	**kupujete** you buy
	kupuje he/she/it buys	**kupují**, ***kupujou** they buy

Examples: **děkovat** – **děkuji/děkuju, děkuješ, děkuje** 'to thank', **pracovat** – **pracuje** 'to work', **potřebovat** – **potřebuje** 'to need', **ukazovat** – **ukazuje** 'to show', **milovat** – **miluje** 'to love', **organizovat** – **organizuje** 'to organise – organises' (many loanwords belong to this category).

The alternative forms are colloquial, least markedly so in the 1st person singular.

Certain monosyllabic verbs fit into this type, where **j** precedes the endings, but the colloquial forms are both less noticeably so and often replace the other forms in writing.

hrát to play	**hra|ji, hra|ju** I play	**hrajeme, *hrajem** we play
	hraješ you play	**hrajete** you play
	hraje he, she, it plays	**hrají, *hrajou** they play

7.4.10 Type 2 – tisknout

tisk|nout	**tisk|nu** I press	**tiskneme, *tisknem** we press
to press	**tiskneš** you press	**tisknete** you press
	tiskne he/she/it presses	**tisknou** they press

Examples: **rozhodnout (se)** pf. 'to decide', **táhnout** 'to pull', **vzpomenout** pf. 'to remember', **zapomenout** pf. 'to forget', **padnout** pf. 'to fall', **vládnout** 'to rule'.

7.4.11 Type 1 – nést, chápat

nést	**nes|u** I carry	**neseme, *nesem** we carry
to carry	**neseš** you carry	**nesete** you pl. carry
	nese he/she/it carries	**nesou** they carry

Examples: **vést** – **vedu, vedeš, vede** 'to lead', **péct/péci** – **peče** 'to bake', **jít** – **jde** 'to go', **číst** – **čte** 'to read'.

Only a few polysyllabic verbs with infinitive **-at** belong to Type 1, e.g. **chápat** – **chápe** 'to understand, grasp', **plavat** – **plave** 'to swim'.

chápu I understand	**chápeme, *chápem** we understand
chápeš you understand	**chápete** you pl. understand
chápe he, she, it understands	**chápou** they understand

The second person plural reduced ending **-em** is substandard again for this group, but common in ordinary speech.

The first-person singular ending **-i** and third-person plural ending **-í** also occur as formal variants in certain Type 1 verbs, following a soft consonant which is produced by a consonant change between the infinitive and present tense:

psát 'to write' – **píši/píšu** 'I write', **píšeš**, **píše**; **píšeme**, **píšete**, **píší/píšou** 'they write'

ukázat pf. 'to show' – **ukáži/ukážu** 'I'll show', **ukážeš**, **ukáže**, **ukážeme**, **ukážete**, **ukáží/ukážou** 'they'll show'

7.5 The past tense – *minulý čas*

Czech has one basic and rather straightforward way of forming the past tense of a verb. This past tense may correspond to any of the past-tense forms of English, e.g. 'he did', 'he was doing', 'he has done', 'he has been doing' etc.

To describe or view actions or states in the past in different ways, Czech employs verb pairs termed imperfectives and perfectives, rather than different tense formations as in English. (See section 7.6 on aspect and aspectual pairs below.)

To obtain the third-person-singular ('he') past-tense form of most verbs, you replace the **-t** of the infinitive by **-l**. Verbs with infinitives ending in **-nout** replace this by **-nul** after a vowel, but have a shorter -l form in standard usage after a consonant (see 7.5.4 below).

dělat to do, make	**dělal**	he did, he made, he was doing, he did, he was making
čekat to wait	**čekal**	he waited, he was waiting
prosit to ask	**prosil**	he asked, he was asking
vařit to cook	**vařil**	he cooked, he was cooking
trpět to suffer	**trpěl**	he suffered, he was suffering

kupovat to buy	**kupoval**	he bought, he was buying
studovat to study	**studoval**	he studied, he was studying
mi|nout to miss, pass	**mi|nul**	he missed, passed
tisk|nout to print, press	**tisk|l**	he printed, pressed

The -l form agrees with its subject in gender as well as number. For 'she waited' you use the ending -la, for 'it waited' you use -lo:

masc.	**Igor/autobus čekal**	Igor/the bus waited
fem.	**Jana/tramvaj čekala**	Jana/the tram waited
neuter	**auto čekalo**	the car waited

For 'they waited' you use the ending -li for masculine animate subjects, but -ly for any others, except that in writing there is a neuter plural ending -la. Note how these endings exactly match the basic plural forms of regular hard-type nouns:

masc. anim.	**studenti čekali**	the students waited
masc. inan./fem.	**vlaky čekaly**	the trains waited
	ženy čekaly	the women waited
neuter	**auta čekala**	the cars waited
	(colloq. **čekaly**)	

Endings -li and -ly are pronounced identically. With mixed-gender plural subjects the masculine animate form -li takes precedence over -ly and -la:

Pavel a Zuzana čekali. Pavel and Zuzana waited.

but:

Jana a Zuzana čekaly. Jana and Zuzana waited.

If any two or more inanimate subjects are present, the ending -ly should also be used, even if the nouns are neuter (!):

Auta a kola čekaly. The cars and bicycles waited.

Present forms of the verb **být** 'to be' are added to the -l forms as an auxiliary verb to indicate singular subjects 'I', 'you' and plural subjects 'we', 'you'.

So the simple full table of the past tense looks like this:

čekal -a jsem	I waited
čekal -a jsi	you waited = familiar sg. sense
čekal, čekala, čekalo	he, she, it waited
čekal|i -y jsme	we waited
čekal|i -y jste	you waited = plural sense
čekal -a jste	you waited = polite sg. sense
čekal|i, -y (neuter -a)	they waited

Add **ne-** to the -l form to make a past-tense verb negative. Never add the negative prefix to the auxiliary verb:

Nečekal(a) jsem.	I didn't wait.
Nečekal.	He didn't wait.
Nečekali jsme.	We didn't wait.

Note that the -l verb form for singular 'you' is always singular, even when the polite singular form of address uses the auxiliary **jste**:

Čekal-a jste.	You (polite sg.) waited.

The familiar second-person sg. **jsi** may be reduced to **-s**:

Čekals, čekalas.	You (familiar sg.) waited.

7.5.1 | *Past tense – word order*

When **jsem, jsi (-s)** and **jsme, jste** are used in past forms they are normally placed in the second possible position or 'slot' in a clause. This happens for example when a subject pronoun is added for emphasis. In colloquial usage the auxiliary is sometimes omitted in the first person (only), if the subject pronoun is present:

já (jsem) čekal-a I waited	**my (jsme) čekali -y** we waited
ty jsi čekal-a you waited	**vy jste čekali, -y** you waited
(or **tys čekal-a**)	(polite sg. **vy jste čekal -a**)
on čekal, ona čekala s/he waited	**oni čekali, ony čekaly** they waited

And if there's a question word or phrase:

| **Jak dlouho jsi čekal-a?** | How long did you (sg.) wait? |

The auxiliary **jsi** may be reduced to **-s**, attached to a preceding pronoun:

Co jsi dělal(a)? or **Cos dělal(a)?**	What were you doing?
Ty jsi tam nebyl(a). or **Tys tam nebyl(a).**	You weren't there.
To jsi mi neřekl(a). or **Tos mi neřekl(a).**	You didn't tell me that.

If **se/si** 'oneself' is needed, it is placed *after* **jsem, jsi, jsme, jste**:

| **My jsme se učili.** | We studied/were studying. |
| **Kde jste se učil-a?** | Where did you study? |

Familiar sg. **jsi** + **se**, **si** regularly become **ses** and **sis**:

| **Učil-a ses?** | Were you studying? |
| **Zpíval-a sis?** | Were you singing (to/for yourself)? |

If other personal pronouns are present, they come after the reflexive pronoun:

| **My jsme se ho na to nezeptali.** | We didn't ask him about that. |

7.5.2 | *Past tense – was and had*

The **-l** form of **být** 'to be' is **byl** and the personal forms are entirely regular:

byl -a jsem I was	**byli -y jsme** we were
byl -a jsi you were	**byli -y jste**, polite sg. **byl -a jste** you were
byl, byla, bylo he, she it was	**byli, byly** (n. **-a**) they were

Byl, byla doma.	S/he was at home.
Nebyli doma.	They weren't at home.
Kde jste byli?	Where were you (pl.)?

The -l form of <u>mít</u> 'to have' is mě̃l and the other forms are entirely regular also:

měl -a jsem I had	**měli -y jsme** we had
měl -a jsi you had	**měli -y jste**, polite sg. **měl-a jste** you had
měl, měla, mělo he, she, it had	**měli, měly** (n. **-a**) they had

Měl/měla knihu.	S/he had a book.
Měli auto.	They (male/mixed) had a car.
Měly auto.	They (female) had a car.
Neměli jsme čas.	We didn't have time.

7.5.3 | Past tense – monosyllabic verbs and vowel shortening

The long vowels of monosyllabic infinitives usually shorten in the past -l forms:

á – a:	**dát – dal** gave, **psát – psal** wrote, **spát – spal** slept
é – e:	**nést – nesl** carried, **vést – vedl** led
í – ě:	**mít – měl** had, **chtít – chtěl** wanted
but also **í – i:**	**pít – pil** drank, **bít – bil** beat
ou – u:	**plout – plul** floated
ů – o:	**růst – rostl** grew
ý – y:	**být – byl** was, **krýt – kryl** covered, **mýt – myl** washed

But sometimes -á- remains long. This particularly applies to Type 3 verbs which have an extra syllable in the present tense:

hrát – hraje – hrál 'played', **stát – stojí – stál** 'stood', **bát se – bojí se – bál se** 'was afraid', **přát – přeje – přál** 'wished'

but also e.g. **zdát se – zdá se – zdálo se** 'it seemed'.

The same shortening or non-shortening of long -á- occurs whenever
a syllabic prefix is added to such a verb:

psát – psal and **napsat – napsal**

dát – dal and **vydat – vydal**

but **hrát – hrál** *and* **zahrát – zahrál**

The most irregular past tense form is šel, šla, šli/šly, the past-tense -l
form of jít 'to go':

Pavel šel domů.	Pavel went/has gone home.
Jana šla domů.	Jana went/has gone home.
Šli jsme domů.	We went home.

7.5.4 | *Past tense – verbs with infinitive -nout*

Verbs with infinitives ending in **-nout** regularly have past tense forms
ending in **-nul** if a vowel precedes this ending:

mi|nout – minul, minula, minuli	missed, passed
ply|nout – plynul, plynula, plynuli	flowed
tr|nout (vocalic r) **– trnul, trnula, trnuli**	become stiff, numb

Similarly, some monosyllabic verbs with a single consonant preceding
(and their compounds), e.g.

hnout (se) – hnul, hnula, hnuli	moved pf.

Other verbs ending in **-nout** preceded by a consonant have shorter
past-tense forms ending in just **-l, -la, -li**. The -l of the masculine sg.
form is pronounced as a separate syllable:

sed|nout si – sed|l si, sedla si, sedli si	to sit down pf. – he, she, they sat down
leh|nout si – leh|l si, lehla si, lehli si	to lie down pf. – he, she, they lay down

Colloquially the masculine sg. -l syllable can be dropped. But in colloquial spoken Czech it is also common to substitute longer **-nul** forms,
especially for the masculine sg.:

***sed si, *sednul si**	he sat down
***leh si, *lehnul si**	he lay down

Other forms such as *sednula si, *sednuli si also occur, but are usually associated with a lower stylistic register.

Occasionally the -nul masculine sg. form is standard, or at least optionally so. This is basically where the pronunciation would otherwise be awkward in some way:

mrznout – mrzl or **mrznul** then **mrzlo** etc. froze

zestárnout – zestárl or **zestárnul** then **zestárla** etc. grew old pf.

zblbnout – zblbl or **zblbnul** then **zblbla** etc. become silly pf.

schnout – schnul only, then **schla, schli** dried

vyschnout – vyschl or **vyschnul** then **vyschla, vyschli** dried pf.

7.6 Imperfective and perfective aspect – *nedokonavý a dokonavý vid*

Czech verbs mostly come in pairs: one 'imperfective', the other 'perfective'. A pair of this kind is called an aspectual pair (**vidová dvojice**). Both verbs in the pair mean basically the same thing, from the point of view of an English verb, but differ in their 'aspect' – i.e. in whether their sense is seen as a completed whole or not.

An *imperfective* verb (**nedokonavé sloveso**) denotes ongoing or general activity, without reference to its completion. The verb may refer to a single state or action in progress, or to the indefinite repetition of a state or action.

A *perfective* verb (**dokonavé sloveso**) denotes a complete act (or complete set of acts).

Most unprefixed basic verbs are imperfective. To make the imperfective verb **psát** 'to write' perfective you add the prefix **na-** (basically 'on, onto') and obtain the perfective verb **napsat** (with a shortened syllable -a-).

Compare:

Chci psát dopis.   I want to write a letter. (activity)

Chci napsat dopis.   I want to write a letter. (complete act)

Other prefixes added to the same basic verb will change the meaning to create a perfective *compound* verb, a 'new verb' or 'lexical item' (in terms of the dictionary), e.g. **podepsat** 'to sign', **popsat** 'to describe'.

These compounds are perfective, just like **napsat**. As a result, they (not very surprisingly) require imperfective counterparts. These are produced by a change of suffix, which alters the ending and type of verb.

The imperfective counterparts of **podepsat** 'to sign' and **popsat** 'to describe' are **podepisovat** and **popisovat**, each using the suffix -ovat.

(Different compounds formed from the same root will normally share the same suffix for this purpose.)

The two main types of aspectual pair, *prefix* pairs and *suffix* pairs, look like this:

psát impf. – **napsat** pf.

podepsat pf. – **podepisovat** impf.

In the second type the more basic form is, as a rule, the perfective one.

7.6.1 | *Prefix pairs*

In *prefix* pairs the perfectives add a prefix to the imperfectives, as in **psát – napsat** 'to write', **dělat – udělat** 'to do, to make'.

In the first example the perfective form is analogous to English 'write down', except that English does not need to add 'down' to indicate a complete act of writing.

In order simply to perfectivise a given verb a relatively neutral prefix is used which does not shift the verb away from the required sense. The most commonly used are:

na-, o-, po-, u-, vy-, s-, z-, za-

Other prefixes occur in this role, but much less often, though certain examples are very frequent, e.g. **pře|číst** read.

If the prefix adds a new syllable then long -á- in a monosyllabic infinitive will shorten, unless it does *not* shorten in the past tense, e.g. **psát, psal – napsat** but **hrát, hrál – zahrát**.

The prefix used is not predictable enough for easy rules to be provided, so this is basically a matter of vocabulary learning:

pře-číst 'to read' ('across', 'through'), **u-vařit** 'to cook', **po-děkovat** 'to thank', **zvát – po-zvat** 'to invite', **za-platit** 'to pay', **u-dělat** 'to do', **vy-pít** 'to drink' ('up'), **s-níst** 'to eat' ('up'), pf. of **jíst** 'to eat'

In prefix pairs the basic imperfective verb is mostly a simple root verb, with no prefix of its own.

For more details, see section 10.9.5 Forming prefix pairs.

7.6.2 | *Suffix pairs*

In *suffix* pairs the two forms end with different suffixes. In this type of pair the perfective form is, as a rule of thumb, derivationally primary, and also shorter.

Most of these verbs are compound verbs, that is to say, those which have a permanently attached prefix which is part of their intrinsic meaning, e.g. **vydělat** pf. 'to earn, make (money)', **podepsat** pf. 'to sign', i.e. 'write your name under':

vydělat pf. – **vydělávat** impf. 'to earn, make (money)'

podepsat pf. – **podepisovat** impf. 'to sign'.

In such pairs the imperfective infinitives will normally have one of these suffixes:

-(á)vat, **-ovat**, **-et** or **-at**

Alongside these typical compound verbs, a few unprefixed verbs have a basic meaning involving immediate completion or instantaneous action which has caused the primary form to be perfective, e.g. **dát** pf. 'to give' and **koupit** pf. 'to buy'. These produce pairs of the suffix type as well:

dát pf. – **dávat** impf.

koupit pf. – **kupovat** impf.

For more details, see section 10.9.6 Forming suffix pairs.

7.6.3 | Irregular aspectual pairs

Some aspectual pairs involve different roots for the two variants. Note especially:

brát, bere, bral impf. – **vzít, vezme, vzal** pf. 'to take' with compounds based on **brát**, e.g. **vybrat** pf. – **vybírat** impf. 'to choose'

klást, klade, kladl impf. – **položit** pf. 'to put (in a lying position)' with compounds such as **skládat** impf. – **složit** pf. 'to put together, compose'

Other pairs involve relatively minor or lesser irregularities, e.g.

čekat impf. – **počkat, počkám** pf. 'to wait'

stavět impf. – **postavit** pf. 'to build'

7.6.4 | Expressing the past with aspectual pairs

Perfective and imperfective verbs form past tenses in the same way, but differ in their precise meaning.

| **Psal jsem dopis.** | I wrote/was writing a letter. (process) |
| **Napsal jsem dopis.** | I wrote/have written a letter. (complete act) |

English has a wide range of past forms with different distinctions. 'Was writing' can be treated as clearly imperfective, but 'wrote' can correspond to either aspect.

Včera psala dopis.	Yesterday she was writing/wrote a letter.
Psala ho celý den.	She was writing/wrote it all day.
Už ho napsala.	Now she has written it.
Dnes napsala další.	Today she wrote/has written another one.

An action which clearly was completed but where the main focus is on the type of action rather than conveying the notion of its completion may be expressed by an imperfective verb:

| **Tento obraz maloval Rembrandt.** | This picture was painted by Rembrandt. |
| **Viděl jsem ho včera.** | I saw him yesterday. |

7.6.5 | Imperfective-only verbs

Some imperfective verbs lack (or usually lack) perfective counterparts. These include imperfectives for fixed states, such as **ležet/ležím** 'to lie, be lying', **sedět/sedím** 'to sit, be sitting'. (Equivalent changes of state are most often perfective, e.g. **lehnout si** 'to lie down', **sednout si** 'to sit down'.)

Other such imperfectives are **být** 'to be', **moct** 'to be able', **muset** 'to have to, must', and **chtít** 'to want'.

Some verbs which are normally perfective can be imperfective in a particular sense:

hodit pf. 'throw', but **hodit se** impf. 'be suitable' (future: **bude se hodit** 'will be suitable')

7.6.6 | Perfective-only verbs

Some verbs are perfective only, e.g. **nadchnout se** 'become enthused'. These include some verbs derived from adjectives and denoting a change of state, e.g. **onemocnět** 'fall ill', **otěhotnět** 'become pregnant'.

7.6.7 | *Bi-aspectual verbs*

Some verbs are 'bi-aspectual', i.e. they can be used as perfective as well as imperfective verbs, e.g. **jmenovat** 'to name, appoint', **organizovat** 'to organise', **věnovat (se)** 'devote (oneself)', **obětovat (se)** 'sacrifice (oneself)'.

Such verbs typically have an imperfective present tense and a past tense which is either perfective or imperfective according to the context:

Organizuje náš seminář.　　S/he is organising our seminar.

Organizovala náš seminář.　　S/he organised our seminar.

Many are loanwords: **informovat** 'inform', **analyzovat** 'analyse', **dezinfikovat** 'disinfect', **konstruovat** 'construct', **riskovat** 'risk'.

Some of these loanwords also have optional prefixed perfectives, often with **z-**, e.g. **zorganizovat, zkonstruovat**.

7.7 Perfective present and future

Only imperfective verbs have a present tense referring to something going on here and now:

Píšu dopis.　　I am writing a letter. (process)

Kupuju knihu.　　I am buying a book.

Teď dělám svou práci.　　Now I am doing my work.

The same tense forms are used for referring to repeated or habitual actions:

Píše romány.　　S/he writes novels.

Kupuje knihy.　　S/he buys books.

However, the present tense forms of perfective verbs can also correspond to an English present tense, if a complete action is described:

Někdy přečte celou knihu za pár hodin!　　Sometimes s/he reads a whole book in a couple of hours!

Někdy to udělá za pět minut!　　Sometimes s/he does it in five minutes!

Narratives can also be delivered at least partly in the present tense, in which case you can use perfective present forms to refer to complete actions which took place in the past:

Přijde domů, sedne si a   S/he comes home, sits down and falls
hned usne.   asleep immediately.

Perfective present forms also regularly occur in stage directions for
plays and the like.

However, these basically present-tense forms of perfective verbs are
also the standard way to refer to complete actions or completion of
acts in the future:

Zítra napíšu dopis.   Tomorrow I will write a letter.
                             (complete act)

Zítra koupím knihu.   Tomorrow I will buy a book.

Udělám to zítra.   I'll do it tomorrow.

In terms of formation, there is really no such thing as a perfective
future tense in Czech. The forms used are the same as those of the
present tense (and moreover, as we have seen, do not even always have
to refer to future events).

7.8   Imperfective future – *budoucí čas nedokonavý*

To express ongoing actions or states in the future, requiring the use of
imperfective verbs, a special future form of the verb **být** 'to be' is used,
followed by the imperfective infinitive of the verb required.

The verb 'to be' uses this special future form on its own. This consists of the root form **bud-**, which gives future meaning, followed by
standard present-tense endings:

budu I shall/will be	**budeme, *budem** we shall/will be
budeš you will be	**budete** you will be
bude s/he will be	**budou** they will be

It is *never* followed by the infinitive **být**!

Budeš bohatý/-á!   You'll be rich!

Nebudou doma.   They won't be at home.

To make an imperfective future of other verbs, but only (!!) imperfectives, just add the infinitive of the verb to the personal forms of
budu:

budu psát I shall/will write	**budeme psát** we shall/will write
budeš psát you will write	**budete psát** you will write
bude psát s/he will write	**budou psát** they will write

Budu psát dopis. I'll write/be writing a letter. (process)

The negative prefix **ne-** is attached to the forms of **budu**:

Nebudeme otvírat okno.	We won't open/be opening the window.

Remember: the perfective future is simply (and only!) the perfective present:

Napíšu dopis.	I'll write a letter.
Neotevřu okno.	I won't open the window.

7.9 The conditional tense – *kondicionál/Podmiňovací způsob*

The conditional corresponds to the English tense 'would do, would make' etc.

It is formed on parallel lines to the past tense, combining its -l form with a special set of auxiliary forms (originally a tense of the verb 'to be', no longer used on its own).

The basic set of forms is as follows:

čekal-a bych I would wait	**čekali-y bychom/** ***bysme** we would wait
čekal-a bys you would wait	**čekal-a/-i, -y byste** you would wait
čekal-a -o by he/she/it would wait	**čekali-y by** they would wait

The form ***bysme** is usual in relaxed usage, where **bychom** may sound too formal.

Mohli bychom/bysme jít na koncert.	We could go to a concert.

The more markedly non-standard forms ***bysem** = **bych** and ***bysi** = **bys** also occur. (This is the result of a tendency to bring the forms of the conditional closer to **by** + the past-tense forms with **jsem, jsi** etc. where the **j** is normally silent.)

Note also the special standard forms for the 'you' sg. **ty** form combined with reflexive pronouns **se, si:**

učil(a) by ses you'd study (i.e. 'teach yourself')

koupil(a) by sis you'd buy for yourself

The conditional tense can be formed from both imperfective and perfective verbs, on the same lines as the past tense:

psal bych 'I would write' (process, repetition – imperfective)

napsal bych 'I would write' (complete act – perfective)

Conditionals on their own typically occur in questions and answers.

Co byste udělali? What would you do?

Kam byste šli? Where would you go?

Šli bychom domů. We would go home.

The conditional tense is also used in 'if' clauses using **kdyby** 'if' and with **aby** 'in order that, so that'. In these cases the auxiliary is written as one word with the preceding syllable, i.e. **kdybych = kdy + by**, **abychom = a + bychom** and so on.

Kdybych měl čas, šel bych do kina.
If I had ('would have') time, I would go to the cinema.

Pospíchali jsme, abychom nezmeškali vlak.
We hurried, so that we wouldn't miss the train.

See 9.11.2 and 9.13 on **kdyby** and **aby** for more details.

| 7.9.1 | *Expressing wishes with the conditional etc.*

The conditional can also express a wish, or a polite enquiry:

Něco bych snědl! I'd like to eat something!

Šel/šla bys se mnou? Would you go with me?

Přeložil(a) byste mi tohle slovo? Would you translate this word for me?

Wishes are also often expressed by **rád by** 'would like, would be glad to', **chtěl by** 'would wish, would like', and **mohl by** 'could':

Rád bych něco snědl!   I'd like to eat something!

Chtěl(a) bys jít se mnou?   Would you like to go with me?

Mohl(a) byste mi přeložit   Could you translate this word for me?
tohle slovo?

Similarly, with **být** 'to be':

Byl(a) bych rád(a).   I would be glad.

Aby can also introduce an exclamatory wish:

Jen abych nespadl!   If only I don't fall! Hope I don't fall!

Už aby ta zima skončila!   Would that winter were over! I
                                wish . . .

A wish may also be expressed by **kéž**, with or without the conditional:

Kéž by přestalo pršet! Kéž přestane pršet!
If only it would stop raining!

7.10   Synopsis of main tenses

Here is the basic scheme of tenses, as described above, taking aspect into account. Past and conditional forms are given as masculine animate only, for clarity's sake.

The first example shows the prefix pair impf. **dělat** – pf. **udělat** 'to make, to do'. Remember: the future with **budu** occurs only with imperfectives.

Infinitive	Present/pf. future		Impf. future	
(u)dělat	(u)dělám	(u)děláme	budu dělat	budeme dělat
	(u)děláš	(u)děláte	budeš dělat	budete dělat
	(u)dělá	(u)dělají	bude dělat	budou dělat
	Past		Conditional	
	(u)dělal jsem	(u)dělali jsme	(u)dělal bych	(u)dělali bychom
	(u)dělal jsi	(u)dělal-i jste	(u)dělal bys	(u)dělal-i byste
	(u)dělal	(u)dělali	(u)dělal by	(u)dělali by

The second example, abridged, illustrates the suffix pair impf. **dávat** – pf. **dát** 'to give'.

Infinitive	Present/pf. future	Impf. future
dávat/dát	**dávám/dám** etc.	**budu dávat** etc.
	Past	Conditional
	dával jsem/dal jsem etc.	**dával bych/dal bych** etc.

The third example illustrates the suffix pair impf. **kupovat** – pf. **koupit** 'to buy'.

Infinitive	Present/pf. future	Impf. future
kupovat/ koupit	**kupuji/koupím** etc.	**budu kupovat** etc.
	Past	Conditional
	kupoval jsem/ koupil jsem etc.	**kupoval bych/ koupil bych** etc.

7.11 Past conditional – *kondicionál minulý*

To talk about what might have been in the past (but wasn't), you can add **byl** or **byl býval** to the conditional, making a 'past conditional', corresponding to 'would have done' in English.

Byl bych (býval) koupil nové auto. I would have bought a new car.

For the past conditional of the verb **být** 'to be' use **byl býval**.

These past conditionals usually occur with 'if' clauses. (See 9.11.2.)

7.12 Pluperfect – *předminulý čas/plusquamperfektum*

Occasionally a pluperfect tense meaning 'had done, had bought' etc. can be formed by adding **byl** to the usual past tense, but this is nowadays semi-obsolete:

Stalo se, jak byl král přikázal.	It happened, as the king had commanded.

7.13 Reported/indirect speech – *nepřímá řeč*

When reporting speech in Czech you don't change the original tense of the verb as you do in English. Often 'would' comes out as 'will'.
If Karel said:

Přijdu zítra.	I will come tomorrow.

This is reported as:

Karel řekl, že přijde zítra.	Karel said that he 'will' (= would) come tomorrow.

Similarly, if Karel said:

Mám hlad.	I'm hungry.

This is reported as:

Karel řekl, že má hlad.	Karel said he 'is' (= was) hungry.

Note how 'that' is often omitted before reported speech in English.

7.13.1 Reported perceptions

The same procedure as for reported speech applies to reported perceptions. If Marie sees Karel and thinks:

Stojí před Evou.	He is standing in front of Eva.
Zpívá.	He is singing.

This is reported in the past as:

Viděla ho, jak stojí před Evou.	She saw him as he 'stands' (= stood) in front of Eva. = She saw him standing in front of Eva.
Slyšela ho, jak zpívá.	She heard him as he 'sings' (= sang). = She heard him singing.

After verbs of perception an infinitive can be used instead. English can also use an infinitive, but only without 'to':

Viděla ho stát před Evou.   She saw him stand in front of Eva.

Slyšela ho zpívat.   She heard him sing.

7.14   The imperative – *imperativ/rozkazovací způsob*

The imperative issues orders or instructions: 'Read!' 'Work!'

The verb may be either imperfective or perfective, depending on whether the activity or a complete act is meant.

The basic imperative is like the present without any ending – more precisely, without the 'they' ending **-í/-ou**.

mluvit – mluví   **Mluv!**   Speak!

Verbs of the regular á-type have **-ej!**

zavolat – zavolají   **Zavolej!**   Call!

dát – dají   **Dej!**   Give!

Verbs of the **-ovat** type have **-uj!**

pracovat – pracují   **Pracuj!**   Work!

Long vowels shorten in the last syllable (note **ou → u**). Final **d, t, n** are always **ď, ť, ň**.

koupit – koupí   **Kup!**   Buy!

vrátit – vrátí   **Vrať!**   Return! Give back!

zaplatit – zaplatí   **Zaplať!**   Pay!

Follow the 'they' form of the present, if there is any divergence from the infinitive:

psát – píšou   **Piš!**   Write!

pít – pijí   **Pij!**   Drink!

For the plural (and formal) imperative you just add **-te!** To say 'let's' add **-me!**

Mluvte! Mluvme!   Speak! Let's speak!

Zavolejte! Zavolejme!   Call! Let's call!

Zaplaťte! Zaplaťme!   Pay! Let's pay!

7.14.1 *Longer imperative*

Czech also has a longer imperative ending in -i! It is used where the imperative would otherwise end in two consonants or lack a syllable.
Parallel plural forms are -ěte/-ete! and -ěme/-eme!

myslet – myslí	**Mysli! Myslete!**	Think!
spát – spí	**Spi! Spěte!**	Sleep!
číst – čtou	**Čti! Čtěte!**	Read!
otevřít – otevřou	**Otevři! Otevřete!**	Open!
zavřít – zavřou	**Zavři! Zavřete!**	Close!
vzít – vezmou	**Vezmi! Vezměte!**	Take!
(colloq. **vemou**)	(colloq. **Vem! Vemte!**)	
říct – řeknou	**Řekni! Řekněte!**	Say!

However, a few consonant sequences are allowed, especially -st':

pustit – pustí	**Pusť mě!**	Let me go!

7.14.2 *Some irregular imperatives*

Note especially:

buď! 'be!', **měj**! 'have!', **jez!**/pf. **sněz**! 'eat!', **stůj** 'stand! cost!'

Nebuď smutný/-á!	Don't be glum! Cheer up!
Nebuď takový/-á!	Don't be like that!
Měj se (dobře)!	Have a nice time! lit. 'have yourself well!'
Nejez to!	Don't eat that!
Sněz to!	Eat it (up)!
Nestůj tam!	Don't stand there!
Stůj co stůj!	Whatever it costs! lit. 'cost what cost!'

Vědět has the relatively uncommon **věz!** 'know!'. **Pomoct** 'to help' has **pomoz!** 'help!', commonly expressed by the noun **pomoc!**

Vidět has **viz!** 'see' (e.g. introducing cross-references). **Podívej(te) se!** 'look! see!' is a neutral equivalent.

Colloquial **hele! heleď'te!** 'look, look here!' invites attention, alongside formal **hle!** 'behold!'

Poslyš! 'hear! listen!' corresponds to **slyšet** 'to hear'.

7.14.3 Negative instructions

Negative instructions tend to be imperfective (unlike positive instructions to carry out a single act), since imperfectives refer to the general activity:

Nekupuj to!	Don't buy it!	*but:* **Kup to!**	Buy it!
Nečekej na mě!	Don't wait for me!	*but:* **Počkej na mě!**	Wait for me!

7.14.4 Other command-like constructions

Instead of an imperative a plain future verb is often used to express firm or peremptory instructions and commands:

Půjdeš hned domů a umyješ se pořádně!
You go straight home and wash yourself properly!

Nezabiješ! Thou shalt not kill!

The infinitive is also used for some brisk, exclamatory, military-style commands:

Stát rovně!	Stand up straight!
Dokouřit!	Finish smoking!
Zastavit stát!	Halt! lit. 'Stop stand!'
Sedět!	Stay sitting!

But imperatives occur also for military commands, e.g.

Pal! Palte!	Fire! (**pálit** 'to fire')
Stůj!	Stand!

A forcefully expressed wish can be introduced by **at'**, providing a kind of third-person imperative:

At' je mír!	Let there be peace!
At' si dělá, co chce.	Let him do what he wants.

At' can also introduce a warning, and the verb need not be third person (for **at'** in subordinate clauses see 9.13.2):

At' nepřijdeš pozdě! May you not be late! = Take care not to be late!

7.15 Participles and passive constructions

A participle combines the meaning – *participates* in the meaning – of both a verb and an adjective. Participles are fundamentally adjectival in form. In Czech they have to agree in gender, case and number with the nouns or pronouns to which they refer.

They may also be *active* or *passive*, distinguishing between active voice (**aktivum, slovesný rod činný**) and passive voice (**pasívum, slovesný rod trpný**):

English verbs form *active* participles in 'ing', which are adjective-like forms referring to a noun, e.g. 'the screaming child', 'the child running in the park', etc. Here the noun described by the '-ing' participle is the doer or agent of the action.

English verbs also form *passive* participles in '-ed', e.g. 'inflated' from 'inflate'. Again the participle can modify a noun ('an inflated balloon'), or it can be used like a predicative adjective ('the balloon is now inflated'). The noun described by this kind of participle is the *passive recipient* of the action of the verb, hence the form is termed *passive*. (Some English passive forms are irregular, e.g. 'broken' from 'to break', as in 'a broken window'.)

The English '-ed' participle and its Czech equivalent are also both used with the verb 'to be' to form *passive* verb constructions.

In these the object of an active verb becomes the grammatical subject of the passive one. The agent may either be omitted, e.g. 'The balloon was inflated yesterday,' or added, in English using 'by', e.g. 'The balloon was inflated by John' = 'John inflated the balloon'.

7.15.1 The passive participle – příčestí trpné

Czech passive participles mostly have long adjectival forms ending in **-ný**, e.g. **zavřený** 'closed, shut', **otevřený** 'open', but a minority end in **-tý** (especially if derived from infinitives ending in **-nout**):

Zavřené okno. Otevřené okno.	A closed/shut window. An open window.
Okno je zavřené, otevřené.	The window is closed/shut, open.
Zapomenutý hrob.	A forgotten grave.

These decline like regular standard adjectives. Their forms are usually predictable according to the infinitive:

-at: -aný	zklamat: zklamaný	to disappoint – disappointed
-it, -et: -ený	překvapit: překvapený viďet: viďený	to surprise – surprised to see – seen
-ovat: -ovaný	organizovat: organizovaný	to organise – organised
-nout: -nutý	zapomenout: zapomenutý	to forget – forgotten

Before **-ený** (mostly verbs with infinitive **-it**) there are sometimes (but not always) consonant changes **d>z, t>c, s>š** and **z>ž**, which have to be learnt for particular roots:

obsadit – obsazený stůl 'an occupied table', **ztratit – ztracený pas** 'a lost passport', **opustit – opuštěný dům** 'an abandoned house', **vymyslet – vymyšlený plán** 'a thought-up, invented plan', **zpozdit se – zpožděný vlak** 'a delayed train'

Passive participles derived from monosyllabic verbs mostly have a short-ened root vowel, as in the past tense. Some further **-tý** forms (e.g. some, but not all monosyllabic Type 3 verbs) just have to be learnt pretty much individually:

zavřít – zavřený 'closed', *but* **zabít – zabitý** 'killed'

Type 1 verbs with infinitives **-st, -zt, -ct/-ci** have passive participles ending in **-ený**. Again, the forms need to be learnt individually:

přinést – přinesený 'brought', **přečíst – přečtený** 'read', **nalézt – nalezený** 'found', **péct – pečený** 'baked, roasted'

Passive participles are derived from both perfective and imperfective verbs, depending on the precise meaning.

Imperfective forms can refer to a type or category of thing, rather than the result of an action, e.g. **vařené nudle** 'boiled noodles', **smažená vejce** 'fried eggs', **pečený pstruh** 'baked trout', **nově otvíraný supermar-ket** 'the newly opened supermarket' (which might be closed, if it is after opening hours).

If the participle is qualified by another phrase it usually follows the noun, as in English, e.g. **dům opuštěný před dvaceti pěti lety** 'the house abandoned twenty-five years ago'.

Some participles have become fully fledged adjectives, even to the extent that they form comparatives and superlatives (which proper participles do not normally do), e.g. **vzdělaný – (nej)vzdělanější** '(well-)educated – more/most well-educated', **otevřený – otevřenější** 'open – more open' (referring to human behaviour).

7.15.2 *Short-form passive participles*

Passive participles also have 'short forms' (**krátké/jmenné tvary**) which regularly occur as the complement of the verb 'to be'. These decline like short-form adjectives (see 4.5).

To make short forms you just drop final **-ý**, but change **-aný** to **-án**:

překvapený – překvapen 'surprised', **napsaný – napsán** 'written', **zakázat – zakázán** 'forbidden', **zapomenutý – zapomenut** 'forgotten'

The short forms nowadays compete with the more colloquial long forms in the complement position, and in speech the long forms predominate:

Okno je zavřeno (zavřené/*zavřený).	The shop is closed.
Dveře jsou otevřeny (otevřené/*otevřený).	The door (pl.) is open.

Sometimes the complement is hardly distinguishable from a passive construction with no agent expressed, and long forms also occur colloquially here as well:

Dopis byl napsán (napsaný/*napsanej) včera.	The letter was written yesterday.
Byli pozváni (pozvaní/*pozvaný) na oběd.	They were invited to lunch.

In fact, only the neuter sg. short forms in **-o** are common in everyday spoken usage, outside certain set phrases. They are commonly used in impersonal phrases requiring neuter agreement such as:

Je otevřeno/zavřeno.	It's open/closed.

Also, idiomatically, after the verb 'to have':

Máme otevřeno/zavřeno.	We are open/closed, lit. 'We have (it) open/closed.'
Máte vybráno?	Have you chosen? lit. 'Do you have (it) chosen?'
Máte zaplaceno?	Have you paid? lit. 'Do you have (it) paid?'

7.15.3 *Passive constructions with participles*

For proper passive constructions, where primarily an action is referred to, rather than a resultant state, the standard language prescribes the short-form participles. Here the agent may also be expressed, with a noun phrase in the instrumental case:

Báseň byla napsána [Seifertem] v roce 1922.
The poem was written [by Seifert] in 1922.

Where the participle is used more like an adjective to express a result-ant state, rather than an action, then the long forms may also be used. In English this distinction can be occasionally made through usage of particular words, e.g. adjective 'open' versus passive participle 'opened':

Dveře byly otevřeny/otevřené.   The doors are/were *open*.

but:

Dveře byly hned otevřeny a šli jsme dovnitř.
The doors were immediately *opened* (= action), and we went inside.

Everyday spoken Czech tends to avoid passive constructions using participles (unlike English). Instead, Czech exploits its use of inflected cases. You can simply say 'Seifert wrote the poem', but reverse the order of words. The meaning is clear, since 'Seifert' will be in the nominative case, not the accusative, and so is clearly the subject of the verb:

Báseň (object) **napsal Seifert** (subject) **v roce 1922.**
= The poem was written by Seifert in 1922.

So it is often best to avoid passives when speaking Czech. Similarly:

Tuto knihu mi dal Petr.
= This book was given to me by Petr.

Where an active verb has an object which is not in the accusative case, but (for example) the genitive, the passive construction leaves the object in that case and makes the verb neuter singular:

Použili různých metod.   They used various methods.

Bylo použito různých metod.   Various methods were used.

This is again formal standard usage.

7.15.4 *Reflexive passive*

Another important, widespread and also more colloquial way of making a passive construction in Czech is to use a third-person reflexive verb (**zvratné sloveso**), with no stated agent:

Jak se to píše?	How is that written?
	lit. 'How does that write itself?'
Kde se prodávají lístky?	Where are the tickets sold?
	lit. 'Where do tickets sell themselves?'
To se nedělá.	That is not done.

Compare some other reflexive examples, where English could (at least conceivably) use either an active or a passive verb:

| **Obchod se zavírá v šest.** | The shop closes ('itself') at six, is closed at six. |
| **Polévka se začíná vařit.** | The soup is starting to boil ('itself'), to be boiled. |

In these examples alternative constructions with participles would be very awkward.

7.15.5 Subjectless constructions

'Subjectless constructions' take a step further beyond the kind of reflexive passive construction outlined above.

This first example is simply a passive construction, as above:

| **Tady se pije pivo.** | Beer is drunk here, lit. 'Beer drinks itself here.' |

But if we remove the subject word **pivo** 'beer', we get a construction, widely used in Czech, where the verb has no specific subject, is 'subjectless'. Compare English statements with 'one', 'people', or even 'we' (like the French use of *on*, and German *mann*):

Tady se pije.	Here drinking goes on. = One drinks here. People drink here.
	lit. '[It] is drinking itself here.'
Tady se nekouří.	One doesn't smoke here.

Even intransitive verbs may occur in such constructions:

| **Jde se domů.** | We're going home. People are going home, lit. '[It] goes itself home.' |

7.16 **Verbal nouns** – *podstatné jméno slovesné*

English can form verbal nouns in '-ing' from almost any verb, e.g. 'reading' from 'to read'. Their direct Czech equivalents end mainly in **-ní**, but sometimes in **-tí**.

Their forms are normally parallel to those of the passive participle ending in **-ný/-tý**. They can also be either imperfective or perfective, according to meaning (impf. for process, pf. for complete act).

Some correspond in use to other kinds of noun in English, i.e. not simply English nouns ending in '-ing':

-at: -ání	čekat: čekání	waiting
-it, -et: -ení	vařit: vaření	cooking
	ležet: ležení	lying
-ovat: -ování	opakovat: opakování	repeating, repetition
-nout: -nutí	zapomenout: zapomenutí	forgetting, oblivion

Verbal nouns are not necessarily listed in dictionaries, as nearly all verbs form them, but normally they should be listed whenever they have become independent items of vocabulary, e.g.

cvičení 'an exercise' (**cvičit** 'to exercise'), **vzdělání** '(an) education' (**vzdělat se** < **vzdělávat se** 'to educate oneself'), **rozhodnutí** 'a decision' (**rozhodnout** 'to decide something')

The same irregularities of formation occur as with passive participles.

Where English has special 'gerund' forms of verbal nouns, which can have objects, Czech usually expresses the idea in another way, without using a verbal noun, e.g.

He likes singing songs.   **Rád zpívá písně.**

lit. 'He glad[ly] sings songs.'

Translating novels is hard work.   **Překládat romány je těžká práce.**

lit. 'To translate novels is hard work.'

7.17 **Frequentatives** – *slovesa opakovací*

Czech verbs sometimes form so-called 'frequentatives' ending in **-vat** (especially **-ávat** from infinitives ending in **-at**, and **-ívat** from **-it**). These refer to repeated tendencies:

být – bývat to be often, tend to be

mít – mívat to have often, tend to have

dělat – dělávat to tend to make, make often

Bývá ospalý.	He is often/tends to be sleepy.
Mívá problémy s češtinou.	He often has problems with Czech.
Dělává chyby.	He tends to make mistakes.

Even indeterminate verbs may form frequentatives, e.g. **chodit** 'to go regularly' has a form **chodívat** meaning 'to go from time to time':

Ano, chodívám do kostela.	Yes, I go to church now and again.

In the past these verbs mean 'used to do':

Býval příjemnější.	He used to be more pleasant.
Míval problémy.	He used to have problems.
Chodíval do kostela.	He used to go to church.

7.18 More participles

7.18.1 Present active participle – příčestí činné

English participles ending in '-ing' have Czech adjectival equivalents ending in **-oucí** or **-ící**.

You form them by adding **-cí** to the third-person plural present form of an imperfective verb, e.g. **běžící** 'running' from **běží** 'they run', **jedoucí** 'going, moving' from **jedou** 'they go, ride'.

Where a verb has a more formal third-person plural present form, after a soft consonant, the '-ing' adjective will regularly match this formal written variant, and use the suffix **-ící**:

píšou/píší gives **píšící** writing

*****hrajou/hrají** gives **hrající** playing

These participial forms can replace a 'who/which' relative clause:

Žena sedící u okna je moje sestra.	The woman sitting by the window is my sister.
Žena, která sedí u okna, je moje sestra.	The woman who is sitting by the window is my sister.

They are also commonly used simply as verbal adjectives:

běžící pás 'a running belt', **jedoucí vlak** 'a moving train', **překvapující účinek** 'a surprising effect', **vedoucí úloha** 'a leading role'

Some are also employed as adjectival nouns, e.g. **vedoucí** 'a manager', **cestující** 'a passenger, traveller'.

Remember, however, that English tenses involving '-ing' participles correspond to simple tenses in Czech. You must not use any present participles here!

The students are reading.	=	**Studenti si čtou.**
The children were playing.	=	**Děti si hrály.**
The children will be reading.	=	**Děti si budou číst.**

7.18.2 Present adverbial participle – přechodník přítomný

In the written language you will sometimes encounter short forms of the present active participles ending in -**íc** or -**ouc**, corresponding to long forms -**ící** or -**oucí** respectively.

These are the feminine and neuter sg. forms of what is called the present **přechodník** or adverbial participle, used for 'doing' in the sense of 'while doing'.

The masculine sg. form looks rather different. It ends in -**ě/e** (instead of -**íc**) and in -**a** (instead of -**ouc**).

The plural forms are -**íce** and -**ouce** respectively, for all genders. Examples:

Leže na trávě, popíjel víno.	Lying/While lying on the grass he drank wine.
Čta noviny, zapomněl na čas.	Reading the paper he forgot the time.
Ležíc na trávě, popíjela víno.	Lying on the grass she sipped some wine.
Čtouc noviny, zapomněla na čas.	Reading the paper she forgot the time.
Ležíce na trávě, popíjeli víno.	Lying on the grass they sipped some wine.
Čtouce noviny, zapomněli na čas.	Reading the newspaper they forgot the time.

This **přechodník** has to agree with the subject of the main verb in gender and number. In today's usage it is nearly always imperfective.

The parallel English constructions with or without 'while' are much more common than their Czech equivalents. Normally, in both spoken and written Czech, you would simply use two clauses connected by 'and':

Leželi na trávě a popíjeli víno.

Četli noviny a zapomněli na čas.

Don't use **přechodníky** when speaking or writing the language in an ordinary relaxed style.

Some have become adverbs or prepositions, and ignore gender/number agreement:

takřka 'so to speak, as it were', **(ne)počítaje/(ne)počítajíc** +acc. '(not) including', **vyjma/vyjímaje/vyjímajíc** + acc. 'excepting', **začínaje/začínajíc** +ins. 'starting with', **konče/končíc** +ins. 'ending with'; also **vsedě** 'sitting, in a sitting position', **v(e)stoje** 'standing, in a standing position'

7.18.3 *Past adverbial participle* – **přechodník minulý**

There is also a past **přechodník**, corresponding to English clauses opening with 'Having . . .' and restricted to very formal writing. It is nearly always formed from a perfective verb, when it occurs, and expresses a complete action preceding the main action. (The Bible is a good place for finding examples of **přechodníky**.)

Form this **přechodník** by replacing the -l of the past-tense form with -v (masculine), -vši (feminine, neuter), and -vše (plural):

Položiv dopis na stůl, vyšel z pokoje.	Having laid the letter on the table, he left the room.
Položivši dopis na stůl, vyšla z pokoje.	Having laid the letter on the table, she left the room.
Položivše dopisy na stůl, vyšli z pokoje.	Having laid/Laying the letters on the table, they left the room

(English often uses a present participle instead, keeping things simpler.)

The verb **být** also has the forms **byv, byvši, byvše** 'having been'.

The consonant **v** is omitted after a consonant, so the forms corresponding to **přivést, přivedl** 'to bring, brought' are:

přived, přivedši, přivedše   having brought

Compounds of **jít** 'to go' have forms with -**šed** etc.:

přišed, přišedši, přišedše   having arrived

Verbs with infinitive -**nout** have forms with -**nuv** etc., e.g. **stisknout**:

stisknuv, stisknuvši, stisknuvše   having pressed, squeezed

Occasionally a long-form participial adjective ending in -**vší** is derived from the **přechodník minulý**:

Muž položivší dopis na stůl byl její otec.
The man who-had-put the letter on the table was her father.

7.18.4 | *Passive equivalent of adverbial participles*

Passive equivalents of the **přechodník** construction can be produced by using forms from the verb 'to be' as auxiliaries:

jsa, jsouc, jsouce 'being'

or:

byv, byvši, byvše 'having been',

These are then accompanied by a short-form passive participle, e.g.

Jsa překvapen/Byv překvapen ...   'Being surprised/Having been
                                            surprised . . .'

However, this is stiff and ultra-formal. Normally the passive participle is used on its own:

Překvapen jejím příchodem, zapomněl vypnout proud.
Surprised by her arrival, he forgot to switch off the current.

7.19   Modal verbs – *modální slovesa*

Modal verbs adjust the sense of another verb in terms of necessity, desire etc., requiring this other verb to be in the infinitive.

In English the verb linked with the modal verb also follows in the infinitive, but often without 'to', e.g. 'John can write', 'John must write', but 'John wants to write'.

7.19.1 | *Can, be able, could, is possible*

Moct (in formal use also the older infinitive **moci**) meaning 'to be able, can' is a slightly irregular e-type verb. The older 'I' and 'they' forms **mohu** and **mohou** are more formal than **můžu** and **můžou**.

můžu/mohu I can, am able	**můžeme** we can
můžeš you can	**můžete** you can
může s/he can	**můžou/mohou** they can

169

Past tense: **mohl** 'could, was able'

Můžeš jít.	You can go.
Nemůžu pracovat.	I can't work. I'm not able to work.
Můžeme čekat.	We can wait.
Mohli pracovat.	They were able to work. They could work. *Also*: They could have worked.
Nemohli pracovat.	They couldn't work. They weren't able to work.

For a polite 'could' use the conditional tense:

Mohl(-a) bych mluvit s Helenou?	Could I speak with/to Helena?
Nemohl(-a) bys mluvit s Láď'ou?	Couldn't you speak with/to Láď'a?
Mohli bychom/*bysme jít na koncert.	We could go to a concert.

English 'can' followed by a passive infinitive often corresponds to **dá se** 'it is possible':

Dá se to koupit prakticky všude.	It can be bought practically anywhere.
Nedá se nic dělat.	Nothing can be done. It's not possible to do anything.
To se nedá říct.	That cannot be said. It's not possible to say that.

A more formal alternative is **lze** 'it is possible', with the more frequent negative **nelze** 'it is impossible, not possible'. In the present tense the verb 'to be' is omitted.

Nelze (less formally: **Nedá se**) **to změnit.**	It cannot be changed. It is impossible to change.
Nebylo lze (or: **Nedalo se**) **to změnit.**	It could not be changed. It was impossible to change.

Another fairly formal alternative for 'it is possible' is **je možno**, using the neuter short form of the adjective **možný** 'possible' (long form **možné** also occurs):

Je/Není možno to změnit.	It is/It is not possible to change it.

The adverb **možná** which usually means 'possibly, perhaps' also occurs as 'possible' in the idiomatic exclamatory phrase (**to**) **není možná!** 'it's not possible!', alongside the expected **to není možné!**

Colloquially **jde** lit. 'it goes' and **šlo** 'it went' can also be used to express something that was or was not achievable, possible to do.

Jde to.	It's possible. It can be done. (*Also*: It's OK. Things are OK.)
To nejde. To se nedá.	That's not possible. It can't be done.
To nešlo. To se nedalo.	That wasn't possible. That couldn't be done.
To by docela šlo.	That would be perfectly 'do-able', OK.
Okno nešlo (se nedalo) zavřít.	The window couldn't be closed.

7.19.2 Know how to

Sometimes 'can' means 'know how to'. Distinguish the use of **umět** 'know how' from **moct** 'can, may':

Umí číst.	S/he can read (knows how to).
Může číst.	S/he can read (may, has the possibility to).
Neumím vařit.	I don't know how to cook.
Nemůžu vařit.	I can't cook (due to some particular circumstances).

7.19.3 Manage to, be capable of, succeed

Related to the above are other verbs such as **dovést – dovede – dovedl** and **dokázat – dokáže – dokázal** 'to manage'. The second perhaps conveys a stronger sense of overcoming obstacles or resistance.

Nedovede pracovat.	He can't manage to work.
Ta to s dětmi dovede.	She knows how to manage with children.
Myslíš, že to dokážeš?	Do you think you can/will manage it?
Nedokáže mlčet.	He can't (manage to) keep quiet.

Note also **být schopen** 'to be able, capable' and **být s to** 'be up to'.

Nebyl schopen mluvit.	He was incapable of speaking.
Nebyl s to pracovat podle plánu.	He wasn't up to working according to a plan.

'Succeed' is often expressed impersonally by **podařit se**, with the person in the dative:

Podařilo se mu najít nové zaměstnání.
He succeeded in finding new employment, lit.
'[It] succeeded to him to find new employment.'

7.19.4 Expressing necessity

Muset (or **musit**) 'to have to, must' is used to express necessity/obligation.

musím I must, I have to	**musíme** we must
musíš you must	**musíte** you must
musí he, she, it must	**musí, musejí** they must

Musím vařit oběd.	I have to cook lunch. I must cook lunch.
Musíte poslouchat rádio.	You have to listen to the radio.

Watch the meaning of the negative!

Nemusíte kouřit.	You don't have to smoke. You needn't smoke.

Other ways of expressing necessity include:

Je/Bylo třeba/potřeba/nutno (něco udělat).	It is/was necessary (to do something).

7.19.5 Expressing permission/prohibition

Smět, smí, směl 'to be allowed, may' expresses the idea of permission:

Smím kouřit?	May I smoke? Am I allowed to smoke?
Smím prosit?	May I ask (for the next dance)?

Moct 'can' is often substituted:

Smím kouřit? Můžu kouřit?	May I smoke? Can I smoke?
Můžu si zapálit?	Can I smoke? lit. 'Can I light up?'

The negative **nesmět** means 'mustn't, not allowed to':

Nesmíte tady kouřit.	You mustn't (aren't allowed to) smoke here.
Tam nesmíš!	You mustn't go there!
To se nesmí!	That is not allowed!
Tady se nesmí kouřit!	You mustn't smoke here!
Nesměla jít ven.	She wasn't allowed to go out.

Note also zakázaný, short form zakázán 'forbidden':

To je zakázané/zakázáno.	That is forbidden.
Kouření zakázáno.	Smoking (lit. 'to smoke') forbidden.
Vstup zakázán!	Entry forbidden!

7.19.6 Am to, ought to, should

'Am to, am supposed to' can be expressed by mít 'to have':

Co mám dělat?	What am I (supposed) to do?
Máš jít domů.	You are (supposed) to go home.

Contrast with **muset** 'to have to, must':

Musíš jít domů.	You have to go home. You must go home.

Conditional **měl bych** means 'ought to, should':

Co bych měl(a) dělat?	What ought I to do? What should I do?
Měl(a) bys jít domů.	You ought to/should go home.
Neměl(a) bys tady zůstat.	You ought not to/shouldn't stay here.

Contrast: **Musel(a) bys jít domů.** You would have to go home.

7.19.7 *Want, wish, would like, feel like*

Chtít 'to want' resembles a Type 1 verb, but note **chci** 'I want' and **chtějí** 'they want':

chci I want	**chceme** we want
chceš you want	**chcete** you want
chce s/he wants	**chtějí** they want

Past tense: **chtěl** 'wanted'

It is followed by infinitives or by nouns:

Jestli chceš, můžeš spát.	If you want, you can sleep.
Chceme jít do kina.	We want to go to the cinema.
Nechtěli jít domů.	They didn't want to go home.
Nechci mléko, chci kávu.	I don't want milk, I want coffee.
Co chcete?	What do you want?
Chci nové kolo.	I want a new bike.

Often it is more polite to say 'wish', using **přát si/přeju si**:

Co si přejete?	What would you like?
Co si přejete k pití?	What would you like to drink?

To express a polite wish the conditional of **chtít** 'to want' is frequently used:

Chtěl(-a) bych mluvit s panem Bednářem.	I would like to talk with Mr Bednář.
Chtěl(-a) byste jít s námi?	Would you like to come with us?

To say a person 'feels' or 'doesn't feel' like doing something the reflexive **chce se** may be used, with the person in the dative:

Chce se mi spát.	I feel like sleeping, lit. 'It wants itself to me to sleep.'
Nechtělo se mu jít do práce.	He didn't feel like going to work.

7.20 Phase verbs – start and stop

Verbs **začít, začne, začal** < **začínat** 'begin' and **přestat, přestane, přestal**
< **přestávat** 'stop, cease' are also followed by infinitives:

Začal zpívat.   He started singing/began to sing.

Přestal zpívat.   He stopped/finished singing.

Začínám tomu rozumět.   I am starting to understand this.

Infinitives after these phase verbs are always imperfective. Modal and
phase verbs can also be combined:

Musím přestat pít.   I have to stop drinking.

7.21 Verbs of motion – *slovesa pohybu*

Several basic verbs of motion do not form imperfective/perfective aspectual pairs. These are simple verbs for 'going', 'carrying', 'leading' etc.
   Instead of forming impf./pf. pairs they distinguish between:

(a) 'determinate' (**determinovaný**) or single, one-directional, goal-
directed, action

and

(b) 'indeterminate' (**indeterminovaný**) or repeated, habitual, multidirectional, and general (non-goal-directed) activity

Pairs of this kind are indicated in this book by a plus sign, e.g. **jít
+ chodit** 'to go'.
   Another distinction made within this group is between (a) motion on
foot, and (b) riding or motion in a vehicle, e.g. **jít + chodit** 'to go on
foot', **jet + jezdit** 'to ride, go by vehicle'.

7.21.1 Jít + chodit, Jet + jezdit

The basic verb **jít/jdu** 'to go on foot' should be distinguished from
jet/jedu 'to go by vehicle, to ride'. Both are Type 1 verbs:

jdu I go	**jdeme** we go
jdeš you go	**jdete** you go
jde s/he goes	**jdou** they go

Past tense: **šel, šla, šli** 'went'

jedu I ride	**jedeme** we ride
jedeš you ride	**jedete** we ride
jede s/he rides	**jedou** they ride

Past tense: **jel, jela, jeli** 'went, rode, drove'

When using **jít** the j in **jd-** can be omitted in casual speech, but not in the negative:

Jde domů.	He is going home.
Nejde domů.	He isn't going home.

Jít and **jet** can also both also mean 'come' – i.e. the 'going' can be in either direction:

Jde/Jede tam.	S/he is going there.
Jde/Jede sem.	S/he is coming here.

Each of these two 'determinate' verbs has a parallel 'indeterminate' verb which refers to habitually repeated or multiple, multidirectional activity:

chodit 'to go' (generally, repeatedly etc.)

jezdit 'to ride, go by vehicle' (generally, repeatedly etc.)

Basically, **jít** and **jet** refer to single acts:

Dnes jdu pěšky.	Today I'm going on foot.
Včera jela vlakem.	Yesterday she went by train.
Vlak jede pomalu.	The train is going slowly.

Chodit and **jezdit** denote repeated, habitual activity, or the activity in general:

Chodí do školy.	S/he goes to school.
Chodíme často do divadla.	We often go to the theatre.
Jezdíme metrem.	We (habitually) go by metro.
Evička se teprve učí chodit.	Evička is just learning to walk.

The futures of **jít** and **jet** are special. You add **pů-** to **jdu,** and **po-** to **jedu:**

Zítra půjdu do školy.	Tomorrow I'll go to school.
Půjdeš se mnou?	Will you go with me?
Zítra pojedu do Brna.	Tomorrow I'll go to Brno.
Pojedeš se mnou?	Will you go with me.

The futures of **chodit** and **jezdit** just use **budu:**

Budu chodit do školy.	I'll be going to school.
Budu jezdit autobusem.	I'll be going by bus.

Imperatives **Jdi! Jděte!** mean 'Go!' while **Pojd'! Pojd'te!** mean 'Come!'

Jdi pryč! Jděte pryč!	Go away!
Pojd' sem! Pojd'te sem!	Come here!
Pojd'me!	is 'Let's go!'
Pojd'me do kina!	Let's go to the cinema!

Negative 'Don't go!' uses **chodit:**

Nechod'! Nechod'te tam!	Don't go! Don't go there!

7.21.2 *Other determinate/indeterminate pairs*

Like **jít + chodit** 'to go', and **jet + jezdit** 'to ride', several other 'determinate', single-action verbs have 'indeterminate' or 'iterative' variants for repeated, habitual or general activity.

Two are verbs for speedy movement, 'run' and 'fly':

běžet + běhat 'to run', **letět + létat**/colloq. **lítat** 'to fly'

Three are verbs for 'carry, take':

nést, nese, nesl + nosit 'to carry' (by lifting)

vést, vede, vedl + vodit 'to lead'

vézt, veze, vezl + vozit 'to carry, convey (by vehicle)'

Again these determinate verbs normally form a future with **po-:**

Poletím. I'll fly. **Ponesu.** I'll carry.

177

Compare the following:

Obvykle jezdí tramvají.	S/he usually goes by tram.
Dnes jde pěšky.	Today s/he's going on foot.
Nerad(a) běhá.	S/he doesn't like running.
Dnes běží do školy.	Today s/he's running to school.
Často létá/lítá do Paříže.	S/he often flies to Paris.
Dnes letí do Ameriky.	Today s/he's flying to America.
Obvykle nosí aktovku.	S/he usually carries a briefcase.
Dnes nese kufr.	Today s/he's carrying a suitcase.
Vozí je často do lesa.	S/he often takes them to the forest.
Dnes je veze na koupaliště.	Today s/he's taking them to the bathing-place.
Obvykle je vodí po městě.	S/he usually takes them about town.
Dnes je vede do muzea.	Today s/he's taking them to the museum.

To these we may add **hnát + honit** 'to chase, drive'. Note the irregular present tense of **hnát – ženu, ženeš, žene**. When reflexive the verb means 'rush'.

Honí krávy na pastvu.	S/he (regularly) drives the cows to the pasture.
Děti se honily po zahradě.	The children rushed about the garden (this way and that).
Žene ho do práce.	S/he chases him to work.
Žene se do práce.	S/he rushes to work.

The indeterminate form **honit** also means 'hunt'.

A couple of other verbs apply the determinate/indeterminate distinction less consistently, e.g. **táhnout** 'pull' and **tahat** 'tug, repeatedly pull'.

A few other verbs also have an optional future with **po-**, e.g. **růst, roste, rostl** 'to grow' – **poroste** 'will grow', **kvést, kvete, kvetl** 'to flower, blossom' – **pokvete** 'will flower'.

7.21.3 Prefixed verbs of motion

Prefixed compounds of the verbs of motion discussed above simply have normal aspectual pairs, of the suffix type.

The patterns are as follows (in the order perfective – imperfective), using as examples verbs with the prefix od- 'away from':

jít + chodit 'go'	**odejít – odcházet** 'go away, leave'
jet + jezdit 'ride'	**odjet – odjíždět** 'ride, go away, leave (by vehicle)'
běžet + běhat 'run'	**odběhnout – odbíhat** 'run off'
letět + létat 'fly'	**odletět – odlétat** 'fly off'
nést + nosit 'carry'	**odnést – odnášet** 'take, carry away'
vést + vodit 'lead'	**odvést – odvádět** 'take, lead away'
vést + vozit 'convey'	**odvézt – odvážet** 'take, convey away'
hnát + honit 'drive, chase'	**odehnat – odhánět** 'drive, chase away'

The opposite prefix **při-** 'reach, come near' produces compound pairs on identical lines, e.g. **přijít – přicházet** 'arrive, come', **přijet – přijíždět** 'arrive, come (riding, by vehicle)', **přinést – přinášet** 'bring (by carrying)', **přivést – přivádět** 'bring (by leading)'.

Jana ještě nepřijela.	Jana hasn't come/arrived yet.
Autobus už odjel.	The bus has left.
Přinesl jí kytici.	He brought her a bouquet.
Odvezl ji domů.	He took her home.
Přivedl ji do kanceláře.	He brought/led her into the office.

7.22 More verbs

7.22.1 Take and get

The most general verb for 'take' is **brát, bere, bral,** with its anomalous perfective **vzít, vezme**/colloq. **veme, vzal.**

But three other verbs discussed above can also correspond to English 'take':

nést + nosit 'to carry'

vézt + vozit 'to convey (by vehicle)'

vést + vodit 'to lead (on foot)'

The meaning of English 'take' is very broad, while **brát/beru** basically means 'pick up and take or use':

Beru knihu ze stolu a čtu.	I take/pick up a book from the table and read.
Beru aspirin.	I take/use aspirin.
Nesu oběd do pokoje.	I take/carry, bring the lunch into the room.
Vezu Ivana do města.	I take/convey, drive Ivan into town.
Vedu Ivana do pokoje.	I take/lead, bring Ivan into the room.

'Get' in the basic sense of 'receive' is generally expressed by **dostat, dostane, dostal < dostávat,** in more formal usage it may be replaced by perfective **obdržet:**

Dostal/Obdržel můj dopis včera.	He got/received my letter yesterday.
Dostává hodně dopisů.	He gets/receives a lot of letters.

In the sense of 'get somewhere' reflexive **dostat se** may be used, especially if there is some sense of difficulty or achievement. Otherwise **přijít** or **přijet** for 'arrive' may be used:

Jak se tam dostanu?	How do I get there? How will I get there?
Jak se dostanu k nádraží?	How do I get to the station?
Dostal se k břehu.	He got to the river bank.
but:	
Přišel domů v pět hodin.	He got (arrived) home at five o'clock.

7.22.2 *Wear*

Nosit 'to carry' also means 'to wear (repeatedly, habitually)'. For single occasions use **mít** 'to have' or **mít na sobě** 'to have on (oneself)':

Obvykle nosí brýle.	S/he usually wears spectacles.
Dnes nemá brýle.	Today s/he's not wearing spectacles.
Co má na sobě?	What is s/he wearing? What has s/he got on?
Dnes má na sobě ten hrozný kabát.	Today s/he's wearing that awful coat.

Another expression for 'wear', in the sense of 'put on', is **vzít si (na sebe),** lit. 'to take (onto oneself)':

Co si mám vzít na sebe?	What should I put on/wear?
Mám si vzít kravatu?	Should I ('have I to') wear a tie?

7.22.3 | *Know and understand*

Vědět/vím 'to know/I know' is an irregular Type 4 verb. Only the 'they' form of the present matches the infinitive.

vím I know	**víme** we know
víš you know	**víte** you know
ví s/he knows	**vědí [!]** they know

Past tense: **věděl** knew

This verb is used for knowing facts and information:

Víme, co děláme.	We know what we are doing.
Nevědí, kde je pan Beneš.	They don't know where Mr Beneš is.

Don't confuse it with **vidět/vidí** 'to see'.

Nevidíte ho? Nevíte, kde je?	Don't you see him? Do you know where he is?

To say you 'know, are familiar with' a person or place use **znát, zná, znal** instead:

Znáte Prahu?	Do you know Prague?
Znáte Karla?	Do you know Karel?
Ne. Karla neznáte.	No. You don't know Karel.

Another verb **umět** is used for 'know how to':

Pan Beneš neumí vařit.	Mr Beneš doesn't know how to cook.
Věra umí číst.	Věra knows how to read.
Neumějí vařit.	They don't know how to cook.

Rozumět/rozumím 'to understand', a compound of **umět** 'to know how', is followed by the dative:

Nerozumíte mi?	Don't you understand me?
Rozumím ti.	I understand you (understand what you are saying).

It is often used with language adverbs.

Rozumíte česky?	Do you understand Czech?
Nerozumějí anglicky.	They don't understand English.

The verb **chápat, chápe – pochopit** 'to grasp/understand' overlaps somewhat in meaning with **rozumět**, but it is followed by the accusative case. It can also mean 'understand' in the sense of 'have fellow-feeling, sympathy for':

Nechápu, proč odešla.	I don't understand why she left.
Chápu tě. Chápu tvoji situaci.	I understand you. I understand your situation.

7.22.4 Like and prefer

There are two competing ways of saying 'to like', using **mít rád** or **líbit se**.

The phrase **mít rád** 'to like' (lit. 'to have glad') is used to express a general, habitual liking for a thing or person. **Rád** is a short-form adjective (see 4.4).

Igor má rád tenis.	Igor likes tennis.
Věra má ráda hokej.	Věra likes ice-hockey.
Dítě rádo spí.	The child likes sleeping.
Rádi spí.	They like sleeping.

The usual negative is **nemít rád**:

Věra nemá ráda tenis.	Věra doesn't like tennis.

With people the meaning can be rather strong, so be careful!

Mám tě rád/Mám tě ráda.	I really like you. I love you.

You can also express active 'dislike' with **nerad, nerada** (short -a- !):

Věra má tenis nerada.	Věra dislikes tennis.

To say that you 'like' or 'dislike' *doing* something you use **rád** or **nerad** with the activity verb (which is NOT in the infinitive):

Rád/ráda poslouchám rádio.   I like to listen to the radio.

Nerad/nerada vařím.   I don't like cooking.

The competing expression **líbit se** 'to please/be pleasing' expresses a more immediate response of liking or not liking than the more fixed, habitual quality of **mít rád** 'to like/love'. The person is expressed in the dative:

Praha se mi (ne)líbí.   Prague pleases/doesn't please me = I don't like it.

Brno se Karlovi líbí.   Brno pleases Karel = he likes it.

Tenhle svetr se matce nelíbí.   Mother doesn't like this sweater.

Jak se ti/vám tady líbí?   How do you like it here?

Moc se mi tady líbí.   I like it here very much.

To say you 'prefer doing' or 'like doing better/best', use **(nej)raději**, colloquially also **(nej)radši** (short i!) and **(nej)radějc**.

Dívám se docela rád(a) na televizi, ale radši čtu a nejradši spím.
I quite like watching TV, but I prefer reading and I like sleeping best.

With a thing, use **mít (nej)radši** or **(nej)raději**. Sometimes the verb **mít** is omitted:

Mám radši/nejradši bavlnu.   I like cotton better/best. I prefer cotton.

Já (mám) radši víno než pivo.   I like wine better than beer.

For immediate preference, again use **líbit se (nej)víc** 'to please more/most':

Ta červená košile se mi líbí víc/nejvíc.   I like that red shirt better/best.

7.22.5 Idiomatic uses of Mít 'to have'

Mít 'to have' is used in a number of other idiomatic phrases. Reflexive **mít se** means 'to be getting on' in phrases such as:

Jak se máte?   How are you?

Mám se dobře.   I am well.

Other idioms include:

Mám hlad.	I am hungry, lit. 'I have hunger.'
Máte hlad?	Are you hungry?
Mám žízeň.	I am thirsty, lit. 'I have thirst.'
Mám pravdu.	I'm right, lit. 'I have truth.'
Nemám pravdu.	I'm not right. I'm wrong.

Mít zpoždění, literally 'to have a delay', is used for 'to be late, delayed':

Vlak má zpoždění.	The train is late, delayed.
Máme dvacet minut zpoždění.	We are twenty minutes late.

For a person being/arriving late simply use **jít/přijít pozdě**:

Jdu pozdě.	I am late.
Přišel jsem pozdě.	I arrived late.

7.22.6 Eat and drink

Jíst 'to eat' is a slightly irregular Type 4 verb (note the related noun **jídlo** 'food'):

jím I eat	**jíme** we eat
jíš you eat	**jíte** you eat
jí s/he eats	**jedí (!)** they eat

Past tense: **jedl** 'ate'

Imperative: **jez!** 'eat!'

Perfective **sníst, sní, snědl** 'eat up' or **najíst se** 'eat one's fill'.

Dát si, literally 'to give oneself' is often used when talking about choosing food:

Co si dáte?	What will you have?
Dám si . . .	I'll have . . .

Note also the commonly used verbs **snídat** 'to have breakfast', **obědvat** 'to have the midday meal, lunch', and **večeřet** 'to have the evening meal, supper'.

Kdy snídáte? V šest (hodin).	When do you have breakfast? At six (o'clock).
Kdy obědváte? Ve dvanáct.	When do you have lunch? At twelve.
Kdy večeříte? V sedm.	When do you have supper? At seven.

Perfectives of these take the form **nasnídat se** 'eat one's fill of breakfast' or **posnídat** 'have some breakfast'.

Pít, pije, pil 'to drink' is a Type 3 verb, with perfectives **vypít** 'to drink up' or **napít se** 'to have a sufficiency of drink'.

'Drink' in general is **pití**. 'Something to drink' is **něco k pití**, but 'a drink, beverage' is **nápoj**.

7.22.7 | *Reflexive usage – wash and dress*

Verbs often add **se** 'oneself' when the action is devoted to the subject/self, e.g. **mýt, myje, myl** 'to wash', perfective **umýt**:

Myju se.	I wash. I wash myself.

but:

Myju nádobí.	I wash the dishes.

'To wash' of clothes is **prát, pere, pral**, pf. **vyprat**:

Peru košile.	I'm washing some shirts.

When the action of **mýt** 'to wash' is devoted to the subject/self, but an associated object is also present, **se** is replaced by **si**:

Myju si ruce.	I wash 'for myself' the hands. I wash my hands.

Compare **oblékat** 'to dress, put on', **svlékat** 'to undress, take off':

Oblékám se.	I dress myself, get dressed, put on my clothes.
Oblékám si kabát.	I put on 'to self' the coat, I put on my coat.
Pavel se svléká.	Pavel gets undressed, takes off his clothes.
Pavel si svléká svetr.	Pavel takes off his sweater.

Similarly, **obouvat** 'to put on shoes', **zouvat** 'to take off shoes':

Obouvám se. Obouvám si boty.	I put on my shoes.
Zouvám se. Zouvám si boty.	I take off my shoes.

7.22.8 Say and tell

Perfective **říct** (older **říci**), **řekne**, **řekl** is the basic verb for 'to say, tell':

Já mu to řeknu.	I'll tell him (say it to him).
Řekl mi to včera.	He told me (said it to me) yesterday.

Its imperfective is **říkat**:

Co říkáš?   What are you saying?

Note the passive use of the reflexive:

Jak se řekne ...?	How do you say ...? lit. 'How is said ...?'
Jak se řekne „school"?	How do you say 'school'?
Jak se řekne anglicky „škola"?	What's the English for 'škola'?

7.22.9 Marry and divorce

The verb **ženit se, oženit se** [s +ins.] is only used of a man getting married:

Pavel se žení.	Pavel's getting married.
Pavel se oženil [s Marcelou].	Pavel got married [to Marcela].

Vdát se, vdávat se [za +acc.] (pf. also **provdat se**) is only used of a woman:

Marcela se vdává.	Marcela's getting married.
Marcela se (pro)vdala [za Pavla].	Marcela got married [to Pavel].

Phrases with **brát, vzít** 'to take' are applicable generally:

Pavel a Marcela se vzali.	Pavel and Marcela got married, lit. 'married each other.'

| **Pavel si vzal (za ženu) Angličanku.** | Pavel married an Englishwoman. |
| **Eva si vzala (za muže) Itala.** | Eva married an Italian. |

To these we may add **rozvést se, rozvádět se** 'to get divorced':

| **Pavel a Marcela se rozvedli.** | Pavel and Marcela got divorced. |

7.22.10 Remember and forget

Two verbs for 'remember' and 'forget' are related compounds. 'Remember' mostly has **si** attached:

| **vzpomenout si, vzpomínat si** | to remember, to recall |
| **zapomenout, zapomínat** | to forget |

Both have special past forms **vzpomněl si** and **zapomněl** (though **vzpomenul** and **zapomenul** also occur).

Both are followed by **na** +acc. when they mean 'remember/forget about', 'think/not think about':

Vzpomněl si na sestru.	He remembered (about), recalled his sister.
Zapomněl na sestru.	He forgot (about) his sister.
Vzpomíná si na Prahu.	He remembers (about), recalls Prague.
Zapomíná na Prahu.	He is forgetting (about) Prague.

But when some item is lost from the memory, 'forget' is followed by a direct object:

| **Zapomněl adresu.** | He forgot the address. |

Another verb **pamatovat si > zapamatovat si** +acc. 'to remember' refers to storage in the memory (rather than active recall):

| **Pamatuje si adresu.** | He remembers the address. |
| **Zapamatoval si adresu.** | He remembered the address. |

Pamatovat se na +acc. (with **se!**) can be used similarly to **vzpomínat si na**:

| **Pamatuje se na Prahu.** | He remembers (about) Prague. |

Compare **pamět'** -ti f. 'memory' and **vzpomínka** 'a memory, a recollection':

| **Mám dobrou/špatnou paměť.** | I have a good/bad memory (ability). |
| **Mám na něj pěknou vzpomínku.** | I have a nice memory of him. |

<h2>7.22.11   Fear and hope</h2>

Bát se/bojím se 'to fear' and **mít strach** 'to be afraid' (lit. 'to have fear') may be followed by either **aby** or **že**. After **aby** the verb is negative!

| **Bojím se, že spadnu.** | I'm afraid I'll fall. |
| **Bojím se, abych nespadl.** | I'm afraid I might fall (i.e. hope I don't). |

A weaker fear can be expressed by **obávat se**:

| **Obávám se, že přijdu pozdě.** | I'm afraid that I'll arrive late. |

'To hope' is **doufat** (but the noun is **naděje** 'hope').

| **Doufám, že nespadnu.** | I hope I won't fall. |

<h2>7.22.12   Happen and become</h2>

The basic imperfective verb for 'to be happening' is **dít se, děje se, dělo se**:

| **Co se děje?** | What is going on? |

But the basic perfective for 'to happen' is **stát se, stane se, stalo se**:

| **Co se stalo?** | What happened? |
| **Co se stane?** | What will happen? |

This has an imperfective counterpart **stávat se**, but this means 'happen repeatedly, regularly':

| **To se stává.** | That happens. |

The pair **stát se** < **stávat se** is also used for 'to become', often followed by a noun in the instrumental:

| **Stal se ředitelem firmy.** | He became manager of the company. |

or: **Stal se z něho ředitel firmy.**

| **Stalo se to zvykem.** | It became a habit. |

Distinguish from **stát – stojí – stál** 'to stand, cost', with a long vowel in the past tense.

Kolik to stojí? Kolik to stálo?   How much does it – did it cost?

7.23   Basic/irregular verbs

This list, and the next, assumes an ability to recognise tenses etc.

být	**jsem**	**jsme**		
to be	**jsi**	**jste**		
	je	**jsou**	**byl**	I am ..., was
	není	isn't, there isn't		
	colloq. **(j)seš = jsi** you are			
	buď!	be!	**bytí** being	
	budu	**budeme**		
	budeš	**budete**		
	bude	**budou**	shall, will be	
	zbýt, zbude (colloq.) **zbyde, zbyl < zbývat** be left (over)			
mít	**mám máme**			
to have	**máš máte**			
	má	**mají**	**měl**	I have ..., had
	měj	have!	**k mání** to be had, available	
chtít	**chci**	**chceme**		
to want	**chceš**	**chcete**		
	chce	**chtějí**	**chtěl**	I want ..., wanted
jíst	**jím**	**jíme**		
to eat	**jíš**	**jíte**		
	jí	**jedí**	**jedl**	I eat ..., ate
	jez!	eat!		
	sníst, sním, snědl pf. eat up			
	najíst se, najím se, najedl se pf. eat your fill			
moct, -ci	**můžu**	**můžeme**		
can	**můžeš**	**můžete**		
	může	**můžou**	**mohl**	I can ..., could, was able

formal: **mohu, mohou** I can, they can

mohl by could, would be able

pomoct, pomoci < pomáhat help

pomoz! help!

vědět	**vím**	**víme**		
to know	**víš**	**víte**		
	ví	**vědí**	**věděl**	I know ..., knew
	věz!	know!		

povědět, povím, pověděl pf. tell

odpovědět, odpovím < odpovídat reply

7.24 Monosyllabic/irregular verbs

Here is a selection of the commoner verbs. Most monosyllabic verbs you encounter will follow similar patterns. Under Type 1 there are also polysyllabic infinitives ending in **-at** (see 7.4.11).

Forms are given in the order: infinitive, third-person singular present tense, past tense. Certain participles/verbal nouns are noted in brackets. Arrowheads point to the perfective form.

Type 5 verbs:

-át: **dát, dá, dal < dávat** give, put

  podat < podávat pass

  prodat < prodávat sell

  vydat < vydávat publish

po|čkat, počká, počkal < čekat wait

tkát, tká, tkal (tkaní) > utkat weave

  po|tkat, potká, potkal < potkávat meet, encounter

  setkat se < setkávat se (s +ins.) meet up with

ptát se, ptá se, ptal se (ptaní) > zeptat se ask

zdát se, zdá se, zdál se (zdání) seem

znát, zná, znal know

  poznat < poznávat recognise, get to know

Type 4 verbs:

-át: **bát se, bojí se, bál se** fear

        spát, spí, spal (spaní) sleep

          vyspat se pf. have a (good) sleep

        stát, stojí, stál (stání) stand, cost

        (see also **stát se, stane se** below, Type 2)

-ět: **smět, smím . . . smějí, směl** may, be allowed to

-ít: **po|hřbít, pohřbí, pohřbil (pohřbený) < pohřbívat** bury

        křtít, křtí, křtil (křtění) > po- christen

        snít, sní, snil (snění) dream

        znít, zní, zněl (znění) > za- 'ring out, sound'

Type 3 verbs:

át: **hrát, hraje, hrál (hraní) > zahrát** play

        vyhrát < vyhrávat win

        prohrát < prohrávat lose

        hřát, hřeje, hřál (hřátí/hřání) > o-, za- warm

          ohřát < ohřívat warm up

        přát, přeje, přál (přání) wish

        smát se, směje se, smál se > za- (zasmání) laugh

          usmát se < usmívat se smile

-ět/-et: **chvět se, chvěje se, chvěl se (chvění)** tremble

-ít: **bít, bije, bil (bití) > uhodit, udeřit** hit

        zabít (zabitý) < zabíjet kill

        dít se, děje se, děl se (dění) happen, be going on

        hnít, hnije, hnil (hnití) > s- rot

        lít/*lejt, lije/*leje, lil (lití) pour

          nalít < nalévat pour out

        pít, pije, pil (pití) > napít se, vypít drink

          opít se < opíjet se get drunk

        sít, seje, sel|sil (setí) > na-, za-, vy- sow

        šít, šije, šil (šití) > u- sew

          vyšít < vyšívat embroider

zrát, zraje, zrál (zrání) > u- ripen

žít, žije, žil live
   užít (užití) < užívat use

-out: **ob|out, obuje, obul (obutý) < obouvat (se)**
put on (shoes)
   zout < zouvat (se) take off (shoes)

plout, pluje, plul (plutí) float, sail
   odplout < odplouvat float, sail away

-ýt: **krýt/*krejt, kryje/*kreje, kryl (krytý)** cover
   skrýt/*skrejt < skrývat conceal, hide

mýt/*mejt, myje/*meje, myl > umýt (umytý) wash

rýt/*rejt, ryje/*reje, ryl (rytí) dig, engrave

Type 2 verbs:

-át: **stát se, stane se, stal se < stávat se** become, happen
   dostat (dostání) < dostávat get
   přestat < přestávat stop, cease
   vstát < vstávat get up, stand up
   zůstat < zůstávat stay

-ít: **vzít, vezme/*veme, vzal (vzatý, vzetí) <** Type I **brát**
take

   za|čít, začne, začal < začínat begin, start
   počít, počne, počal (počatý, početí) conceive, begin

-out: **do|tknout se, dotkne se, dotkl se (dotknutí/dotčení)**
< dotýkat se touch

hnout, hne, hnul (hnutí) < hýbat, hýbu (se) move
   vyhnout se < vyhýbat se +dat. avoid

při|jmout, přijme, přijal (přijatý, přijetí) < přijímat
receive
   obe|jmout, obejme, objal/obejmul (objetí/obejmutí)
   < objímat embrace, hug

za|mknout, zamkne, zamkl (zamknutí/zamčení) <
zamykat lock
   odemknout < od(e)mykat unlock

za|pnout, zapne, zapnul (zapnutý) < zapínat fasten, switch on

> **rozepnout < rozpínat** unfasten, undo
>
> **vypnout < vypínat** switch off

tnout (†tít), tne, tnul/t'al (tnut, tnutí/t'at, †tětí) cut, slash

žnout (†žít), žne, žnul/žal (žat/žnut, žnutí) reap, mow

-ct/ci: **říct/říci, řekne, řekl (řečený) < říkat** say, tell

Type 1 verbs:

-át: **brát, bere, bral (braní) >** Type 2 **vzít** take
> **vybrat < vybírat** choose

hnát, žene, hnal (hnaní) + honit drive
> **vyhnat < vyhánět** drive out

lhát, lže, lhal (lhaní) > zalhat lie = tell lies

prát, pere, pral (praní) > vyprat wash clothes

psát, píšu/i ... píšou/í, psal (psaní) > napsat write
> **podepsat < pod(e)pisovat** sign
>
> **popsat < popisovat** describe

poslat, pošle, poslal (poslání) < posílat send

rvát, rve, rval (rvaní) tear

řvát, řve, řval (řvaní) > za- 'roar'

*** srát, sere, sral (sraní) > vysrat se shit

zvát, zve, zval (zvaní) > pozvat invite
> **nazvat < nazývat** call, name

-at: **česat, češe/česá, česal (česání) > učesat** comb

hýbat, hýbe/-á, hýbal > hnout (se) move, bend

chápat, chápe chápal (chápání) > pochopit understand

kašlat, kašle, kašlal > zakašlat cough

kázat, káže, kázal preach
> **ukázat < ukazovat** show

klamat, klame, klamal > oklamat deceive
> **zklamat** pf. disappoint

koupat, koupe/-á, koupal (koupání) > vykoupat (se) bathe

lámat, láme, lámal > zlomit break

mazat, maže, mazal > na- etc. spread, oil

plakat, pláče, plakal cry, weep

plavat, plave, plaval (plavání) > zaplavat (si) swim

skákat, skáče, skákal (skákání) > skočit jump

vázat, váže, vázal > s-, u- etc. tie, bind

-ět/-et: **jet, jede, jel + jezdit** ride, go

    přijet < přijíždět arrive

    odjet < odjíždět leave

    přejet (přejetí) < přejíždět run over

-ít: **jít, jde, šel/šla/šli + chodit** go

    přijít < přicházet arrive

    odejít < odcházet leave, go away

mlít, mele, mlel (mletý) > u- grind

o|přít (se), opře, opřel (opřený) < opírat lean, prop

ote|vřít, otevře, otevřel (otevření) < ot(e)vírat open

    zavřít < zavírat close

u|mřít, umře, umřel (umření) < umírat die

-ct|-ci: **moct|moci, může, mohl** be able, can
1sg. **mohu/můžu**, 3pl. **můžou/mohou**

    pomoct < pomáhat +dat. help

péct/*píct/péci, peče, pekl (pečený, pekoucí) > upéct bake

téct/*týct/téci, teče, tekl (tečení, tekoucí) flow

    utéct < utíkat run away

tlouct/tlouci, tluče, tloukl (tlučení, tlukoucí) thump

vléct/*vlíct/vléci, vleče, vlékl (vlečený, vlekoucí) drag

    ob|léct/*(v)oblíct/obléci, obleče, oblekl (oblečený)
    or regular **obléknout/*(v)oblíknout < oblékat/**
    ***oblíkat (se)** put on (clothes)

svléct/*svlíct/svléci, svleče, svlekl (svlečený)
or regular **svléknout/*svlíknout < svlékat/*svlíkat (se)**
take off (clothes)

-st: **číst, čte, četl(a)/čtla, četl (čtení) > přečíst** read

klást, klade, kladl (kladení) > položit put, lay

krást, krade, kradl (kradení) steal
pf. **ukrást/ukradnout, ukradne, ukradl (ukradení)**

kvést/*kvíst, kvete, kvetl (kvetení) blossom, flower

nést/*nýst, nese, nesl (nesení) + nosit carry
  přinést < přinášet bring

plést/*plíst, plete, pletl (pletení) > uplést knit, confuse

růst, roste, rostl grow

třást (se), třese, třásl (třesení) shake

vést/*víst, vede, vedl (vedení) + vodit lead
  přivést < přivádět bring

-zt: **lézt/*lízt, leze, lezl (lezení)** climb, crawl
  nalézt, nalezne, nalezl < nalézat find

vézt/*vízt, veze, vezl (vezení) + vozit convey (by vehicle)
  přivézt < přivážet bring

Chapter 8

Cases and prepositions –
pády a předložky

The basic roles of the seven cases were introduced in Chapter 3, but will now be considered in a little more detail. Their functions are often covered by prepositions in English.

A preposition (**předložka**) is a word like 'on', 'onto', 'for', 'across', which links up with nouns to define place, time, purpose etc.

Czech prepositions are always followed by nouns in particular cases.

The first part of this chapter focuses on the use of cases themselves, without prepositions.

8.1 The nominative case

The basic (dictionary) form of a Czech noun is the subject form, habitually called the nominative case. This is used for the subject (agent, doer) of a verb:

Otec vaří.	Father is cooking.
Voda je dobrá.	The water is good.

8.2 The accusative

A noun directly affected by the action or other meaning of a verb is called its object. If you say 'The dog bites Peter' then the object is Peter. But if you say 'Peter bites the dog', then the object is the dog.

Masculine inanimate and neuter nouns always stay the same in the accusative case:

Máme kufr. Máme auto.	We have a suitcase. We have a car.
Otec vaří oběd.	Father is cooking lunch.

The accusative and genitive of masculine animate nouns are normally identical:

Znáte Igora. Dopis od Igora.   You know Igor. A letter from Igor.

Note that the verb 'to be' is *not* followed by the accusative! It is usually followed by the nominative case:

To je Jana/David.   That is Jana/David.

Adverbially, the accusative expresses time duration:

Mluvil celou hodinu.   He spoke for a whole hour.

8.3   The genitive

To say 'of' you regularly use the genitive case on its own:

voda – sklenice vody	glass of water
víno – sklenice vína	glass of wine
autor – jméno autora	name of the author
papír – kousek papíru	piece of paper

The preposition z 'out of' + genitive may be required when 'of' means 'out of' a group. Compare:

Dva studenti šli domů.   Two students went home.

Dva ze studentů šli domů.   Two of the students went home.

Genitive phrases do not normally precede the nouns they accompany, except in poetical usage, e.g. **lásky čas** 'love's time'.

An exception is when possession is expressed using an adjectival noun, or other nouns which cannot form possessive adjectives (see 4.6):

Škvoreckého romány 'Škvorecký's novels' – cf. **Kunderův román** 'Kundera's novel'

Certain verbs, especially reflexive verbs are followed by the genitive case, where an English speaker might expect the accusative, e.g. **bát se** 'to fear, be afraid of', **ptát se** 'to ask', **všimnout si** 'to notice':

Bál se trestu.   He was afraid of punishment.

Všimli si jeho strachu.   They noticed his fear.

Zeptal se Jany (genitive), **kde je Karel.**   He asked Jana where Karel was.

Váží si jejího názoru.	S/he respects her opinion.
Dosáhla vysokého věku.	She reached a great old (lit. 'high') age.
Dosáhli velmi dobrých výsledků.	They achieved very good results.
Užili vhodného okamžiku.	They took advantage of a suitable moment.
Užila (si) pěkného počasí.	She enjoyed the fine weather.

Sometimes the genitive expresses 'some, a (notable) quantity of'. This may occur in everyday colloquial phrases:

Ta dostala dárků!	That one got [a lot] of presents! What a lot of presents she got!
Tady je lidí!	What a lot of people there are here!

In fixed phrases after a negative verb the genitive occasionally denotes 'not any'. This usage is largely confined to idioms in present-day speech:

Neřekl ani slova/slovo.	He didn't say a word. He said not a word.
Není divu.	It's no wonder.

8.4 The dative

The dative basically means 'to/for' and corresponds to what is habitu-ally called the 'indirect object' in English grammar.

Used without a preposition the dative case has its basic meaning of 'to/for', e.g. giving 'to' or doing 'for':

Dávám Věře knihu.	I'm giving a book to Věra.
Vařím Igorovi oběd.	I'm cooking lunch for Igor.

Note that in English instead of saying 'to Věra' and 'for Igor' you can say 'I give Věra the book' and 'I cook Igor lunch.'

Some Czech verbs are followed by a dative where 'to/for' is never used in English, e.g. **pomáhat** 'to help', **věřit** 'to believe':

Pomáháme Honzovi.	We're helping (giving help 'to') Honza.
Věříme tátovi.	We believe (give trust 'to') Dad.

Sometimes the dative actually means taking something 'from' someone, someone 'to' whom the thing belonged or was associated:

Ukradl mému kamarádovi padesát korun.	He stole fifty crowns from my friend.
Vzal mu také pas a peněženku.	He also took from him his passport and wallet.
Vzal mu míru/teplotu.	He took his measure/ temperature.

The dative of the person also occurs in 'impersonal' verb constructions, where the verb is given a subjectless third-person sg. form with neuter agreement, e.g.

Je/Bylo mi (dative) **Věry** (genitive) **líto.** I was sorry for Věra, lit. 'It was to me of Věra sorry.'

Podařilo se Věře (dative) **utéct.** Věra succeeded in running away. Věra managed to run away, lit. 'It succeeded itself to Věra to run away.'

Nechtělo se Věře jít domů. Věra did not feel like going home, lit. 'It did not want itself to Věra to go home.'

8.5 The locative

The locative case is used only after prepositions – especially to denote location, but also for time or topic.

Igor bydlí v Ostravě.	Igor lives in Ostrava.
Praha je na Vltavě.	Prague is on the Vltava.
Po obědě spí.	After lunch s/he sleeps.
Mluvíme o Evě.	We are talking about Eva.

8.6 The instrumental

On its own the instrumental case denotes the means or instrument 'by' or 'with' which something is done:

vlak, auto – Cestujeme vlakem, autem.	We travel by train, by car.
nůž – Krájíme chleba nožem.	We cut bread with a knife.
pero – Píšeme perem.	We write with a pen.
tužka – Píšeme tužkou.	We write with a pencil.

The instrumental can also have the spatial meaning 'through':

| **Půjdeme parkem.** | We'll go through the park. |

Some verbs are habitually followed by the instrumental, e.g. **hnout** pf. 'to move', **stát se** pf. 'to become', **jmenovat** impf./pf. 'to appoint', **chlubit se** 'boast of':

Nemohl hnout rukou.	He couldn't move his hand.
Stal se důležitým politikem.	He became an important politician.
Jmenovali ho předsedou.	They appointed him (as) chairman.
Chlubil se svými známostmi.	He boasted of his acquaintances.

Moving a thing or part of the body may also be expressed by the instrumental:

Mávl rukou.	He waved his hand.
Nehnul ani prstem.	He did not move even a finger.
Pokrčil rameny.	He shrugged his shoulders.
Hodil po něm kamenem.	He threw a stone at him. He used a stone to throw at him.
but: **Hodil knihu na stůl.**	He threw the book on the table.

The instrumental may also be used after the verb 'to be' instead of the nominative, to indicate that something or someone acts 'as' or occupies some role:

Kniha je vždycky dobrým dárkem.	A book is always a good present.
Výhodou je levná cena.	The advantage is the cheap price. The cheap price acts as an advantage.
Čím byl váš otec?	What (instrumental) was your father?
Otec byl učitel(em).	Father was a teacher.

A number of instrumental forms have become adverbs, e.g. **náhodou** 'by chance', **většinou** 'mostly', **cestou** 'on the way', **mimochodem** 'by the way'.

Others have become prepositions with the genitive, e.g. **během** 'during', **kolem** 'around', **pomocí** 'with the help of, by means of', **prostřednictvím** 'through, by means of'.

8.7 The vocative

For addressing one person (masculine or feminine), the vocative must regularly be used. In English we simply use intonation: 'Tom!'

Ivan – Ivane! Jana – Jano! Pepík – Pepíku!

In informal usage a masculine surname may be left in the nominative when preceded by **pan** 'Mr', e.g.

pane Novák! – in formal standard usage: **pane Nováku!**

Czechs use titles when addressing people more than is the habit in English, e.g.

pane inženýre! 'Mr engineer!' **paní inženýrko!** 'Mrs engineer!'

pane doktore! 'Mr doctor!' **paní doktorko!** 'Mrs doctor!'

8.8 Prepositions

Czech prepositions are always followed by nouns in particular cases. For example, the accusative case is used after:

na in the sense of 'for (a purpose)' or 'onto'

Čekám na Věru, na Milana. I'm waiting for (on, 'onto') Věra, Milan.

Dávám oběd na stůl I put ('give') lunch onto the table.
(acc. = nom.).

pro meaning 'for' in the sense of 'for the benefit of'

Kniha pro Irenu, pro Igora. A book for Irena, for Igor.

přes meaning 'across, despite'

Most přes řeku. A bridge across the river.

8.8.1 On – onto, in – into

Sometimes the case taken by a preposition changes its meaning. One common example is **na** 'on' or 'onto'.

When **na** means location 'on' it takes the locative, but when it means 'onto' (with motion towards the place) it takes the accusative:

Kniha leží na stole. The book is lying on the table.

Dávám knihu na stůl. I give/put the book onto the table.

201

However, for 'in' and 'into' you normally use two different prepositions.
V + locative means location 'in', while **do** + genitive means motion 'into':

Marta je v Brně.   Marta is in Brno.

Marta jede do Brna.   Marta goes to/into Brno.

Notice how with some places you say 'on', and then 'onto' for motion,
instead of 'in, (in)to':

Slovensko, Morava: Jsou na   They are in (lit. 'on') Slovakia,
Slovensku, na Moravě.   Moravia.

Jedou na Slovensko/na   They are going to Slovakia/
Moravu.   Moravia.

pošta: Je na poště.   S/he's at the post-office.

Jdu na poštu.   I'm going to the post-office.

Ulice 'street' uses either, depending on whether the houses are included,
but **náměstí** 'square' always uses **na** 'on':

Čekám na ulici/na náměsti.
I am standing on the street, on the square.

Bydlím v Karlově ulici/na Karlově náměstí.
I live in 'Charles Street'/on 'Charles Square'.

Similarly, with districts of Prague such as **Žižkov, Smíchov:**

Bydlím na Žižkově, na   I live in Žižkov, in Smíchov.
Smíchově.

Jedu na Žižkov, na Smíchov. I'm going to Žižkov, to Smíchov.

Various places which are not considered as enclosed spaces use **na**,
whereas those which are treated as buildings or enclosed spaces use **v**
instead:

na koncertě at the concert – **na koncert** to the concert

v kině at the cinema – **do kina** to the cinema

It is ultimately just a matter of usage.

8.8.2 | *Prepositions – case usage and forms*

Many prepositions are followed by one case only, but some are followed
by more than one case. We have listed these below under the case
which for practical purposes we may consider the basic one for the
preposition concerned.

Many prepositions have a fundamentally spatial meaning, but are used also for other purposes, such as designating time.

Certain prepositions which you may like to think of as basically '+ locative' or '+ instrumental' switch to being '+ accusative' when they describe motion relative to the place described.

The most essential prepositions are listed in capitals. Only a selection of usages beyond the most basic are listed here.

Some non-syllabic, i.e. single-consonant, prepositions often have an appended -e. Generally this occurs as follows:

> before a consonant cluster, e.g. **ve škole** 'in school', **ze školy** 'from/out of school'

> before an identical consonant, e.g. **ve vodě** 'in the water', **ze zahrady** 'from/out of the garden'

> or its voiced/voiceless pair, e.g **ve filmu** 'in the film', **se Zorou** 'with Zora'

Some ending in consonants add -e before **mě, mne, mně** 'me' and case forms of **všechno, všeho** etc. 'all', e.g. **ode mě** 'from me', **ode všech** 'from all'.

8.8.3 | *Prepositions + accusative only*

mimo	outside, apart from, except for	**Bydlí mimo Prahu.** He lives outside Prague.
		Všichni tam byli mimo něho. Everyone was there apart from him.
ob	every other	**Chodili ob dům.** They went to every other house.
		Ob týden. Every other week.
PRO	for (sake, benefit of)	**Tohle je pro tebe.** This is for you.
		Četba pro děti. Reading-matter for children.
	for, due to (a reason)	**Pro nemoc zavřeno.** Closed for illness.
	for (to fetch)	**Jdu pro mléko.** I'm going for some milk.
	for, in favour of (cf. **proti** + dat. against)	**Rozhodli se pro druhou možnost.** They decided in favour of the second option.
		Jsem pro. I am in favour.

PŘES	across, through	**Běžel přes ulici.** He ran across the street.
	via	**Vlak jede přes Berlín.** The train goes via Berlin.
skrz	through	**Díval se na něj skrz brýle.** He looked at him through his glasses.

8.8.4 | *Prepositions + genitive only*

BEZ	without	**Piju kávu bez cukru.** I drink coffee without sugar.
		Beze mě. Without me.
DO	into, to	**Jdu do města.** I'm going into/to town.
	until, till	**Zůstanu do ledna.** I'll stay till January.
OD	away from, from	**Odešla od okna.** She went away from the window.
	from (person)	**Dostal dopis od Petra.** He got a letter from Petr.
		Ode mě. From me.
U	at (house, place of)	**Bydlím u tety.** I live at my aunt's.
	near, at	**Sedí u okna.** S/he sits at the window.
Z, ZE	out of	**Vyšel z pokoje.** He went out of the room.
		Ze mě. Out of me.
	off, down from – also spelt **S(e)**	**Kniha spadla ze/se stolu.** The book fell off the table.

8.8.5 | *Prepositions + dative only*

| **K, KE** | towards | **Jdu ke kostelu.** I go towards the church. |
| | to | **Jak se dostanu k řece?** How do I get to the river? |

	to (house, place of)	**Jdu k tetě.** I'm going to my aunt's.
AŽ K(e)	as far as	**Jdu až ke kostelu.** I go as far as the church.
PROTI	against, opposite	**Jste proti mně.** You are against me.

8.8.6 | Preposition + locative only

| **při** | at, during | **Při obědě mlčeli.** At lunch they were silent. |

8.8.7 | Prepositions + locative/accusative

| **NA** | on | **Kniha leží na stole.** The book is lying on the table. |

NA + accusative

onto	**Položil knihu na stůl.** He put the book on(to) the table.
on (instrument)	**Hraji na housle.** I play the violin.
for (purpose)	**Čekám na tramvaj.** I'm waiting for the tram.
	Kartáček na zuby. A brush for your teeth. A toothbrush.
for (intended time)	**Jsem tu jen na týden.** I'm here only for a week.

O	about (topic)	**Mluví o politice.** They're talking about politics.
	at, in (certain fixed time phrases)	**O víkendu.** At the weekend.
		O prázdninách. In the holidays.

O + accusative

on, against	**Opírá se o stůl.** He is leaning on the table.
by (difference)	**Jsi o rok starší než já.** You're a year older than me.
for, after, in (with certain verbs)	**Starala se o matku.** She looked after/cared for her mother.
	Zajímám se o kulturu. I am interested in culture.

PO	after	**Po obědě četl noviny.** After lunch he read the paper.
		Toužil po ní. He yearned after her. He longed for her.
	along	**Běžela po ulici.** She ran along the street.
	about, around, all over	**Běhala po zahradě.** She ran about the garden.
	. . . each	**Dala jim po koruně.** She gave them one crown each.

PO + accusative

as far as, up to	**Sníh mu byl až po kolena.** The snow was right up to his knees.
for, during, throughout	**Pršelo (po) celý den.** It rained all day.

V, VE	in	**Sedím v autě.** I'm sitting in the car.
		Byl ve straně. He was in the party.
	in (month etc.)	**V lednu sněží.** In January it snows.

V(e) + accusative	
on (day)	**V pondělí.** On Monday.
	Ve středu, ve čtvrtek. On Wednesday, Thursday
in (with some verbs)	**Nevěříš v Boha?** You don't believe in God?

8.8.8 | Prepositions + instrumental/accusative etc.

Most of these also require the <u>accusative</u> in some senses, see below. **ZA** is also followed by the <u>genitive</u>.

MEZI	between	**Mezi oknem a stolem.** Between the window and the table.
	among(st)	**Mezi kamarády.** Amongst friends.
NAD	above, over	**Letěl nad městem.** He flew over the town.
		Nade mnou. Above me.
POD	below, under	**Stál pod hradem.** He stood below the castle.
		Pode mnou. Below me.
PŘED	in front of	**Stál před domem.** He stood in front of the house.
	before	**Před válkou bydlel v Brně.** Before the war he lived in Brno.
		Přede mnou. In front of me.
	ago	**Byl tu před rokem, před týdnem.** He was here a year ago, a week ago.
S, SE	with	**Jdu tam s Petrem.** I'm going there with Petr.
		Se školou. With the school.
	+ acc. in idioms only:	**Nejsem s to (rozhodnout se).** I am not up to (deciding), able (to decide).

+ gen. 'down from'
more often **Z(e)**

Jeli s/z kopce dolů. They drove down the hill.

ZA behind, beyond

Stojí za stromem. S/he is standing behind a tree.

after (following after)

Běžela za ním. She ran after him.

ZA + accusative

---

for (in exchange for)

Koupil to za pět korun. He bought it for five crowns.

in (time taken)

Udělám to za hodinu. I'll get it done in an hour.

in (after time elapsed)

Přijdu za hodinu. I'll come in a hour's time.

ZA + genitive

---

during the time of

Za války byl doma. During the war he was at home.

Za Karla Čtvrtého. In the reign of Charles IV.

MEZI, NAD, POD, PŘED and **ZA** are also followed by the accusative when they mean 'motion towards' the place:

Spadl mezi židle. He fell between the chairs.

Spadl pod stůl. He fell under the table.

Vyběhl před dům. He ran out in front of the house.

Schovala se za strom. She hid behind a tree.

Figuratively also **nad** 'above, more than' and **pod** 'below, less than':

Nad třicet (stupňů). Above thirty (degrees). **Pod osmnáct.** Below eighteen.

8.8.9 | More prepositions

Most other prepositions take the genitive:

> **během** 'during', **blízko** 'near', **daleko od** 'far from', **kromě** 'except for, apart from', **nedaleko** 'not far from', **kolem/okolo** 'around, about', **místo** 'instead of', **na rozdíl od** 'in contrast to, unlike', **podél** 'along', **podle** 'according to', **pomocí** 'with the help of', **uprostřed** 'in the middle of', **vedle** 'next to'

A few take the dative:

> **díky** 'thanks to', **kvůli** 'for the sake of, because of', **naproti** 'opposite', **navzdory** 'despite', **vůči** 'towards, with respect to'.

Chapter 9

Syntax and conjunctions – syntax a spojky

9.1 Sentences – *věta a souvětí*

A sentence (**věta**) may be said to be simply a string of words containing at least one finite verb, ending in a full stop (**tečka**), e.g.

Ptáci létají. Birds fly.

Prší. It is raining.

If there is more than one finite verb, then each forms its own 'clause', in Czech also called **věta**. The more complex sentence is now called **souvětí**.

The following sentence has two clauses, connected by a conjunction (**spojka**), which here is the word **a** 'and':

Ptáci létají a lidé chodí. Birds fly and people walk.

Syntax (**syntax** f., **skladba**) is the study of how words are put together to form different kinds of clauses and sentences.

9.2 Yes and no

The basic words for yes and no are:

Ano./colloquially **Jo.** Yes.

Ne. No.

'Yes' with questioning intonation can also act as a response, as in English, e.g.

Ano? Jo? Yes?

Another common colloquial term for 'yes . . .' or 'mmh . . .' is **no . . .**, expressing agreement, often to a list of things or statements, with level or rising intonation. The concluding yes might switch to **jo** instead, with a dropping intonation.

Tenhleten salám? – No . . .	This salami? – Mmh . . . / Yes . . .
Takovýhle kus? – No . . .	A piece like this? – Mmh . . . / Yes . . .
Krájet? – No . . .	Slice it up? – Mmh . . . / Yes . . .
Všechno? – Jo.	Is that all? – Yes.

Or, with a rising intonation, **no!** might express an emphatic, satisfied agreement:

Máš to s sebou? – No!	Do you have it with you? – I do! Yes I do!

Otherwise **no** is commonly used as 'well, um', with varying intonations, and in the common phrase **no jo** 'oh well'.

No, nevím.	Well, I don't know.
No jo. Ale teď musím domů.	Oh well. But now I have to go home.

Emphatic positives are terms such as:

Ano! Jo!	Yes!
Samozřejmě! Ovšem!	Obviously! Of course!

An emphatically rejecting negative is:

Kdepak!	No! Definitely not!

Also:

Vůbec ne!	Absolutely not! Not at all!
Ovšemže ne!	Of course not!
Samozřejmě že ne!	Obviously not!
Jistěže ne!	Certainly not! Indeed not!

A slightly lengthier answer than simply yes or no may be dealt with by repeating the verb in the question, which can be the past-tense **-l** form, modal verb on its own or future auxiliary **bude**:

A máš čas? – Ano, mám.	And do you have time? – Yes, I do.
A vaříš pro všechny? – Ano, vařím.	And you cook for everyone? – Yes, I do.
Napsal jste to? – Ano, napsal.	Did you write it? – Yes, I did.

A musel odejít? – Ne, nemusel.	And did he have to leave? – No, he didn't.
A budeš tam chodit každý den? – Jo, budu.	And will you be going there every day? – Yes, I will.

> **9.2.1** | *Negative clauses* – záporné věty

To make a verb in a clause negative you just add **ne-**:

Nečekám.	I'm not waiting.
Nemám čas.	I don't have time. I haven't got time.

Negative adjectives also add the prefix **ne-**, e.g. **neinteligentní** 'unintelligent'. In other contexts, when negating a single word, **ne** can be a separate word for 'not' (as well as 'no', the opposite of **ano** 'yes').

Ne dnes, zítra.	Not today, tomorrow.

Note how Czech uses double negatives, unlike standard English. Verbs in sentences with **ni-** words have to be made negative:

Nikoho nemá rád. lit. 'He doesn't like nobody.' = He likes nobody/ He doesn't like anybody.

Nemluví o ničem. lit. 'He doesn't talk about nothing.' = He talks about nothing/He doesn't talk about anything.

A contrastive word for 'but' following a negative clause is **nýbrž**, though **ale** does also occur:

Nejel domů, nýbrž do města.	He did not go home, but into town.

The word *sice* 'albeit', placed second in its clause, sets up a following clause of concession with a less contrastive **ale** for 'but':

Nejel sice domů, ale hned tam zavolal.
He didn't [albeit] go home, but he did telephone there immediately.

Nemá [sice] hodně peněz, ale má hodně štěstí.
He doesn't have a lot of money, but he has plenty of good luck.

> **9.2.2** | *Neither . . . nor, either . . . or*

The negative contrast of 'neither . . . nor' is regularly expressed by **ani**
. . . ani:

Nejel ani domů ani do město.   He went neither home nor to town.

The first **ani** may be omitted, for a less explicit contrast:

Nejel domů ani do město.   He didn't go home or go to town.

The parallel pair 'either . . . or' is often expressed by **bud' . . . nebo**:

Bud' jel domů nebo do města/Jel bud' domů nebo do města.
Either he went home or to town.

Nebo (sometimes occurring as **anebo**) is also used independently:

Jel domů nebo do město.   He went home or to town.

9.2.3 | No, not . . . any

'No, not . . . any' with a noun is usually expressed by **žádný**, with a negative verb (see also 5.15):

Nemá žádné jídlo.   S/he has no food. S/he doesn't have any food.

9.3   Questions – otázky

Questions without a question word at the beginning can be expressed simply by a change of intonation, signalled in writing only by the question mark (**otazník**):

Máš kufr?   Do you have a suitcase?

Vy jste Jana?   You are Jana? Are you Jana?

Jste Angličanka?   Are you English?

Nejsou doma?   Aren't they at home?

Sometimes the order of subject and verb is reversed, as in English questions with 'is'. This can add a more emphatic questioning tone:

Věra je Češka?/Je Věra Češka?   Is Věra (a) Czech?

To je hrad?/Je to hrad?   Is it a castle?

Věra má dceru?/Má Věra dceru?   Does Věra have a daughter?

| **Nemůže nám Pavel říct, kdy přijde?** | Can't Pavel tell us when he's coming? |
| **Nemohl by nám říct, kdy přijde?** | Couldn't he tell us when he's coming? |

An emphatic question is sometimes introduced by **copak**, an enquiring, wondering one by **zdalipak** or **jestlipak**:

Copak nevíš, že Robert je už zase doma?
Don't you know that Robert is back at home again?

Zdalipak/Jestlipak se na mě ještě pamatuješ?
Do you still remember me, I wonder?

9.3.1 | Polite questions

In Czech the negative form of an enquiry is often politer.

Promiňte. Nevíte, kde je nádraží?
Excuse me. Do you know where the railway station is?

Unless this is delivered with an emphatic intonation, this does *not* correspond to the slightly scornful English question 'Don't you know where the station is?' In Czech a question which suggests that the person ought to know can however be positive:

| **Víte, kde je nádraží?** | You know where the station is? |

A negative question in Czech can often mean the same as the corresponding positive question in English:

| **Nevíte, kde je pan Beneš?** | Do you know where Mr Beneš is? |
| **Neřekl byste mi, kdo to je?** | Could you tell me who that is? |

In English 'Don't you know . . . ?' etc. would express surprise or even sarcasm.

The difference between negative and positive questions is however often reduced or even neutralised when some other form of politeness is present, e.g. by saying 'could you' etc. Intonation also has to be taken into account, not surprisingly:

Nemohl/Mohl byste mi (laskavě) říct, kdo to je?
Could you (kindly, possibly) tell me who that is?

| *Question tags*

English often tags a whole variety of little phrases on to questions, which ask for a response of agreement or disagreement, e.g. 'are you?', 'aren't you?', 'does he?', 'doesn't he?', 'will they?', 'won't they?', 'would she?', 'wouldn't she?'

The briefest Czech equivalents for all of these tags are simply:

že? or **viď'?**, both amounting to 'is that not so?'

But you can also say, more explicitly:

že ano?/colloquially **že jo?** if the expected answer is yes

že ne? if the expected answer is no

Vy mě neznáte, že?/že ne?	You don't know me, do you?
Nechce jít domů, že?/že ne?	S/he doesn't want to go home, does s/he?
David je nemocný, že?/že ano/jo?	David is ill, isn't he?
Přijeli jste včera, že?/že ano/jo?	You arrived yesterday, didn't you?

Notice how in English the tag is positive if the preceding verb is negative, and vice versa. This does not happen in the equivalent Czech tags.

A slightly different usage of **ano?/jo?** and **ne?** at the end of sentences is used to turn what started out as a suggestion into a brief question. There isn't a great deal of difference here between adding a negative or a positive tag, but the negative tag suggests more strongly that the person being asked should agree to the suggestion:

Půjdeme domů, ne?	We'll go home, shall we not? Let's go home, no? Let's go home, OK?
Půjdeme domů, ano/jo?	We'll go home, is that all right?

9.4 Exclamations – *zvolací věty*

As in English, exclamatory statements (**zvolací věty**) are habitually indicated in speech by intonation, and in writing by an exclamation mark (**vykřičník**).

Nemám čas!	I have no time!

Word order – *slovosled*

Znáte Karla?   Do you know <u>Karel</u>?

Ne. Karla neznáte.   No. You <u>don't know</u> Karel.

Note the flexible word order of Czech. You habitually put the word or phrase you want to emphasise more at the end. This is normally the new information.

Sentences and clauses usually begin with what is already known from the context, the 'theme' – **téma**, or 'starting point', and go on to deliver what is new, the 'rheme' – **réma**, or main point of the statement or utterance.

There can be several word-order variants of the English sentence 'Pavel killed Petr', depending on the previous context. This is enabled by the case system of the language, which puts **Petr** in the accusative form **Petra**, as the object of the verb. As a result the word **Petr** does not need to be in a particular position in the word order simply to indicate that it is the object. Its position depends on the known context and what is new information.

If we know that Pavel killed someone, but the question is 'Who did Pavel kill?', the new information is **Petr** and the sentence might come out as:

Pavel zabil <u>Petra</u>.   Pavel killed <u>Petr</u>.

On the other hand, if we know that Petr was killed, but not who did it, then the sentence would come out as:

Petra zabil <u>Pavel</u>.   <u>Pavel</u> killed Petr. = It was <u>Pavel</u> who killed
                               Petr. = Petr was killed by <u>Pavel</u>.

(Note how English can use a passive construction to achieve this re-ordering of sentence elements. Czech does not need to do this.)

If we know about Pavel (our starting point) and also that he has done something to Petr, but we don't yet know exactly what, then the statement could come out as:

Pavel Petra <u>zabil</u>.   Pavel <u>killed</u> Petr.

Similarly, if we have the same information, but take Petr as our starting point, the statement could also come out as:

Petra Pavel <u>zabil</u>, ale Jiřího jenom <u>zranil</u>.
Petr was <u>killed</u> by Pavel, but Jiří was only <u>wounded</u> by him.

The arrangement of sentence and clause word order dependent upon context is termed Functional Sentence Perspective – **Funkční větná perspektiva** or **Aktuální členění větné**.

9.5.1 | Enclitics – příklonky

An enclitic (**příklonka**) is a word which does not normally carry its own stress, but follows after another stressed word.

Enclitics in Czech are typically unstressed auxiliary verbs and pronouns, which are habitually placed early in the sentence or clause, following an initial stressed word or phrase.

When **jsem, jsi (-s)** and **jsme, jste** are used in past-tense forms they normally come in the second possible position in a sentence. So, if a subject pronoun is added for emphasis, you say:

| **Já jsem čekal-a.** | I waited. |

If there's a question word or phrase:

| **Jak dlouho jsi čekal-a?** | How long did you wait? |
| **Co jsi dělal-a?** or **Cos dělal-a?** | What were you doing? |

If **se/si** 'oneself' is needed, it is placed *after* jsem, jsi, jsme, jste:

| **My jsme se učili.** | We studied/were studying. |
| **Kde jste se učil-a?** | Where did you study? |

Familiar sg **jsi** + **se, si** regularly become **ses** and **sis**:

| **Učil-a ses?** | Were you studying? |
| **Zpíval-a sis?** | Were you singing (to/for yourself)? |

The position for other personal pronouns is also after the auxiliary, but also after any reflexive pronoun **se/si**:

| **Věra ji hledala.** | Věra was looking for her. |
| **Jan se ho pořád ptal, kam chce jít.** | Jan kept asking him where he wanted to go. |

'Him'/'her'/'it' come after 'me'/'you'/'us':

| **Dejte mi ho! Já vám ho nedám!** | Give me him/it! I won't give you him/it! |
| **Dej mi ji! Já ti ji nedám!** | Give me her/it! I won't give you her/it! |

Demonstratives regularly follow after the other pronouns. The typical order of enclitics, taking account of the above, is thus:

Stressed item	Auxiliary	Reflexive	Pronoun	Pronoun	Continuation
Já	**bych**	**se**	**ho**	**na to**	**nezeptal(a)**
Včera	**jste**		**mi**	**ho/to**	**ukázal(a)**

= I would not ask him (about) that.

= Yesterday you showed me it/that.

9.6   Conjunctions – *spojky*

A conjunction (**spojka**) is a word which connects two clauses together (cf. **spojit** pf. connect, join).

Coordinating conjunctions connect together principal or main clauses which could be independent sentences on their own:

Šel do města a koupil lístky do divadla.
He went to town <u>and</u> bought some theatre tickets.

Subordinating conjunctions, e.g. **když** 'when', 'that', introduce subordinate clauses, which, as their name indicates, are subordinate to the main clause to which they are attached and modify it in some way.

Often such clauses are adverbial in function, e.g. they may indicate the time of an action in the main clause:

<u>Když přišel domů</u>, našel její dopis.   <u>When he got home</u>, he found her letter.

They may also have the function of a noun phrase, e.g.

Co (object) **řekl Petr?**   What did Petr say?

Řekl, <u>že nemá čas</u>.   He said <u>that he didn't have time</u>.

9.6.1 | *Enclitics with conjunctions*

Normally conjunctions will count as the first word in a clause, and enclitics will follow after them, in their usual internal sequence:

Když jsem ho včera viděl, stál před divadlem.
When I saw him yesterday, he was standing in front of the theatre.

Coordinating conjunctions meaning 'and' or 'but', however, may be regarded as standing outside the clause which follows them. Some other word or phrase must precede the enclitics in such clauses, as if the clause were standing on its own:

Přišel jsem domů a řekl jsem jí, co se mi stalo.
I came home and told her what had happened to me.

Šel jsem do obchodu, ale neměl jsem s sebou peníze.
I went into the shop but I did not have any money with me.

The subordinating conjunction že is regularly followed by any enclitics, but sometimes a stressed word, especially a stressed pronoun or noun, may also precede the enclitics:

Řekl mu, že Jana mu řekla (*or:* že mu Jana řekla), že ho navštíví zítra.
He said that Jana had told him that she would visit him tomorrow.

9.7 Commas – *čárky*

The use of the comma (**čárka**) is more rigidly codified in Czech than in English.

Subordinate clauses are regularly demarcated by commas, at both ends if one of these does not coincide with the beginning or end of the sentence. This happens regardless of whether there would be a pause in speech:

Starý dům, který stál na náměstí, shořel.	The old house which stood on the square has burnt down.
Zavolám, až přijdu.	I'll call when I arrive.
Řekl, že nebude mít čas.	He said that he wouldn't have time.
Řeknu mu, aby ti zavolal.	I will tell him to call you.

However, subordinate clauses connected by **a** 'and' are not themselves divided by commas:

Řekl, že nebude mít čas a že zítra odjíždí.
He said that he wouldn't have time and that he was leaving tomorrow.

An adverb or similar qualification may precede a subordinating conjunction, without being followed itself by a comma:

Teprve když prišel domů, uvědomil si, že ztratil klobouk.
Only when he reached home did he realise that he had lost his hat.

There is usually no comma before **a** 'and' (unless there is a very long narrative chain of clauses repeatedly connected by **a** 'and'):

Kluci šli domů a máma jim uvařila oběd.
The boys went home and mum cooked them lunch.

This also normally applies to phrases and clauses connected straight-forwardly, non-contrastively, with **i** 'and also', **nebo/anebo**, **či** 'or', **ani** 'or' (used after a negative verb):

Smál se i plakal.	He laughed and also wept.
Chodili se koupat nebo hráli tenis.	They went bathing or played tennis.
Hrál si anebo četl.	He played or read.
Nejedl ani nepil.	He did not eat or drink.

But when used with a noticeable pause, or if another clause linking word follows, e.g. **a tak/proto** 'and so/therefore', **a přece** 'and yet', commas are added:

Nechtěl jít domů, a čekat v dešti také nechtěl.	He didn't want to go home, and he also didn't want to wait in the rain.
Chceš kávu, nebo čaj?	Do you want coffee, or tea?
Půjdeme, nebo zůstaneme doma?	Shall we come, or stay at home?
Napíšu, anebo zavolám.	I will write, or else I will phone.
Bylo už jaro, a přece ještě mrzlo.	It was spring now, and yet it was still freezing.

Also with **ani . . . , . . . ani** 'neither . . . , nor':

Nemám ani čas, ani chuť.	I have neither the time, nor the appetite. I do not have either the time, or the appetite.

Ale 'but' requires a comma:

Navštívil jsem ho, ale nebyl doma.	I visited him, but he wasn't at home.

9.8   Quotation marks – *uvozovky*

Quotation marks are usually printed like this: „takto"
Double ones are frequently used to mark direct speech:

„Nemám čas," řekl pan Novák.	'I don't have time,' said Mr Novák.

Single quotation marks may be used inside a pair of double ones:

„Takové ‚cocktail parties' vůbec nemám rád,“ řekl Libor.
'I really don't like "cocktail parties" of that kind,' said Libor.

9.9 Reported speech – *nepřímá řeč*

Direct speech (**přímá řeč**) simply is, or purports to be, the actual words spoken.

Reported or indirect speech (**nepřímá řeč**) is typically introduced by 'that', in Czech by the conjunction **že**.

When reporting speech in Czech you do not alter the original tense of the verb as you do in English. If Karel said:

Přijdu zítra.   I will come tomorrow.

this is reported, using the same tense, as:

Karel řekl, že přijde zítra.   Karel said (that) he 'will' (= would) come tomorrow.

Note how in English 'that' is often omitted before reported speech.

9.10 Time

9.10.1 When

Když is the usual word for 'when', introducing an adverbial clause of time.

Když přišla, začali pracovat.   When she came, they started to work.

With future reference, **až** is used instead (**když** means 'if' in such a context):

Až odejdou, začnu pracovat.   When they leave, I'll start to work.

Questions however require the interrogative form **kdy?**

Kdy přijde?   When will s/he come?

Nevím, kdy přijde.   I don't know when s/he will come.

Kdy is only used for non-questions if a time word precedes it, introducing a relative clause, not an adverbial one:

Přišel čas, kdy museli začít.   The time had come when they had to begin.

| 9.10.2 | *Until and before* |

Až often means 'until', referring to an oncoming boundary point, after a verb with future reference:

Počkám, až bude mít čas.   I'll wait until s/he has ('will have') time.

Otherwise, **dokud . . . ne-** (i.e. with a negative verb) is regularly used for 'until', in the sense of 'while something is not yet the case' and may be more emphatic:

Počkám, dokud nebude mít čas.
I'll wait until s/he has time (i.e. as long as necessary, while s/he is not yet free).

Dokud nezavoláš, nepřijdu.   I will not come until you call me.

Dokud nezavolala, nevěděl, kde je.   Until he called, he did not know where she was.

Another word for 'until' is **než**, in the temporal sense of 'before and until':

Zůstal na nástupišti, než odjel vlak.   He stayed on the platform until the train left.

or: . . . **dokud neodjel vlak.**

It may also translate as simply 'before':

Než odjel vlak, šel si koupit noviny.   Before the train left, he went to buy a newspaper.

This is a shortened form of **dřív než**, literally 'earlier than':

Dřív než odjel vlak, jeho přítelkyně už byla doma.
Before the train had left, his girlfriend was already back at home.

9.11 Conditions

| 9.11.1 | *If and when* |

Když 'when' also often carries a sense of 'if':

Když jsme měli čas, šli jsme do kina.   When (if) we had time, we went to the cinema.

In fact, in talking about the future **když** *only* means 'if and when' (followed by a future verb). To say a clear 'when' in the future use **až** instead:

Když budeme mít čas, půjdeme do kina.
If we have ('will have') time, we'll go to the cinema.

Až budeme mít čas, půjdeme do kina.
When we have ('will have') time, we'll go to the cinema.

9.11.2 If and would

'If' is often expressed by **kdyby**. This consists of **kdy-** followed by the conditional tense, where the forms of **by** are fused with **kdy-** in a single word:

kdybych if I	**kdybychom**/colloq. **kdybysme** if we
kdybys if you	**kdybyste** if you
kdyby if he/she/it	**kdyby** if they

Kdyby is used for 'if' when the main statement has a conditional 'would', referring to something which is seen as not necessarily ever going to be true.

Kdybych měl čas, šel bych do kina.
If I had time, I would go to the cinema.

Kdyby měla peníze, koupila by dům.
If she had money, she'd buy a house.

Co byste dělali, kdybyste neměli peníze?
What would you do, if you didn't have money?

To talk about what might have been in the past (but wasn't), you may add **byl** or **byl býval** to the conditional, making a 'past conditional' (section 7.11):

Kdybych byl (býval) měl peníze, byl bych koupil nové auto.
If I had had ('would have had') money, I would have bought a new car.

Kdyby byl býval rychlejší, byl by chytil vlak.
If he had been quicker, he would have caught the train.

There is a tendency however not to use two past conditionals in a row, which seem clumsy, but replace one (or both) by an ordinary conditional:

Kdybych (byl býval) měl peníze, koupil bych nové auto.

9.11.3 *If and would with the infinitive*

Another (colloquial) way of saying 'if' is with the infinitive:

Mít čas, šel bych na ten film.	'To have time' = If I had time, I'd go to that film.
Být na tvém místě, šel bych domů.	Were I in your place, I'd go home.

After **být** you find persons in the instrumental:

Být tebou, já bych to nedělal.	If I were you, I wouldn't do it.

After negative **nebýt** you use the genitive:

Nebýt jeho, chytili by vlak.	Were it not for him, they'd have caught the train.

9.11.4 *Other words for if*

Where there is no 'would', 'if' may be conveyed explicitly by **jestli**, **jestliže** or **-li**:

Jestli(že) bude pršet, zůstaneme doma.	If it rains ('will rain'), we'll stay at home.

or:

Bude-li pršet, zůstaneme doma.

But 'if' in the sense of 'insofar as' is very often **pokud**:

Pokud bude pršet, zůstaneme doma.	If it rains, we'll stay at home.
Pokud budeš mít čas, přijď' mě navštívit.	If you have time, come and visit me.

'As long as' may be expressed by **dokud**, which carries a different meaning. In the following example the rain *is* falling, not merely anticipated as a possibility:

Dokud bude pršet, zůstaneme doma.	As long as it is raining/carries on raining, we'll stay at home.

9.12 If meaning whether

'If' in the sense of 'whether' (regarding a question) is normally expressed by **jestli** (and *not* by **jestliže**):

Ptal se, jestli přijdu. He asked me if I would come.
(The question was: **Přijdete?** Will you come?)

Nevím, jestli přijde. I don't know if he will come.
(**Přijde?** Will he come?)

In formal usage, **jestli** is replaced by **zda,** or an appended **-li:**

Nevěděla, zda přijdou/   She did not know whether they
přijdou-li.   would come.

9.13 Aby etc.

9.13.1 Expressing purpose with aby

Aby means literally something like 'that/in order that ... would', and is used to express purpose. Like **kdyby**, it is shaped from **a-** followed by the conditional auxiliary **bych** etc., producing:

abych that I . . .   **abychom**/colloq. **abysme** that
                                        we . . .

abys that you . . .   **abyste** that you . . .

aby that he/she/it . . .   **aby** that they . . .

Aby is *never* followed by infinitives! In English however we usually say 'to' or 'in order to' to express purpose:

Potřebuju peníze, abych si koupil dům.
I need money to buy a house (lit. 'in order that I would buy a house').

Šel tam, aby mu řekl pravdu.
He went there to tell him the truth (lit. 'in order that he would tell him the truth').

A plain infinitive *can* be used in Czech after a verb of motion:

Přišel jsem tě navštívit.   I have come (in order) to visit you.

A related use of **aby** is with the phrase **je čas** 'it is time', in the sense of 'the time is ripe for this purpose':

Už je čas, abych šel domů.   It is time for me to go home now.

The infinitive may occur if the person is not expressed:

Je čas jít domů.   It is time to go home.

Instructions and wishes with aby and at'

Aby 'that would/should' is also used for instructions, wishes and advice, after verbs of wanting or telling:

Chci, abys přišel.	I want you to come (lit. 'that you would come').
Chtějí, abych studoval medicínu.	They want me to study medicine.
Řekli mu, aby si koupil nové auto.	They told him to buy a new car.

But with verbs meaning 'want' the infinitive is used, not **aby**, where both verbs have the same subject:

Chci přijít. I want to come.

After imperatives **at'** is often used in the sense of a warning:

Řekni mu, at' nepřijde pozdě. Tell him not to be late.

Infinitive versus aby

Sometimes the infinitive and a clause with **aby** can be alternative constructions. The infinitive may sometimes be preferable where the statement is briefer, **aby** where it is longer and more elaborate.

Radila nám, abychom už radši hned šli domů.
She advised us to go home preferably right away.
or: **Radila nám jít domů.** She advised us to go home.

Požádala ho, aby do Francie jel v létě spolu s ní.
She asked him to go together with her to France in the summer.
or: **Požádala ho jet spolu s ní.** She requested him to go with her.

Dovolit < dovolovat 'allow' and zakázat/zakáže < zakazovat 'forbid' often occur with infinitives.

Lékař mu zakázal kouřit.	The doctor forbade him to smoke.
Učitel mu taky nedovolí kouřit.	The teacher also won't let him smoke.

But **aby** may also be used:

Nedovolila mi/Zakázala mi, abych tam jel spolu s ní.
She did not allow me/she forbade me to go there with her.

Dovolit is commonly used with **aby** in phrases of introduction (lit. 'allow me to . . .'):

Dovolte, abych se (vám) představil.	May I introduce myself.
Já jsem/Jmenuju se Jean Smith.	I am/My name is Jean Smith.
– Těší mě.	Pleased to meet you.

Dovolte, abych vám představil svého kolegu pana Millera.
Let me introduce you to my colleague Mr Miller.

9.14   List of coordinating conjunctions

These conjunctions join together equally important words, phrases or clauses:

a	and	**Jedli a pili.** They ate and drank.
		Měli pivo a víno. They had beer and wine.
i	and also	**Měli pivo i víno.** They had beer and wine also.
i . . . i	both . . . and	**Měli i pivo i víno.** They had both beer and wine.
ale	but	**Petr je tady, ale Jana je doma.** Petr is here, but Jana is at home.
nebo, anebo	or, or else	**Chcete červené nebo bílé víno?** Do you want red or white wine?
buď . . . nebo	either . . . or	**Buď mu zavolej, nebo napiš.** Either call him, or write.
ať . . . nebo	whether . . . or	**Ať mladí, nebo staří, všichni se smáli.** Whether young or old, everyone was laughing.
ani . . . ani	neither . . . nor	**Nemám ani víno, ani pivo.** I have neither wine nor beer.

9.15 List of subordinating conjunctions

These introduce subordinate clauses of time:

když	when	**Když přišel, začalo pršet.** When he came, it started to rain.
kdykoli(v)	whenever	**Kdykoli přišel, začalo pršet.** Whenever he came, it started to rain.
až	until	**Počkám, až přijdeš.** I'll wait till you come.
	when (future)	**Až přijdou, půjdeme ven.** When they come, we'll go out.
dokud	while, as long as	**Rozhodni se, dokud je čas.** Decide while there's time.
dokud ne	until	**Dokud nepřijdeš, zůstanu tady.** Until you come, I'll stay here.
než	until	**Zůstal tam, než přišla.** He stayed there till she came.
než	before	**Než přišla, začalo pršet.** Before she arrived, it started to rain.
od té doby, co	(ever) since	**Prší od té doby, co přišla.** It's rained ever since she came.
po té, co	after	**Po té, co odešla, začalo sněžit.** After she left, it started to snow.
sotva(že)	scarcely	**Sotva odešla, začalo sněžit.** Scarcely had she left when it started to snow.
jakmile	as soon as	**Jakmile zavoláš, přijdu.** As soon as you call, I'll come.
jen co	as soon as	**Přijdu, jen co tohle napíšu.** I'll come as soon as I've written this.

mezitímco	while	**Mezitímco/zatímco psala dopis, uvařil jí čaj.** While she wrote the letter, he made her some tea.
zatímco	= mezitímco	
pokud	as long as	**Pokud měl peníze, utrácel.** As long as he had money, he spent it.

These indicate purpose, reason, condition, result etc.:

aby	in order to	**Šel domů, aby se umyl.** He went home in order to wash.
aby, ať	to	**Řekni mu, aby přišel/ať přijde.** Tell him to come.
protože, poněvadž	because	**Vrátil se, protože zmeškal vlak.** He returned because he had missed the train.
neboť	for	**Zůstal doma, neboť pršelo.** He stayed at home, for it was raining.
s tím, že	on the grounds that, saying that	**Odmítl s tím, že nemá čas.** He refused, saying that he didn't have time.
když	if (and when)	**Když budu mít čas, přijdu.** If I have time, I'll come.
kdyby	if	**Přišel bych, kdybych měl čas.** I'd come if I had time.
jestli(že), -li	if	**Jestli(že) máš čas/Máš-li čas, přijď.** If you have time, come.
jestli, zda, -li	if, whether	**Zeptal se, jestli (zda) půjdu s nimi/půjdu-li s nimi.** He asked if I would go with them.
i když, ač(koli)(v)	although	**Ačkoli/I když pršelo, šli ven.** Though it was raining, they went out.
třebaže	even though	**Šel pěšky, třebaže ho bolely nohy.** He went on foot, even though his feet were hurting.

přestože	despite the fact that	**Byla mu zima, přestože svítilo slunce.** He was cold, despite the fact that the sun was shining.
aniž	without, though not	**Šel tam, aniž (by) ho pozvali.** He went there without being invited, though they hadn't invited him.
jak	how	**Vyprávěl, jak zmeškal vlak.** He told how he missed the train.
	colloq. if	**Jak budeš zlobit, nepůjdeš nikam.** If you're bad, you're not going anywhere.
jako by	as if	**Šel dál, jako by mě nepoznal.** He walked on as if he didn't recognise me.
jen(om)že	only	**Šla bych s tebou, jenže nemám čas.** I'd go with you, only I don't have time.
kdežto	whereas	**Ráda plavala, kdežto on se vždycky bál.** She liked swimming, whereas he was always afraid.
zatímco	while	**Ráda plavala, zatímco on se vždycky slunil.** She liked swimming, while he always sunbathed.
pokud	as far as	**Pokud vím, není tady.** As far as I know, s/he isn't here.
	if, insofar as	**Pokud budeš mít čas, přijď'.** If you have time, come.
takže	so (that)	**Pršelo, takže jsme nemohli jít ven.** It was raining, so we couldn't go out.
že	that	**Řekla mi, že přijde.** She told me that she would come.
(proto), že	that, because (often preceded by **proto** 'for the reason')	**Urazil se (proto), že ho nepozvali.** He was insulted (for the reason) that they had not invited him/because they hadn't invited him.

Chapter 10

Word formation

Many Czech words can be analysed into three elements:

prefix + root + suffix

e.g. **před-** + **-škol-** + **-ní** 'pre-school'

= prefix 'pre' + root 'school' + adjectival suffix

Not all elements are necessarily present. Less common are compound words containing more than one root, e.g.

knih|kup|ec 'book merchant, bookseller'

derived from **kniha** 'book' (**knih** 'of books') + **kup|ec** 'merchant'

where **kup|ec** is itself derived from the root **kup-** in **kupovat** 'to buy'

Sometimes certain sounds regularly alternate in words derived from the same root. For example, the same root **kup-** 'buy' has a variant form **koup-**, found in the noun **koup|ě** 'a purchase' and the perfective verb **koupit** 'to buy'.

10.1 Vowel alternations

Alternations between long and short vowels have been mentioned in other chapters of this book, e.g. **dům** 'house' – **domu** 'of the house', **být** 'to be' – **byl** 'was'.

These alternations also often occur in related words with common roots, e.g.

á – a: **láska** 'love' – **laskavý** 'kind, loving'

é – e: **jméno** 'name' – **jmenovat** 'to name'

í – i: **knížka** dim. '(little) book' – **kniha** 'book' í – e/ě: **svítit** 'to shine' – **světlo** 'light'

dítě 'child' – **děti** 'children', **dětský** 'children's'

dívka 'girl' – **děvče** 'girl'

hlídat 'to watch, guard' – **hledat** 'to look for'

jízda 'a ride', **jízdenka** 'travel ticket' – **jezdit** 'to ride, go'

ou – u: **koupit** pf. 'to buy' – **kupovat** impf. 'to buy'

kousek dim. '(small) piece' – **kus** 'piece'

ú – u: **účes** 'hairdo' – **učesat** pf. 'to comb'

ů – o: **dům** 'house' – **doma** 'at home', **domácí** 'domestic'

hrůza 'horror' – **hrozný** 'horrible'

ý – y: **být** 'to be' – **byt** 'flat, apartment'

jazýček dim. '(little) tongue' – **jazyk** 'tongue'

Prefixes **na-, pro-, při-, u-, vy-** and **za-** sometimes have lengthened vowels. Prefixed nouns often have this when derived from verb roots with a masculine zero suffix or the feminine suffix **-a**:

náhoda 'chance', **průvod** 'procession', **příklad** 'example', **účin** 'effect' (hence **účinný** 'effective'), **výhoda** 'advantage', **zájem** 'interest'

Only a few verbs have lengthened prefixes themselves, e.g. **závidět** impf. 'to envy', **nenávidět** impf. 'to hate'.

Less obvious are some root alternations involving **ě/e** (sometimes lengthened to **í**) alongside forms with **a** or **á**, e.g.

devět nine	**devítka** a number nine	**devátý** ninth
		devatenáct nineteen
		devadesát ninety
pět five	–	**pátý** fifth
pětka a number five		**patnáct** fifteen
		padesát fifty
úřední official	**řídit** to direct, drive	**úřad** office
úředník an official		**pořádek** order

Inserted **-e-**, as in the genitive plural of nouns, is another common feature, e.g.

kapsa 'pocket' – **kapesní** 'pocket' adj., **kapesník** '(pocket-)handkerchief'

barva 'colour' – **barevný** 'coloured'

Finally, colloquial variants of long vowels (see 2.9) occur in certain words, sometimes co-existing in standard usage with formal variants, e.g.

é – ý/í: **polévka** 'soup' – informal **polívka**

okno 'window', formal diminutive **okénko** – usually **okýnko**

kámen 'stone', formal diminutive **kamének** – usually **kamínek**

ý – ej: **brýle** 'spectacles' – often **brejle**

ú – ou: **úřad** 'office' – colloq. **ouřada** 'bureaucrat' (pejorative)

ucho 'ear' – diminutive **ouško** (only)

10.2   Consonant alternations

Some alternations of consonants have also been detailed in earlier chapters.

The following are particularly relevant to word formation:

h/g – ž: **jih** 'south' – **jižní** 'southern'; **kniha** 'book', **knížka** dim.

Praha 'Prague' – **pražský** 'Prague' adj.

soudruh 'comrade' – **soudružka** 'female comrade'

k – č: **ruka** 'hand' – **ruční** 'hand' adj., **ruční̇k** '(hand-)towel'

park 'park' – dim. **parčík**

ch – š: **strach** 'fear' – **strašný** 'fearful, terrible'

suchý 'dry' – **sušenka** 'biscuit', **sušit** 'to dry'

Čech 'Czech' – **čeština** 'Czech language'

c – č: **ulice** 'street' – dim. **ulička, uliční** 'street' adj.

noc 'night' – **noční** 'nocturnal'

konec 'end' – **konečný** 'final'

d – z: **narodit se** pf. 'to be born' – **narození** 'birth', **narozeniny** 'birthday'

chodit 'to walk' – **chůze** 'gait, walk'

t – c: **psát** 'to write' – **psací** 'writing' adj., **psací stroj** 'typewriter'

s – š: **vysoký** 'tall, high' – **výše** 'height'

z – ž: **vozit** 'to convey, cart, carry' – **přivážet** 'to bring'

sk – šť: český 'Czech' – **čeština** 'Czech language'

ck – čť: německý 'German' – **němčina** 'German language'
anglický 'English' – **angličtina** 'English language'

10.3 Forming nouns

For recognising the meaning and derivation of nouns and adjectives a knowledge of suffixes is particularly useful.

Prefixes are particularly typical of verb derivation. Those attached to nouns and adjectives are often part of the verb from which they are derived, but see also 10.10.

10.3.1 Holders of occupations

Czech personal nouns usually have separate male and female forms. Female forms usually add -ka, e.g. ředitel, ředitelka 'manager, director'. Some terms for occupations (práce 'work', zaměstnání 'employment') are close to English:

> **architekt, -ka** 'architect', **bankéř, -ka** 'banker', **diplomat, -ka** 'diplomat', **doktor, -ka** 'doctor', **ekonom, -ka** 'economist', **inženýr, -ka** 'engineer', **žurnalista, -istka** 'journalist'

With others, it helps to note how related words have shared roots:

> **lékař, -ka** 'physician, doctor' – **lék** 'a medicine'

> **novinář, -ka** 'journalist', **nový** 'new', **noviny** 'newspaper'

> **právník, právnička** 'lawyer' – **právo** 'law, justice, right'

> **překladatel, -ka** 'translator' – **překládat** 'to translate'

> **učitel, -ka** 'teacher' – **učit** 'to teach', **učit se** 'to learn'

> **podnikatel, -ka** 'entrepreneur' – **podnik** 'an enterprise'

Some female forms end in -ice or -yně:

> **dělník, dělnice** 'worker, industrial worker' – **dělat** 'to do, make'

> **pracovník, pracovnice** 'worker, employee' – **pracovat** 'to work'

> **hudebník, hudebnice** 'musician' – **hudba** 'music'

> **umělec, umělkyně** 'artist' – **umění** 'art'

| 10.3.2 | *Languages, countries, nationalities* |

Adjectives for languages and nationalities, as well as places, typically end in **-ský**, **-cký**, e.g. **český dopis** 'a Czech letter', **anglická kniha** 'an English book', **ruský román** 'a Russian novel', **pražský hotel** 'a Prague hotel', cf. **Praha** 'Prague'.

Nouns for languages end in **-ina**:

> **čeština** 'Czech', **slovenština** 'Slovak', **angličtina** 'English', **němčina** 'German', **mad'arština** 'Hungarian', **polština** 'Polish', **ruština** 'Russian', **francouzština** 'French'.

Jazyk 'language/tongue' may also be used with the adjectives, e.g. **český jazyk** 'the Czech language'.

The Czech Republic, **Česká republika**, is also called **Česko** – in fact there is no other acceptable one-word form, although some speakers still dislike this term. Other country names commonly end in **-sko**, **-cko** or **-ie** [-ije]:

> **Anglie** [-ije] 'England', **Francie** 'France', **Velká Británie** 'Great Britain'

> **Slovensko** 'Slovakia', **Německo** 'Germany', **Rakousko** 'Austria', **Mad'arsko** 'Hungary', **Polsko** 'Poland', **Rusko** 'Russia'. Also former **Československo** 'Czechoslovakia'.

Note **Amerika** 'America' and **Spojené státy** 'the United States'.

The names for the Czech historic provinces are: **Čechy** (plural!) 'Bohemia', **Morava** 'Moravia', **Slezsko** 'Silesia'.

Nouns for members of nationalities often have masculine forms ending in **-an**, sometimes **-ec**, less often **-ák**, and most have female forms in **-ka**:

> **Čech/Češka** 'a Czech', **Moravan/-ka** or, colloq., **Moravák/ Moravačka** 'a Moravian', **Slovák/Slovenka** 'a Slovak', **Angličan/ Angličanka** 'an Englishman/-woman', **Američan/Američanka** 'an American', **Japonec/Japonka** 'a Japanese man/woman', **Němec/ Němka** 'a German', **Rakušan/Rakušanka** 'an Austrian', **Mad'ar/ Mad'arka** 'a Hungarian', **Polák/Polka** 'a Pole', **Rus/Ruska** 'a Russian', **Francouz/Francouzka** 'a Frenchman/-woman'.

Similarly, **cizinec/cizinka** 'a foreigner, a stranger', from **cizí** 'foreign'.

Language adverbs are formed from **-cký**, **-ský** adjectives with **-cky**, **-sky**, e.g. **česky** '(in) Czech', **anglicky** '(in) English' etc.

> **Mluvíte česky? Umíte anglicky?** Do you speak Czech? Do you know English?

To say 'in the Czech manner' etc. the preposition **po** can be used with a special, originally short-form ending -**cku**, -**sku**, e.g. **vařit po česku** 'to cook in the Czech manner, like a Czech'.

10.3.3 Masculine noun suffixes

Most masculine suffixes produce animate nouns; some also produce inanimates.

-áč/-ač, **-eč**, **-ič**	agent nouns (esp. manual jobs), tools, instruments (the suffix vowel follows the verb type)

hráč 'player' – **hrát** 'to play'

prodavač 'salesman, shop assistant' – **prodávat** 'to sell'

řidič 'driver' – **řídit** 'to drive'

počítač 'computer' – **počítat** 'to count'

vysavač 'vacuum-cleaner' – **vysávat** 'to vacuum, suck up'

-ák	agent nouns, inhabitants (mostly colloq.), bearer of qualities

divák 'spectator, onlooker' – **dívat se** 'to look'

kuřák 'smoker' – **kouřit** 'to smoke'

Polák 'Polish' – **Pol|sko** 'Poland'

Pražák colloq. 'Praguer' (= **Pražan**) – **Praha** 'Prague'

chudák 'poor thing, poor fellow' – **chudý** 'poor'

zpěvák 'singer' – **zpívat** 'to sing'

otvírák 'opener' – **otvírat** 'to open'

květák 'cauliflower' – **květ(ina)** 'flower'

věžák 'tower block' – **věž** 'tower'

also used for some slang abbreviations

Marxák – 'Marxism-Leninism'

zdroják – 'source code' (computers)

-an	inhabitants of countries and towns etc. (**-ák** is more colloquial for towns)

Pražan 'Praguer' (colloq. **Pražák**) – **Praha** 'Prague'

Brňan 'someone from Brno' (colloq. **Brňák**) – **Brno**

Angličan 'Englishman' – **Anglie** 'England', **anglický** 'English'

Evropan 'a European' – **Evropa** 'Europe'

-ář, -ař   agent nouns, long **-ář** in monosyllabic nouns and those with three or more syllables; in two-syllable words usually short **-ař** following a long syllable, either form following a short syllable, but short **-ař** usually in newer words

lhář 'liar' – **lhát** 'to lie'

funkcionář 'functionary, official' – **funkce** 'function'

houbař 'mushroom picker' – **houba** 'mushroom'

pekař 'baker' – **péct** 'to bake'

rybář 'fisherman' – **ryba** 'fish'

čtenář 'reader' – **čtení** 'reading', **číst, čte** 'to read'

filmař 'film maker' – **film** 'film'

related suffixes in some other words, e.g.

malíř 'painter' – **malovat** 'to paint'

bankéř 'banker' – **banka** 'bank'

-ce   agent nouns, less frequent

vůdce 'leader' – **vodit** 'to lead'

průvodce 'guide' – **provést, provádět** 'to guide'

soudce 'judge' – **soudit** 'to judge'

-čí   some agent nouns, adjectival nouns

krejčí 'tailor' – **krájet** 'to cut'

průvodčí 'guard, conductor' – cf. **průvodce** 'guide' (above)

rozhodčí 'referee, umpire' – **rozhodnout** 'to decide'

-ec   agent nouns, bearers of qualities, some bearers of nationalities

herec 'actor' – **hra** 'a play' (gen. pl. **her**)

stařec 'old man' – **starý** 'old'

slepec 'blind man' – **slepý** 'blind'

zaměstnanec 'employee' – **zaměstnaný** 'employed'

Japonec 'a Japanese person' – **Japon|sko** 'Japan'

-(n)ík   agent nouns, bearers of qualities, things

dělník 'manual worker' – **dělat** 'to do, work'
básník 'poet' – **báseň** 'poem'
mladík 'young man, youth' – **mladý** 'young'

rychlík 'express train' – **rychlý** 'fast'
rohlík 'crescent shaped roll' – **roh** 'horn, corner'

-tel   agent nouns, generally non-manual

učitel 'teacher' – **učit** 'to teach'
ředitel 'manager' – **řídit** 'to direct, manage'
zaměstnavatel 'employer' – **zaměstnávat** impf. 'to employ'

10.3.4 Feminine noun suffixes

-ka   feminine equivalents of masculine animate nouns, commonest
suffix for 'gender switching' (**přechylování**)

kamarádka – **kamarád** 'friend'
kuřačka – **kuřák** 'smoker'
Pražanka, colloq. **Pražačka** – **Pražan**, **Pražák** 'Praguer'
prodavačka 'saleswoman' – **prodavač** 'salesman'
čtenářka – **čtenář** 'reader'
herečka 'actress' – **herec** 'actor'
Němka 'German woman' – **Němec**
Japonka 'Japanese woman' – **Japonec** 'Japanese man'
Češka 'Czech woman' – **Čech**
učitelka – **učitel** 'teacher'

-ina   languages, activities etc.

čeština 'Czech' – **český** 'Czech' adj.
angličtina 'English' – **anglický** 'English'
latina 'Latin' – **latinský** 'Latin' adj.
řečtina 'Greek' – **řecký** 'Greek'

dřina 'drudgery' – **dřít se** 'to drudge, work hard'

-na   rooms, buildings, enclosed spaces

koupelna 'bathroom' – **koupel** 'a bathe', **koupat se** 'to
bathe'

jídelna 'dining room' – **po-jídat** 'to eat (a bit)', **jíst, jí, jedl** 'to eat'

čekárna 'waiting room' – **čekat** 'to wait'

knihovna 'library' – **kniha** 'book'

herna 'gaming room' – **hra** 'game' (gen. pl. **her**)

-ná   adjectival nouns, native words for sports

kopaná (= **fotbal)** 'football' – **kopat** 'to kick'

odbíjená (= **volejbal)** – **odbíjet** 'to hit away'

házená 'handball' – **házet** 'to throw'

similarly, **košíková** (= **basketbal)** – **košík** 'small basket'

-(n)ice   feminine equivalents of masculine animates, esp. from **-ník**

dělnice – **dělník** '(industrial) worker'

lvice 'lioness' – **lev** 'lion'

tygřice 'tigress' – **tygr** 'tiger'

-ost   qualities, nouns derived from quality adjectives, very common prefix

hloupost 'silliness, stupidity' – **hloupý** 'silly, stupid'

slabost 'weakness' – **slabý** 'weak'

(ne)trpělivost '(im)patience' – **(ne)trpělivý** '(im)patient', cf. **trpět** 'to suffer'

-(k)yně some feminine equivalents of masculine animates

přítelkyně – **přítel** 'friend'

průvodkyně – **průvodce** 'guide'

žákyně – **žák** 'pupil'

mistryně – **mistr** 'sports champion'

zaměstnankyně – **zaměstnanec** 'employee'

10.3.5 | *Neuter noun suffixes*

-dlo   means, instruments, tools etc.

mýdlo 'soap' – **mýt** 'to wash'

umývadlo 'washbasin' – **umývat** 'to wash'

sedadlo 'seat' – **sedět** 'to sit'

divadlo 'theatre' – **dívat se** 'to look'

pravidlo 'rule' – **pravý** 'true'

letadlo 'plane' – **letět** 'to fly'

prostěradlo 'sheet' – **prostírat** 'to stretch out'

-í, -oví   collective nouns

listí 'foliage' – **list** 'leaf'

kvítí 'flowers, blossom' – **květ, květina** 'flower'

dříví '(quantity of) timber' – **dřevo** 'timber, wood'

kamení 'stones' – **kámen** 'a stone'

uhlí 'coal' – **uhel** 'a coal'

stromoví 'group of trees' – **strom** 'tree'

křoví 'shrubbery, bushes' – **keř** 'bush'

-isko   points

hledisko 'point of view' – **hledět** 'to look'

stanovisko 'standpoint' – **stanovit** 'to establish', **stát** 'to stand'

ohnisko 'focus' – **oheň** 'fire'

-iště   open place, site

nástupiště 'platform' – **nastoupit** 'to board'

hřiště 'playground, playing field' – **hrát** 'to play'

letiště 'airport' – **letět** 'to fly'

pracoviště 'workplace' – **pracovat** 'to work'

parkoviště 'car park, parking lot' – **parkovat** 'to park'

-ivo   materials for a purpose, collective nouns

topivo 'fuel' (for heating) – **topit** 'to heat'

palivo 'fuel' (for burning) – **pálit** 'to burn'

pečivo 'bakery goods' (rolls, pastries, biscuits) – **péct, peče, pekl** 'to bake'

zdivo 'masonry' – **zeď** 'wall'

-ní, -tí   verbal nouns and their derived senses

překvapení 'surprise' – **překvapit** 'to surprise'

pití 'something to drink, a drink' – **pít** 'to drink'

-ství, -ctví   abstract qualities, professions, industries, shops, often with associated adjectives ending in **-ský**, **-cký**

hrdinství 'heroism' – **hrdina** 'hero'

vlastenectví 'patriotism' – **vlastenec** 'patriot', **vlast** 'homeland'

bohatství 'wealth, riches' – **bohatý** 'rich'

pekařství 'baker's shop, trade' – **péct, peče, pekl** 'to bake'

(but **pekárna** 'a bakery, bakehouse')

řeznictví 'butcher's shop, trade' – **řezník** 'butcher', **řezat** 'to cut'

novinářství 'journalism' – **novinář** 'journalist'

strojírenství 'machine engineering' – **stroj** 'machine'

knihkupectví 'bookshop' – **knihkupec** 'bookseller'

-stvo, -ctvo non-abstract, collective nouns, esp. groups of people

obyvatelstvo 'population' – **obyvatel** 'inhabitant'

lidstvo 'humanity, mankind' – **lidé** 'people'

členstvo 'the membership, members' – **člen** 'member'

(but **členství** 'membership, state of being a member')

-tko instrument, tool, esp. if smaller (dim. of **-dlo**)

pravítko 'ruler' – **pravý** 'true' (cf. **pravidlo** 'rule')

razítko 'date stamp, official stamp' – **razit** 'to strike, stamp'

10.4 Adjective suffixes

Adjective suffixes include the following (there are plenty more):

-cí denotes function (derived from infinitives)

psací stroj 'typewriter' – **psát** 'to write'
plnicí pero 'fountain pen' – **plnit** 'to fill'

-čí derived from from nouns with suffixes **-ec, -ce**

vůdčí 'leading' – **vůdce** 'leader'
also adjectival nouns (see also above)
mluvčí 'speaker, spokesman' – **mluvit** 'to speak'

-í   generic adjectives from animal words

  ptačí 'bird's', e.g. **ptačí hnízdo** 'a bird's nest' – **pták** 'bird'

  čapí 'stork's' – **čáp** 'stork'

  lví 'lion's', e.g. **lví podíl** 'lion's share' – **lev** 'lion'

  also **dívčí** 'girl's' – **dívka** 'girl'

-ící, -oucí   present participial adjectives, and derived senses

  překvapující 'surprising' – **překvapovat** 'to surprise'

  vedoucí 'leading' – **vést, vede** 'to lead'

-lý   derived from past tense forms ending in **-l**

  zestárlý 'aged' – **zestárnout** 'to age'

  zastaralý 'antiquated' – **zastarat** 'to become antiquated'

  zvadlý 'withered' – **zvadnout** 'to wither'

-ní   extremely common suffix, often noun attributes in English

  lesní 'forest' adj. – **les** 'forest'

  školní 'school' adj., e.g. **školní budova** 'school building' – **škola** 'school'

  hudební 'music(al)' – **hudba** 'music'

  hlavní 'main' – **hlava** 'head'

  střední 'middle, neuter' adj. – **střed** 'centre, middle'

-ný   also common, used in various ways

  bolestný 'painful' – **bolest** 'pain'

  silný 'strong' – **síla** 'strength'

-ový   'of, made of', highly productive, often noun attributes in English

  kovový 'metal, metallic, made of metal' – **kov** 'metal'

  lidový 'popular, of the people' – **lid** 'the people', **lidé** 'people'

-ský, -cký   typical for nationalities, towns and places, many loanwords

  český 'Czech' – **Čechy** 'Bohemia'

  ruský 'Russian' – **Rus** 'a Russian'

  americký 'American' – **Amerika** 'America'

pražský 'of Prague' – **Praha** 'Prague'

brněnský 'of Brno'

olomoucký 'of Olomouc'

mužský 'male, masculine' – **muž** 'man'

ženský 'female, feminine' – **žena** 'woman'

bratrský 'fraternal' – **bratr** 'brother'

fyzický 'physical' – **fyzika** 'physics'

chemický 'chemical' – **chemie** 'chemistry'

geografický 'geographical' – **geografie** 'geography'

psychologický 'psychological' – **psychologie** 'psychology'

-telný   '-able', '-ible'

(ne)srozumitelný '(in)comprehensible' – **rozumět** 'to comprehend'

(ne)čitelný '(il)legible' – **číst**, **čte** 'to read'

pochopitelný 'understandable' – **pochopit** 'to understand'

-ův, -in   possessive adjectives, see 4.6.

Karlův most 'Charles' Bridge' – **Karel** 'Charles'

bratrův 'brother's' – **bratr** 'brother'

sestřin 'sister's' – **sestra** 'sister'

See also 7.15 for adjectival past participles ending in -ný, -tý:

překvapený 'surprised', **vzdělaný** 'educated', **zapomenutý** 'forgotten'

See 10.7 for diminutive adjectives such as **maličký** 'tiny little'.
Loanwords often use suffixes -cký, -ní, -ový:

fyzický 'physical', **mediální** 'media', **individuální** 'individual', **golfový** 'golf' etc.

10.5   Adverbs

Adverbs are mostly derived regularly from adjectives using the suffix -e/-ě as detailed in Chapter 3, e.g. **dobrý** 'good' – **dobře** 'well', **špatný** 'bad' – **špatně** 'badly'.

The suffix **-sky/-cky** is used however for adjectives ending in **-ský/** -cký, e.g. **cynický** 'cynical' – **cynicky** 'cynically', **český** 'Czech' – **česky** 'in Czech'.

Some less regular adverbs use the neuter sg. short form of the adjective ending in **-o**, e.g. **daleký** 'far' – **daleko** 'far away', **dlouhý** 'long' – **dlouho** 'for a long time'.

Others are derived from prepositional phrases with short-form adjectives, e.g. **odedávna** 'from time immemorial' (**dávný** 'ancient', **dávno** 'long ago').

10.6 Foreign suffixes

A good number of foreign suffixes are used in noun and adjective formation, but most of these are common to many European languages, and easy for English speakers to recognise, e.g.

-ace	**navigace** 'navigation'
-ační	**navigační** 'navigational'
-olog	**archeolog** 'archeologist', **biolog** 'biologist'
-ologický	**archeologický** 'archeological', **biologický** 'biological'
-ologie	**archeologie** 'archeology', **biologie** 'biology', **geologie** 'geology'
-ální	**individuální** 'individual', **mediální** 'media', **globální** 'global'
-ista	**materialista** 'a materialist', **feminista** 'a feminist' (but **feministka**, if female!)
-istický	**materialistický** 'materialist', **feministický** 'feminist'
-ismus/-izmus	**feminismus** 'feminism', **materialismus** 'materialism', **komunismus** 'communism'

10.7 Diminutives – *zdrobněliny*

Nouns ending in **-(č)ek**, **-(č)ka**, or **-(č)ko** are regularly used for something small(er). They are termed 'diminutives' (**zdrobnělina** – diminutive). They express basically either (a) 'smallness', or (b) 'niceness, affection, endearment'.

Their gender matches the nouns from which they are derived.

Familiar forms of personal names are often diminutives. 'Double' diminutives end in **-ček, -čka, -čko**. These may (but do not always) intensify the expression of 'smallness' or 'endearment'.

Masculine diminutives end in **-ek/-ík** or **-eček, -íček**:

dům – domek, domeček 'small house, tiny house', **kus – kousek,
kousíček** 'small piece, tiny little piece', **list – lístek, lísteček** 'small
leaf, tiny leaf', **talíř** 'plate' – **talířek** 'small plate' = 'saucer', **ubrus**
'tablecloth' – **ubrousek** 'napkin, serviette', **Karel – Karlík, Karlíček**
'Charlie, wee Charlie'

Feminines end in -ka or -ečka, -ička:

kniha – knížka, knížečka 'little, tiny book', **lžíce** 'spoon' – **lžička**
'teaspoon', **ulice – ulička** 'little street', **ruka – ručka, ručička** 'little
hand', **Zuzana – Zuzka** 'Sue, Susie', **Jana – Janička** 'Jany'

Neuters end in -ko or -(e)čko:

okno – okénko/okýnko 'little window', **město – městečko** 'little
town', **slovo – slovíčko** 'little word', **víno – vínečko** 'nice wine',
pivo – pivečko 'nice beer'

Some adjectives, occasionally other words, have similar diminutive
forms:

malý – maličký, malinký '(nice) little, tiny'

sladký – slaďounký 'nice and sweet'

trochu – trošku, trošičku '(just) a little bit'

Diminutives may have particular neutral meanings:

list – lístek 'little leaf' = 'ticket', **jídelní lístek** 'menu'

kniha – knížka 'little book', **šeková knížka** 'cheque book'

ruka – ručička 'little hand' = 'clock/watch hand'

strom – stromeček 'little tree', **vánoční stromeček** 'Christmas
tree'

Diminutives turn up a lot in folksongs. Speech involving children tends
to be full of them. Waiters often say **řízeček** for **řízek** 'schnitzel', **pivko**
for **pivo** 'beer' etc. Diminutives are conveniently mainstream in declension, e.g. **sluníčko** 'sun' as opposed to **slunce**, **ručičky** 'hands' as opposed to **ruce**. They are also used similarly to lovey-dovey language in
English, to express endearment and intimacy.

10.8 Personal names

Many common personal names have familiar shortened variants with
the suffix -a (either masculine or feminine). They also have diminutives,
often several of these.

Such names are used familiarly, casually, between friends, family and closer colleagues. The diminutives especially tend to express affection (they may also be used with irony or sarcasm, of course). They can be used more or less neutrally when referring to small children.

Some (mostly the less obvious) English equivalents are shown in the lists below. Some sample familiar forms follow in brackets.

Certain Slav names (revived in the nineteenth century) consist of two elements. These may have shared familiar forms as follows:

> Names with the initial element **Bohu-** (= 'to God') may have familiar forms **Bohuš**, **Boža**, **Božka**.

> Names with the initial element **Miro-** or final element **-mír(a)** (= 'peace') may have familiar forms **Mirek**, **Míra**, **Mirka**.

> Names with **Milo-** or **-mil(a)** (= 'dear') may have **Milek**, **Míla**, **Milka**.

> Names with **Slavo-** or **-slav(a)** (= 'glory') may have **Slávek**, **Sláva**, **Slávka**.

Those forms are additional to any given below.

Male personal names:

> **Alexandr (Saša), Antonín (Tonda, Toník), Bohumil (Bohuš etc.), Bohumír (Mirek etc.), Bohuslav (Slávek etc.), Břetislav (Břeťa), Čeněk** = Vincent, **Dalibor (Borek, Libor), David (Davídek), Eduard (Eda), Emil (Emílek), Ferdinand (Ferda), Filip (Filípek), František** = Francis, Franz **(Franta, Fráňa, Fanda), Hynek** = Ignatz, Ignatius, **Ivan, Jakub** = James **(Kuba, Kubík, Kubíček), Jan** = John **(Jeník, Jeníček, Honza, Honzík, Jenda), Jaromír (Jarda, Jára, Mirek), Jaroslav (Jarda, Jára, Slávek), Jindřich** = Henry **(Jindra), Jiří** = George **(Jirka), Josef (Pepa, Pepík, Pepíček, Josífek), Karel** = Charles **(Karlík), Ladislav (Láďa), Libor/Lubor (Borek), Lubomír (Luba, Mirek), Ludvík** = Louis, Lewis **(Luděk), Lukáš** = Luke **(Lukášek), Marek** = Mark, **Martin, Matěj** = Matthew, **Michal (Míša), Milan, Miloslav, Miloš, Miroslav, Mojmír, Oldřich** = Ulrich **(Olda), Ondřej** = Andrew **(Ondra), Otakar (Ota), Pavel** = Paul **(Pavlík), Petr (Péťa, Petřík)** = Peter, **Přemysl, Radomír (Radek), Rostislav (Rosťa), Řehoř** = Gregory, **Stanislav (Stáňa, Standa), Svatopluk (Sváťa, Svatek), Šimon (Šimek), Štěpán** = Stephen, **Tomáš** = Thomas **(Tomášek), Václav** = Wenceslas, Wenzel **(Váša, Vašek, Vaněk), Vilém** = William **(Vilda), Vítězslav (Víťa, Vítek), Vladimír (Vláďa), Vladislav (Vláďa), Vlastimil (Vlasta), Vlastislav (Vlasta), Vojtěch** = Adalbert **(Vojta), Vratislav (Vráťa), Zbyněk, Zdeněk (Zdena).**

Female personal names:

Alena (Alenka, Lenka), Alexandra (Saša), Alžběta = Elizabeth
(Eliška, Líza, Běta), Anna (Anička, Andulka, Anka, Anča),
Barbora (Bára, Bárka, Baruška), Blanka, Bohdana, Bohumila,
Božena (Božka, Boženka), Daniela (Dana), Drahomíra, Elena,
Eva (Evička, Evinka, Evka), Hana, Irena, Ivana, Jana, Jarmila,
Jiřina, Jitka = Judith, **Julie, Karolína, Kateřina** = Catherine
(Katka, Káťa, Káča), Klára, Lidmila/Ludmila (Lída), Lucie
(Lucka, Lucinka), Magdalena (Magda, Madla, Madlena, Léna,
Lenka), Marcela, Marie = Mary **(Máňa, Mařenka, Maruška,**
Máša), Milada, Milena, Naděžda (Naďa), Olga (Olinka), Petra
(Petruška), Renata, Růžena = Rose, **Soňa, Sylvie, Šárka,**
Taťána (Táňa), Tereza, Vendula (Vendulka), Věra, Vlasta,
Zdeňka/Zdenka, Zuzana = Susan(na) **(Zuzka), Žofie** = Sophia
(Žofka).

10.8.1 Surnames

Masculine surnames are either nouns or adjectival nouns, e.g. **Beneš,
Novotný.**

Female surnames ending in **-ová** are derived from their masculine
equivalents and behave like adjectives. Male adjectival surnames ending
in **-ý** have female forms ending in **-á.**

pan Beneš a paní Benešová Mr Beneš and Mrs Benešová

pan Novotný a paní Novotná Mr Novotný and Mrs Novotná

Only a few surnames are indeclinable, notably those like **Martinů, Janů,**
which have no feminine variants.

10.9 Derived verbs

Verbs are formed from other simpler verbs using prefixes and suffixes.
Compound verbs are derived from simple verbs using prefixes. Verb
prefixes and suffixes are both involved in the formation of aspectual
pairs. These are all treated separately further below.

Verbs derived from other parts of speech regularly use one or other
of the standard infinitive types. The **-ovat** type is productive for foreign
loanwords and other new formations, the **-nout** type is common for
changes of state ('become, turn') and perfective momentary actions.

-at   **červenat se** 'blush' – **červeny** 'red'

-et   **slzet** 'weep, drop tears' – **slza** 'tear'

     zlidovět pf. 'become popular' – **lidový** 'popular'

-it   **rybařit** 'go fishing, be a fisherman' – **rybář** 'fisherman', **ryba** 'fish'

-nout **blednout > z-** 'turn pale' – **bledý** 'pale'

     rudnout > z- 'turn red, blush deeply' – **rudý** 'red'

     risknout pf. 'risk, take a risk'

-ovat **lyžovat** 'to ski' – **lyže** 'skis'

     organizovat 'organise'

     telefonovat 'telephone'

     riskovat impf./pf. 'risk'

10.9.1 Baby verbs

It is notable that a group of childish verbs used in 'baby' language – i.e. initially when children are learning to speak Czech – belong to the highly regular **-at** type, e.g. **papat** 'to eat', **bumbat** 'to drink', **spinkat** 'to sleep', **čůrat** 'to pee' and **kakat** 'to do a poo'. (The adult equivalents are more irregular.)

10.9.2 Perfectivising prefixes

Any of the following prefixes will normally make an imperfective verb perfective:

do-, na-, nad-, o-/ob-, od-, po-, pod-, pro-,

pře-, před-, při-, roz-, s-, u-, v-, vy-, vz-, z-, za-

Each adds its own meaning to the verb (though less obviously so where a neutral perfective is formed from a simple verb). They are fundamental to the way in which Czech verbs are formed and used.

If the prefix adds a new syllable then long -á- in the simple infinitive will shorten, unless it does *not* shorten in the past tense, e.g. **psát, psal** 'write' – **podepsat, podepsal** 'sign', but **hrát, hrál** 'play' – **vyhrát, vyhrál** 'win'.

10.9.3 Prefixed compound verbs

English verbs often have words like 'in'/'out' after them: 'He went out. He came in.' Often these verb phrases have idiomatic meanings, e.g. 'He shut up. He piped down.'

In Czech prefixes are habitually attached to the front of verbs instead, just like many English verbs of Latin origin, e.g. 'circum|navigate' = 'sail round' etc.

Most of the prefixes in use are the same as, or closely related to, certain basic common prepositions.

In the list which follows the first example is most often a perfective compound of **jít** 'to go'. Most of these have imperfective counterparts with **-cházet**.

The first meanings given for each prefix are basic, usually spatial, ones, followed by further examples (all perfectives) illustrating some other relatively frequent and easily identifiable areas of usage.

Many have imperfective counterparts, formed in ways outlined in the immediately following section on suffixes.

For full details of each verb you will need a good dictionary, preferably one which properly records the aspectual pairs (unfortunately not all do this).

---

do- 'finish/reach'

---

dojít, dojde, došel < docházet 'reach, go for/fetch'

Došel do školy.   He reached (finished the journey to) school.

Došel pro chleba.   He went to get/fetch some bread.

similarly: **dodat** 'add, deliver', **dojet** 'reach' (by vehicle, riding), **donést** 'bring', **doručit** 'deliver', 'complete (final phase of)':

dočíst 'finish reading', **dojíst** 'finish eating', **dodělat** 'finish, complete making'

'achieve':

dohodnout se 'reach an agreement', **dokázat** 'prove', **dosáhnout** 'achieve'

---

na- 'upon, onto'

---

najít, najde, našel < nacházet 'come upon, find'

Našel jsem pěknou knihu.   I found a nice book.

similarly, but more literally: **nastoupit** 'get on, board', **natřít** 'paint'

'stretch, fill, extend':

natáhnout 'stretch out'

'quantity', with **se** 'enough, sufficiently':

nacpat 'stuff (a quantity)', **napadnout** 'fall (in a quantity)', **napéct** 'bake a quantity'

najíst se 'eat one's fill', **napít se** 'drink one's fill'

'partially, a bit', often occurs as adjectives from -l forms of verbs

nakousnout 'bite into', **nahnout se** 'bend over a bit'

nahluchlý 'a bit deaf', **nahnilý** 'a bit rotten'

> **nad(e)-** 'over, above, up'

---

nadejít (si), nadejde, nadešel < **nadcházet** 'get ahead (via a shortcut); come (of time)'

Nadešel mu uličkou.   He overtook him via a side-street.

Nadešel si pěšinou.   He took a shortcut via a path.

Nadešla chvíle, kdy se musíme rozhodnout.   The time has come for us to decide.

similarly: **nadjet** 'take a shortcut (by vehicle, riding)' and, more literally, **nadepsat (stránku)** 'head (a page, write at the top of it)', **nadhodit** 'throw up, toss', **nadskočit** 'leap up a bit, bounce'

> **ne-** 'not', also shortens -**á**- in a following infinitive syllable; does *not* perfectivise

---

nejít, nejde, nešel + nechodit 'not to go'

similarly: **nepsat** 'not to write' (**psát** 'write'), **nedbat** 'not to heed' (**dbát** 'heed') and, less obviously, **zanedbat** pf. 'neglect'; **nechat** pf. 'let, leave alone' is also said to be negative in origin, though it has no positive counterpart

also **nedo-** 'insufficiently, incompletely'

nedoslýchat be hard of hearing

---

o-, ob(e)- 'round'

---

obejít, obejde, obešel < obcházet 'go round'

Obešel dům.　　　He went/walked round the house.

similarly: **objet** 'drive round, bypass', hence **objížďka** 'a detour', **obklopit** 'surround', **otočit (se)** 'turn (around)'

also: 'around the surface'

ohřát 'heat up, warm up', **okopat zeleninu** 'dig around vegetables', **okopat boty** 'kick and damage shoes', **obložit chléb** 'garnish bread', i.e. make sandwiches (**obložené chlebíčky**), **obtěžovat** 'encumber, trouble'

'concerning, about'

oplakat 'lament, weep over'

Intransitive verbs from adjectives, with changes of human state:

onemocnět 'fall ill', **otěhotnět** 'get pregnant', **osiřet** 'be orphaned'

---

od(e)- 'away, away from' (opposite of **při-** 'up near, arrive')

---

odejít, odejde, odešel < odcházet 'go away, leave, depart'

Karel už odešel.　　　Karel has now left, departed.

Anna odejde zítra.　Anna will go away, leave tomorrow.

similarly: **odjet** 'go, drive, ride away', **odnést** carry/take away', **oddělit** 'separate', **odstoupit** 'step away, step aside'

'respond', 'off, get done'

odpovědět 'reply' (hence **odpověď** 'an answer'), **odepsat** 'write back, write off', **odříkat báseň** 'recite a poem', **odčinit** 'undo, redress, make up for', **odbýt** 'get rid of, get done', **odkvést** 'finish blossoming', **odbít** 'finish striking' (bells)

---

pa- 'as a substitute, falsely', which does not perfectivise

---

padělat impf./pf. 'forge, fake, make falsely'

---

po- 'over a surface'

---

popsat < popisovat 'to cover with writing, describe'

Popsal všechen papír.   He wrote all over the paper.

Popsal život na venkově.   He described life in the countryside.

similarly, often damaging: **pokrýt** 'cover', **podupat** 'trample', **pomalovat** 'paint', **pošpinit** 'dirty'

'a bit'

poodejít 'go off, move away a bit', **poopravit** 'correct slightly, adjust', **pootevřít** 'open a bit', **poblednout** 'turn a bit pale', **pohrát si** 'play about, fiddle', **posnídat** 'have some breakfast', **poobědvat** 'have some lunch', **povečeřet** 'have some supper', **poohlédnout se** 'have a look around', **pootočit klikou** 'turn the handle a bit', **povyskočit** 'leap up a bit'

with reflexive **si**: 'enjoy a certain quantity of, have a (good)'

počíst si 'have read', **popovídat si** 'have a chat', **posedět si** 'have a sit'

'successively, one after another'

pozamykat 'lock one after another', **pomřít** 'die off'

'to make, -ise', transitive verbs from adjectives

počeštit 'Czechise', **poněmčit** 'Germanise'

In special senses with **-jít:**

pojít, pojde, pošel (pf. only) 'die' (of animals), 'snuff it' (vulgar, of humans)

pocházet (impf. only), 'come from, originate from'

Pes nám pošel.   Our dog has died.

Je tu nuda, že by člověk pošel.   It's deadly boring here.

Pochází z Brna.   He comes from Brno.

---

popo- 'a little bit' (= **po-** + **po-**)

---

popojít, popojde, popošel < popocházet 'move along a bit'

Popošel k oknu.   He moved up a bit closer to the window.

similarly: **popojet** 'inch along a little (in a vehicle)', **poposednout** 'move away a bit, to another seat'

---

pod- 'under' in various senses

---

podejít, podejde, podešel (pf. only) 'go under'

Podešla most.   She went under the bridge.

similarly: **podjet** 'drive under', hence **podjezd** 'underpass', **podepsat** 'sign', hence **podpis** 'signature', **podplatit** 'bribe, pay underhand money', **podléhat** 'succumb', **podpálit dům** 'set fire to a house'

also: **podnapít se** 'get a bit drunk, tipsy', **podcenit** 'underestimate', **podniknout** 'undertake'

---

pro-   'through'

---

projít, projde, prošel < procházet 'go through', **projít se** 'have a walk'

Prošla tunelem.   She walked through the tunnel.

Šla se projít.   She went to have a walk.

similarly: **projet** 'drive, ride through', **proniknout** 'penetrate', **prohřát** 'heat through', **procestovat** 'travel through', **prostoupit** 'permeate'

'lengthen, extend'

prodloužit 'lengthen, extend', **protáhnout se** 'stretch oneself'

'wear out, through'

prošlapat 'wear out (shoes, by walking)', **prosedět** 'wear out (trousers, by sitting)'

'through and through, thoroughly'

pročíst 'read through', **proměnit** 'transform, alter, change'

'here and there, partly'

Prošedivět, vlasy mu   His hair became streaked with grey.
prošedivěly.

'be rid of, lose'

prodat 'sell', **prohrát** 'lose (match, game)', **prominout** 'forgive, excuse', **promárnit** 'squander, waste'

'get to place or achieve by passing through'

probojovat se 'fight one's way through'

> **pře-** 'across, over'

přejít, přejde, přešel < přecházet 'go across, cross'

Přešli most/přes most. They crossed the bridge.

similarly: **přejet** 'ride, drive across; run over', **přelétat** 'fly across', **překousnout** 'bite across', **přelepit** 'stick, paste over', **přemalovat** 'paint over'

'move across, transfer'

přelít 'decant, pour across', **přemístit** 'relocate, move', **přenést** 'carry across, transfer', **přeměnit** 'change, convert, transform'

'too far, too much, over-'

přelít se přes břehy 'spill over, overflow its banks', **přezrát, ovoce přezrálo** 'the fruit overripened', **přepepřit** 'overpepper', **přesolit** 'oversalt', **přelidnit** 'overpopulate'

're-, again'

přebalit 'rewrap', **přetisknout** 'reprint', **přemalovat** 'repaint', **přepsat** 'rewrite', **přestylizovat** 'restyle, rephrase'

'get over, get upper hand'

přebolet 'stop hurting', **přelstít** 'trick', **přemoct** 'overcome'

> **před(e)-** 'in front of, before'

předejít, předejde, předešel pf. 'overtake, pass, forestall', also předcházet impf. 'precede'

Předešla ho u pokladny. She beat him getting to the till.

Pýcha předchází pád. Pride comes before a fall.

similarly: **předjet** 'pass (driving), overtake', **přednášet** 'hold forth, lecture', **předpovědět** 'predict, forecast'

> **při-** 'at, near, arrive' (opposite of **od(e)-** 'away, away from')

přijít, přijde, přišel < přicházet 'come, arrive'

Karel ještě nepřišel.   Karel hasn't come/arrived yet.

Přijd'te zítra!   Come tomorrow!

similarly: **přijet** 'come, arrive (by vehicle, riding)', **přinést** 'bring by carrying', **přistoupit** 'step, walk up to'

'bring right up to'

přistrčit (stůl k oknu) 'push up (the table to the window)', **přihrát míč** 'play the ball to'

'attach, add'

přidat 'add', **přiložit** 'attach', **přišpendlit** 'pin on' (**špendlík** 'a pin'), **přivydělat si** 'earn a bit extra', **přisolit** 'add salt', **připsat** 'ascribe'

'do a little'

přivřít 'partly close', **přičesat** 'comb a bit', **přihřát** 'heat up a bit' (**trochu ohřát**), **připít** 'drink to'

> **roz(e)-** 'apart', separate, scatter, spread out (opposite of **s(e)-** 'together')

rozejít se, rozejde se, rozešel se < rozcházet se 'part, separate'

Rozešli se u stanice metra.   They separated, parted at the metro station.

similarly: **rozjet se** 'drive off in different directions', **rozkrájet** 'cut up into pieces', **rozprodat** 'sell off', **rozpustit** 'dismiss, dissolve'

'disperse, damage'

rozdupat 'trample', **rozladit** 'put out of tune, annoy', **rozčarovat** 'disenchant'

'untie, resolve, settle'

rozvázat 'untie', **rozhodnout (se)** 'decide, resolve'

'get going, start'

rozesmát 'make laugh', **rozesmát se** 'burst out laughing', **rozveselit** 'cheer up, make happy', **rozjet** 'set in motion', **rozjet se** 'drive off, start moving'

Auto se hned rozjelo. The car set off immediately.

---

s(e)- 'together' (esp. reflexive, opposite of **roz(e)-** 'apart'), sometimes **sou-**; 'down' (opposite of **vy-** 'up')

---

sejít se, sejde se, sešel se < scházet se 'come together, meet'

Sešel se s kamarádem. He met with a friend.

Sešli se před divadlem. They met in front of the theatre.

similarly: **sběhnout se** 'run together', **shodnout se** 'agree', **spojit** 'join, connect', **složit** 'put together, compose', **skoupit** 'buy up (all together)'

sejít, sejde, sešel < scházet 'go/come down'

Sešli dolů. They went down.

Sešla ze schodů. She went down the stairs.

similarly: **sjet** 'drive down', **sklonit** 'bend, droop', **sklesnout** 'fall, drop down', **snést z půdy** 'bring down from the loft', **svést** 'lead down, seduce'

---

spolu- 'co-, jointly, together' (adverbial prefix – does *not* perfectivise)

---

spolupracovat 'cooperate', spolupůsobit 'contribute'

---

u- 'off, away' (abrupt, dynamic)

---

ujít, ujde, ušel < ucházet 'get away, escape' (+dat.)

Ušel smrti. He escaped death.

Uchází plyn. Gas is escaping. There is a gas leak.

similarly: **uniknout** 'escape', **utéct** 'run away', **unést** 'carry off, kidnap', **ujet** 'drive off', **ustoupit** 'step aside, step back, retreat'

Vlak nám ujel.	We have missed the train, lit. 'The train has left on us.'

'cover a distance, manage to do'

> **ujet sto kilometrů** 'drive a hundred kilometres', **unést** 'manage to carry'

'smooth, settle'

> **urovnat** 'straighten', **uklidit** 'tidy up', **ulehčit** 'lighten', **usnout** 'fall asleep'

'wear away, harm'

> **umazat** 'soil, stain', **unavit** 'tire', **usmrtit** 'kill, cause death of', **umřít** 'die', **upít se** 'drink oneself to death'

'do a little'

> **usmát se** 'smile', **upít** 'sip'

occasionally = **v-**:

> **umístit** 'place, locate, put'

---

v(e)- 'into' (opposite of **vy-** 'out, out of')

---

vejít, vejde, vešel < vcházet 'go/come in, enter'

Vešel dovnitř.	He went in(side).
Vešla do obchodu.	She went into the shop.
Právě vcházeli do domu.	They were just going into the house.

similarly: **vložit** 'put in, insert', **vnutit své názory** 'impose one's own views'

= **vz-** in:

> **vstát** 'get up, stand up'

---

vy- 'out, out of' (opposite of **v(e)-** 'into'); 'up' (opposite of **s(e)-** 'down')

---

vyjít, vyjde, vyšel < vycházet 'go/come out, exit; go up'

Vyšla ven. She went out.

Vyšel z obchodu. He came out of the shop.

Právě vycházeli z domu. They were just coming out of the house.

similarly: **vyjet** 'drive out', **vynést** 'carry out', **vyběhnout** 'run out', **vystoupit** 'step out of, get off, alight; appear (on stage)', also **vyměnit** 'exchange, take out and change, replace'

Vyšel do prvního patra. He went up to the first floor.

Vyšli nahoru. They went up.

similarly: **vyskočit** 'jump up'; **vyrůst** 'grow up', **vynést na půdu** 'carry up to the loft', **vyhrnout rukávy** 'roll up sleeves', **vystoupit (na kopec)** 'go up, ascend, climb up (a hill)'

'pick out, separate off, enumerate one by one'

vybrat 'choose, select', **vyjmenovat** 'list, name'

'empty out, use up, complete'

vylidnit 'depopulate', **vyhubit** 'wipe out, exterminate'; **vyplakat si oči** 'cry one's eyes out', **vystudovat** 'complete one's studies, graduate in'

'fill'

vyplnit 'fill, fill in, fulfil', **vykrmit** 'feed up, fatten'

'achieve by effort, create'

vydělat 'earn, make (money)', **vyhrát** 'win (game, match)', **vyžebrat si** 'scrounge, get by begging', **vyběhat** 'obtain by effort, by running about', **vynalézt** 'invent', **vyrobit** 'produce, manufacture'

---

vz-	'up', but more dynamic/abrupt than **vy-** in the sense of upwards

---

vzejít, vzejde, vzešel < vzcházet 'come up, sprout (e.g. a crop); arise'

Vzešla pšenice. The wheat came up, sprouted.

Ze schůze vzešel návrh. A proposal arose from the meeting.

similarly: **vzletět** 'fly up', **vznést se** 'rise up, be carried up' also: **vzdychnout** 'sigh', **vzpomenout si** 'remember', **vzplanout** 'flare up', **vzniknout** 'arise'

'up against', followed by **proti** 'against'

> **vzbouřit se** 'rebel, rise up (like a storm)', **vzepřít se** 'resist, oppose'

---

z(e)- rarely 'out of', but usually just perfectivises, carries out the action

---

zběhnout pf. 'desert, run away'

also: **zříct se** 'renounce, give up', **zbýt** 'be left (over)', **zbít** 'thrash, beat up'

pf. verbs from adjectives denoting a change of state:

> **zlidovět** pf. 'become popular, of the people', **zpevnit** 'strengthen, make firmer', **zevšeobecnit** 'generalise', **zneklidnit** 'make uneasy', **zneklidnět** 'become uneasy', **zpřesnit** 'specify, put more exactly', **zpříjemnit** 'make pleasant'

perfective multiple action, 'one after another'

> **zpřeházet** 'throw into disorder, jumble', **zpřetrhat** 'sever, cut off one after another'

occasionally = **vz-**:

> **zvednout** 'lift, pick up', **zdvihnout** 'lift up, raise'

also, not infrequently: **z|ne-** 'mis-, make un-, not'

> **znečistit** 'defile, make unclean', **znemožnit** 'make impossible', **zneužít** 'misuse', **zneuctít** 'dishonour', **znehodnotit** 'devalue'

---

za- behind, off (as in going offstage, out of the field of view)

---

zajít, zajde, zašel < **zacházet** 'go behind, go in (for a purpose)'

Zašel za strom.	He went behind a tree. (**za** + acc. = motion 'behind')
Zašel za roh.	He went round ('behind') the corner.
Slunce zašlo.	The sun has set (gone down/'behind').
Zašli si na pivo.	They went in, called in, popped in for a beer.

similarly: **zajet** 'go behind (riding, by vehicle)'

'turn aside into, get into'

> **zahnout** 'turn' (**doleva** 'left'), **zabodnout** 'stab', **zamilovat se** 'fall in love'

only occasionally 'begin':

> **začít** 'begin', **zatopit** 'kindle, light' (**v kamnech** 'stove'), **zapálit** 'light, ignite'

'put away, lose, destroy'

> **zahodit** 'throw away', **zapomenout** 'forget', **založit** 'put away', **zabít** 'kill', **zastřelit** 'shoot and kill'

'cover over, block'

> **zarůst** 'become overgrown', **zabalit** 'wrap up', **zakrýt** 'cover', **zamalovat** 'paint over', **zastínit** 'overshadow', **zakouřit** 'make smoky', **zastoupit někomu cestu** 'block someone's way', **zastavit (se)** 'stop'

'instead of, in place of'

> **zastoupit** 'stand in for, represent', **zaměnit** 'mix up, swap'

with **si**, to do with zest, with enjoyment, **s chutí**:

> **zaplavat si** 'have a swim', **zatančit si** 'have a dance', **zakouřit si** 'have a smoke'

| 10.9.4 | *Aspectual pairs* |

Aspectual pairs were introduced in basic outline in Chapter 7, especially sections 7.6–7.6.2. The following assumes a general grasp of the two types described there.

> The sign > is used here to point *forwards* to the perfective

> The sign < is used to point *back* to the more basic perfective form

prefix pairs – imperfective verbs (mostly simple) with prefixed perfectives

> e.g. **psát > napsat** 'write', **číst > přečíst** 'read', **zpívat > zazpívat** 'sing'

suffix pairs – perfective verbs, usually prefixed (but sometimes not), with suffixed imperfectives

> e.g. **popsat < popisovat** 'describe', **dát < dávat** 'give', **koupit < kupovat** 'buy'

| **10.9.5** | *Forming prefix pairs* |

Prefixes used to make a simple verb perfective often restrict or further qualify the meaning in some way, and their employment for this purpose draws on the lexical senses outlined in the section above.

Sometimes, as a result, there is no neutral perfective, and one simple verb has to be thought of as having more than one prefixed perfective, each with a different meaning, e.g. **pít – vy|pít** 'drink up', **napít se** 'drink one's fill'.

In other verbs there are alternative perfectives, with no very clearly distinct or obvious differences between them, at least in some contexts, e.g.

> **končit > dokončit, skončit, ukončit, zakončit (práci)** 'end, finish (work)'

No hard and fast rules can be laid down for which prefix will be used with a given verb. The following account attempts to identify certain more widespread patterns, but in the end these pairs are simply a matter of usage and vocabulary learning.

The most commonly used prefixes for this purpose are **na-, o-, po-, u-, vy-, s-, z-, za-,** but a few others also occur, e.g. **číst – přečíst** 'to read'.

NA- is used for recording onto a surface, or providing a sufficient quantity (reflexive perfective where the subject is affected):

> **psát > napsat** 'write', **na|kreslit** 'draw', **na|malovat** 'paint', **na|diktovat** 'dictate'

> **na|plnit** 'fill', **na|lít** 'pour (drink)', **pít – na|pít se** 'drink', **jíst > na|jíst se** 'eat', **obědvat > na|obědvat se** 'have lunch', **snídat > na|snídat se** 'have breakfast', **večeřet > na|večeřet se** 'have supper'

Others: **na|učit** 'teach', **na|učit se** 'learn', **na|rodit se** 'be born'

O- may occur for an action around or over a surface:

> **o|holit** 'shave', **o|razítkovat** 'rubber-stamp', **o|slepnout** 'go blind', **o|sprchovat se** 'have a shower', **o|mládnout** 'grow younger'

PO- indicates a certain (modest) quantity of action, is often used with verbs involving an evaluative response, and frequently with other common verbs:

> **po|snídat** 'have (some) breakfast', **po|obědvat** 'have (some) lunch', **po|večeřet** 'have (some) supper'

> **po|chválit** 'praise', **po|děkovat** 'thank', **po|divit se** 'be surprised', **po|trestat** 'punish', **po|radit** 'advise, counsel', **po|litovat** 'be sorry

for' (also **za|litovat**), **po|gratulovat** 'congratulate', **po|blahopřát** 'congratulate'

po|dívat se 'look', **zvát > pozvat** 'invite', **čekat > počkat** 'wait', **po|trvat** 'last', **po|sloužit** 'serve', **po|starat se** 'take care of', **po|hovořit** 'talk, chat', **po|bavit** 'amuse', **po|těšit** 'please', **po|prosit** 'ask, request'

S- may indicate using up/destroying, or other kinds of completeness (phonetically it is identical to the commoner prefix Z- before voiceless paired consonants, and this can lead to confusion, if one is not careful enough about spellings):

jíst > sníst 'eat, eat up', **s|hořet** 'burn down', **s|pálit** 'burn', **s|končit** 'end, finish', **s|trávit** 'spend (time)', **s|tvořit** 'create'

U- indicates achievement of a result, actions involving dirt or harm, and is used with some other common verbs:

u|dělat 'do, make', **u|činit** 'do, act', **u|vařit** 'cook, boil', **u|péct** 'bake, roast', **u|plést** 'knit', **u|šít** 'sew', **u|tvořit** 'form, create', **u|končit** 'finish, end', **u|zrát** 'ripen', **u|věřit** 'believe' **u|vítat** 'welcome' (or **při|vítat**)

u|špinit (also **po-, za-, ze-**) 'dirty', **u|škodit** 'harm, damage', **u|mazat** 'make greasy'

also: **u|slyšet** 'hear, suddenly hear', **u|vidět** 'see, catch sight of', **u|cítit** 'feel' (also **po|cítit**)

VY- may be used for more extended, elaborate achievements, and for emptying/using up:

vy|pěstovat 'cultivate', **vy|tvořit** 'form, create' (also **u|tvořit**), **vy|řešit** 'solve' (also **rozřešit**), **vy|luštit** 'decipher, solve' (also **rozluštit**), also **vy|čistit** 'clean, brush (teeth)'

vy|pít 'drink up', **vy|kouřit** 'smoke'

Z- occurs often, for negative actions, change of state (-**nout**) verbs, and many loanwords (often -**ovat**):

z|kazit 'spoil', **z|klamat** 'disappoint', **z|děsit** 'horrify', **z|rušit** 'annul', **z|ničit** 'destroy'

z|blednout 'turn pale', **ze|stárnout** 'grow old', **z|bohatnout** 'become/grow rich', **z|mrznout** 'freeze'

z|komplikovat 'complicate', **z|korumpovat** 'corrupt', **z|likvidovat** 'liquidate', **z|rentgenovat** 'X-ray', **z|organizovat** 'organise'

also: **ptát se – ze|ptat se** 'ask', **z|měnit** 'change', **z|opakovat** 'repeat'

ZA- is often used for a certain duration of sounds or sights, also for killing:

za|volat 'call', **za|smát se** 'laugh', **za|zvonit** 'ring', **za|zpívat** 'sing', **za|šeptat** 'whisper', **za|kašlat** 'cough', **za|křičet** 'shout', **za|telefonovat** 'telephone' (by analogy with **za|volat**), **za|hřmít** 'thunder', **za|troubit** 'trumpet', **za|znít** 'resound'

za|blikat 'flash', **za|jiskřit** 'spark', **za|zářit** 'glow', **za|svítit** 'shine', **za|tmít se** 'be darkened', **za|rdít se** 'blush', **za|červenat se** 'blush', **za|chvět se** 'tremble'

also: **za|platit** 'pay', **za|hrát** 'play', **za|chovat se** 'behave', **lhát >** **zalhat** 'lie, tell lie'

za|vraždit 'murder', **za|škrtit** 'strangle'

| **10.9.6** | **Forming suffix pairs** |

Czech dictionaries often list suffix pairs under their more basic, usually shorter, perfective forms.

In suffix pairs the imperfective infinitive will normally have one of these suffixes:

-(á)vat, -ovat, -et or **-at**

Each suffix type is quite strongly associated with certain kinds of perfective verb.

Related verbs of the suffix-pair type also tend to form little families with parallel aspectual forms. The pairs can be predicted more and more reliably, as one's vocabulary grows.

The sign < is used here to point back to the perfective form.

(a)   suffix type (-á-)vat, typically goes with Type 5 infinitives ending in -at or -át:

vydělat < vydělávat	'earn, make (money)'
dát, dá, dal < dávat	'give'
vydat < vydávat	'publish'
objednat < objednávat	'order (food, things)'
překonat < překonávat	'overcome'
potkat < potkávat	'meet, encounter'
získat < získávat	'gain'
zanedbat < zanedbávat	'neglect'
poznat < poznávat	'recognise, come to know'
přiznat < přiznávat	'confess, admit'

Also verbs of other types with infinitive -at, -át and -ovat:

vyhrát, vyhraje, vyhrál < vyhrávat	'win'
prohrát < prohrávat	'lose'
stát se, stane se, stal se < stávat se	'become'
dostat, dostane < dostávat	'get, obtain'
vstát, vstane, vstal < vstávat	'get up'
přestat, přestane, přestal < přestávat	'stop, cease'
přepracovat < přepracovávat	'rework, redo'
zpracovat < zpracovávat	'process'

Various other verbs have similar forms with -vat, e.g.

usmát se, usměje se, usmál se < **usmívat se**	'smile'
skrýt, skryje, skryl < skrývat	'hide'
užít, užije, užil < užívat	'use'
zbýt, zbude, zbyl < zbývat	'be left (over)'
obout, obuju, obul < obouvat (se)	'put on (shoes)'
zout < zouvat (se)	'take off (shoes)'
přezout < přezouvat (se)	'change (shoes)'

(b) Suffix type -ovat, typically goes with Type 4 infinitives ending in -it:

dokončit < dokončovat	'finish, complete'
představit < představovat	'present, represent'
vysvětlit < vysvětlovat	'explain'
zjistit < zjišťovat	'find out, ascertain'
přesvědčit < přesvědčovat	'convince'
překvapit < překvapovat	'surprise'
půjčit < půjčovat	'lend'
vypůjčit < vypůjčovat	'borrow'
koupit < kupovat	'buy'
spojit < spojovat	'join, connect, unite'
slíbit < slibovat	'promise'

But also with other types, e.g.

podepsat, podepíše, podepsal < pod(e)pisovat   'sign'

  popsat < popisovat   'describe'

ukázat, ukáže, ukázal < ukazovat   'show'

rozhodnout (se) < rozhodovat (se)   'decide'

obsáhnout < obsahovat   'contain'

  dosáhnout < dosahovat   'reach'

(c)   Suffix type **-et** goes with some other Type 4 infinitives ending in **-it**:

vrátit (se) < vracet (se)   'return'

  obrátit < obracet   'turn'

ztratit < ztrácet   'lose'

pustit < pouštět   'let go'

  vypustit < vypouštět   'let out'

otočit < otáčet   'turn, rotate'

pokusit se < pokoušet se   'try, attempt'

  zkusit < zkoušet   'try out'

probudit (se) < probouzet (se)   'awaken'

But also sometimes with other types, e.g.:

zabít, zabije, zabil < zabíjet   'kill'

opít, opije, opil < opíjet   'intoxicate'

prohlédnout < prohlížet   'look through'

The third-person plural present-tense ending **-ejí** is preferable in standard usage for these <u>derived</u> imperfectives, e.g. **ztrácejí** 'they lose'.

(d)   Suffix type **-at,** goes especially with infinitives ending in **-nout**:

vzpomenout si, vzpomene, vzpomněl   'remember'
< vzpomínat si

  zapomenout < zapomínat   'forget'

  připomenout < připomínat   'remind'

padnout < padat   'fall'

vzniknout < vznikat   'arise'

265

zvednout < zvedat	'raise, lift'
všimnout si < všímat si	'notice'
hnout (se) < hýbat (se)	'move'
obléknout < oblékat (se)	'put on (clothes)'
svléknout < svlékat (se)	'take off (clothes)'
převléknout < převlékat (se)	'change (clothes)'

Others include:

poslat, pošle, poslal < posílat	'send'
nazvat, nazve, nazval < nazývat	'name, call'
umřít, umře, umřel < umírat	'die'
vybrat, vybere, vybral < vybírat	'choose'
začít, začne, začal < začínat	'begin'
říct, řekne, řekl < říkat	'say'
pomoct, pomůže, pomohl < pomáhat	'help'
otevřít, otevře, otevřel < otevírat	'open'
zavřít, zavře, zavřel < zavírat	'close, shut'
odpovědět, odpoví, odpověděl < odpovídat	'answer'
nalézt, nalezne, nalezl < nalézat	'find'
utéct, uteče, utekl < utíkat	'run away, flee'
přijmout, přijme, přijal < přijímat	'receive'
dotknout se, dotkne se, dotkl se < dotýkat se	'touch'

10.9.7 Single/momentary versus multiple action

Sometimes the range of perfective verb forms available allows a distinction to be made between single and multiple (repeated) actions.

In particular, the suffix **-nout** often forms a perfective verb expressing a single/momentary event, e.g.

riskovat impf./pf. 'risk' – **risknout** pf. 'risk (something once)'

bodat impf. 'stab' – **bodnout** pf. 'stab (once)'

Sometimes alternative perfective counterparts to a verb are produced as a result:

probodávat impf. 'stab through' – **probodnout** pf. (once), **probodat** pf. (multiple action)

křičet impf. 'shout' **zakřičet** pf. 'shout' (for a certain complete length of time)

křiknout pf. 'give a single shout'

Another example occurs with compounds of the pair **hodit** < **házet** 'throw', where pf. **hodit** stands for the single action. Perfective compounds may be formed by adding prefixes to each of these, but there is only one corresponding imperfective, using the suffix type **-ovat**:

vyhazovat impf. 'throw out' **vyhodit** pf. 'throw out' (single act)

vyházet pf. 'throw out' (multiple act, e.g. one after another)

10.9.8 Overlapping pairs

Perfectivising prefixes often restrict or colour the meaning of a simple verb, so that different prefixes have to be used for different senses. These may also form their own derived imperfectives, which then retain that narrower meaning:

dělit 'divide, separate' > **rozdělit** 'divide', **oddělit** 'separate'

rozdělit < **rozdělovat** 'divide'
oddělit < **oddělovat** 'separate'

Sometimes derived verbs which seem superfluous are produced:

impf.	pf.	impf.	
blížit se	**přiblížit se**	**přibližovat se**	'approach, come near'
budit (se)	**probudit (se)**	**probouzet (se)**	'awaken, wake, wake up'
	vzbudit (se)	**vzbouzet (se)**	ditto
	but **vzbudit**	**vzbuzovat**	'arouse (interest, mistrust, love)'
končit	**dokončit**	**dokončovat**	'end, complete, bring to an end'
	ukončit	**ukončovat**	'end, finish'

skončit	**skončovat**	ditto, *also*: 'end up'
zakončit	**zakončovat**	ditto

Such verbs often hardly differ in their essential meaning, or differ in minor ways which may not be simple to define.

10.10 Prefixes with other parts of speech

Prefixed elements used with nouns, adjectives and adverbs are often again those derived from basic prepositions. Others are compounding elements using independent parts of speech, e.g. **mnoho-, málo-, samo-**.

The following alphabetical list mingles the various types. Use a dictionary to identify the basic words from which the examples are derived.

arci-   'arch-'

         arcibiskup 'archbishop', **arcivévoda** 'archduke', **arcilotr** 'arch rogue', **arcidílo** 'great masterpiece'

bez(e)-   'without'

         bezvědomí 'unconsciousness', **bezdomovec** 'homeless person', **bezvětří** 'calm', **bezzubý** 'toothless', **bezvadný** 'perfect, faultless', **beznaděj** 'despair', **bezmocný** 'powerless'

do-   'up to, until'

         dopoledne 'morning', **doživotní** 'life(long)' **doživotí** 'life imprisonment'

jedno-   'mono-, uni-, single'

         jednoslabičný 'monosyllabic', **jednoduchý** 'simple', **jednotvárný** 'monotonous, uniform'

málo-   'little'

         málomluvný 'taciturn'

mezi-   'between, inter-'

         mezipatro 'mezzanine floor', **mezistupeň** 'intermediate stage', **mezinárodní** 'international'

místo-   'deputy, vice-'

         místopředseda 'vice-chairman, deputy chairman', **místopředsedkyně** 'vice-chairwoman'

mnoho-	'poly-, multi-, many'
	mnohomluvný 'talkative', **mnohobarevný** 'multi-coloured, polychromatic', **mnohoslabičný** 'polysyllabic'
na-, ná-	'on, upon, somewhat, slightly'
	nábřeží 'embankment, quay', **nahnilý** 'partly rotten'
nad(e)-	'over, above, super-'
	nadjezd 'flyover, overpass', **nadpřirozený** 'supernatural', **nadlidský** 'superhuman', **nadprůměrný** 'above-average', **nadvýroba** 'overproduction'
ne-	'not, non-, un-, in-'
	nesmysl 'nonsense', **Nečech** 'a non-Czech', **nemarxista** 'a non-Marxist', **nepřítel** 'enemy' (lit. 'non-friend'), **nemotorný** 'clumsy', **neschopný** 'incapable', **nesmrtelný** 'immortal', **nestranický** 'non-party', **nespolehlivý** 'unreliable', **nemoc** 'illness', lit. 'not-power'
nedo-	'insufficiently, incompletely', usually verb roots
	nedouk 'half-educated person', **nedopalek** 'cigarette end'
nej-	'most, -est', superlative prefix, added to comparatives (see 4.15.4)
	nejlepší 'best', **nejstarší** 'oldest', **nejdřív** 'first of all, soonest'
o-, ob(e)-	'around, every other'
	okvětí 'outer part of a flower, perianth', **obden** 'every other day', **občas** 'from time to time'
od(e)-	'from, since'
	odvěký 'age-old', **odpoledne** '(in the) afternoon'
pa-	'substitute, false, inferior, pseudo-'
	paklíč 'master key', **pavěda** 'pseudoscience', **pachuť** 'aftertaste', **padělek** 'forgery, fake'
po-	'after, post-; along; somewhat, a bit'
	poválečný 'postwar', **pobřeží** 'shore', **pobledlý** 'somewhat pale'

pod- 'sub-, under'

podzemí 'underground', **podsvětí** 'the underworld',
podprůměrný 'sub-average', **podhůří** 'foothills',
poddůstojník 'non-commissioned officer', **podzim**
'autumn' (**zima** 'winter'), **podvědomí** 'the subconscious',
podpaždí 'armpit'

pra- 'pre-, ancient, original state, proto-, very (negative or
ancient), great- (relations)'

prales 'primeval forest', **pravěk** 'prehistoric times',
pračlověk 'ancient man, primeval man', **pradávný**
'ancient', **pramálo** 'very little', **pranic** 'absolutely
nothing', **pravnuk** 'great-grandson', **prababička**
'great-grandmother', **praotec** 'forefather', **praslovanský**
'Proto-Slavonic'

reduplicated: **prapradědeček** 'great-great-grandfather'

proti- 'against, anti-, counter-'

protilék 'antidote', **protiválečný** 'anti-war',
protiteroristický 'anti-terrorist', **protiútok**
'counter-attack', **protiváha** 'counterpoise,
counterweight', **protizákonný** 'illegal', **protireformace**
'the Counter-Reformation'

pře- 'over, very'

přesila 'superior strength, superiority', **překrásný**
'magnificent, very fine', **převeliký** 'very great', **přemíra**
'surfeit, excess'

před- 'in front of, before, pre-, fore-'

předválečný 'pre-war', **předměstí** 'suburbs', **předehra**
'overture, prelude', **předloktí** 'forearm', **předkrm**
'starter, hors d'oeuvres', **předmanželský** 'premarital',
předpotopní 'antediluvian', **předprodej** 'advance
booking, sale', **předškolní** 'pre-school'

přes- 'over, excessive'

přesčas 'overtime', **přespolní** 'cross-country, from out
of town, from the next village', lit. 'from across the fields'

při-, pří- 'at, near, attached, partial, weak, semi-'

přízemí 'ground floor', **příchuť** '(added) flavour,
tinge', **příjmení** 'surname', **přihlouplý** 'simple-minded,
half-witted', **příkrm** 'side-dish', **přítmí** 'semi-darkness'

roz-   'separate, asunder'

rozcestí 'parting of the ways, crossroads'

samo-   'self-'

samohláska 'vowel', **samopal** 'sub-machinegun', **samozřejmý** 'self-evident, obvious', **samozvaný** 'self-styled', **samouk** 'self-taught person', **samostatný** 'independent'

sou-   'with, con-'

souhvězdí 'constellation', **souhláska** 'consonant', **současný** 'contemporary', **sourozenec** 'sibling', **soutok** 'confluence'

spolu-   'co-'

spolupracovník 'fellow-worker, colleague', **spoluautor** 'co-author', **spolubydlící** 'room-mate', **spolužák** 'fellow pupil, student'

ú-   can represent the prefix **v-** 'in' as well as **u-** 'at', and it is not always clear which it is

úrok 'interest (payment)', **údolí** 'valley', **úpatí** 'foot' (**kopce** 'of a hill'), **úplný** 'entire, complete', **území** 'territory'

vele-   'great, superior'

veletrh 'trade fair', **velvyslanec** 'ambassador', **velmistr** 'grand master' (**šachový** 'chess'), **velmoc** 'world power', **velryba** 'whale' (**ryba** 'fish'), **veledílo** 'masterpiece', **velekněz** 'high priest', **velezrada** 'high treason'

vý-   'out'

výročí 'anniversary', **výsluní** 'sunny place, sunny side'

zá-, za- 'beyond'

zahraničí 'foreign countries, abroad', **zákeřný** 'insidious', lit. 'behind a bush' (**keř** 'bush'), **záňadří** 'bosom', **zámořský** 'overseas'

There are also compound words where a neuter short-form adjective is the first element, e.g.

velkostatek 'large farm, estate', **velkoobchod** 'wholesale trade', **maloobchod** 'retail trade', **maloměšťák** 'petty bourgeois',

starověk 'antiquity, ancient times', **staropramen** lit. 'old source', 'Urquell (beer)', **novotvar** 'neologism, coinage', **novomanželé** 'newly married couple, newly-weds', **novodobý** 'modern-day', **středozemní** 'Mediterranean', **středoškolský** 'secondary-school', **středověk** 'Middle Ages', **středověký** 'medieval', **středoevropský** 'Central European'

The list above omits prefixes in loanwords, often instantly recognisable to English speakers, e.g. **re|konstrukce** 'reconstruction', **post|graduální** 'postgraduate', **inter|pretace** 'interpretation'. Some do not match their English equivalents, e.g. **interpunkce** 'punctuation', **interrupce** 'abortion'.

Index

References are to section numbers.